OREGON'S
Greatest *Natural*
DISASTERS

Above: Lightning strikes Salem.   Below: The January 1862 Flood in Portland.

OREGON'S Greatest Natural DISASTERS

William L. Sullivan

Navillus Press

Eugene, Oregon

Mt. St. Helens began building a second lava dome within its crater in October 2004. Similar dome-building eruptions occurred at Mt. Hood in 1781 and about 500 AD (photo by Randy Wilson).

The articles in the foldout newspaper inside the front cover of this book are entirely fictional. The name "Oregon Times" represents a fictitious newspaper of the future, and is not intended to reflect any existing or historic periodical. The final chapter of this book, "A Fictional Epilogue: A Week of the Future" is also entirely fictional. The characters described are purely products of the author's imagination and are not based on real people, alive or dead. The events described are hypothetical and fictional. The Marquam Bridge, for example, received an earthquake retrofit in the 1980s and is unlikely to collapse as described. Although the specific impacts of the coming earthquake and tsunami are unpredictable, the goal has been to depict the overall scale of the disaster realistically.

Published by the Navillus Press
1958 Onyx Street
Eugene, Oregon 97403   *www.oregonhiking.com*

Printed in USA

Contents

A Newberg grain elevator lies in ruins after the Columbus Day windstorm of 1962.

Introduction

Oregon has long seemed an eerily safe place to live—an Eden immune to the terrible earthquakes of California, the hurricanes of the Caribbean, the tornadoes of the Great Plains, and the many natural misfortunes of the world outside our gentle garden.

The deadliest natural disaster to befall the state in historic times has traditionally been listed as a flash flood that killed 259 people in the small eastern Oregon town of Heppner in 1903.

But now we have learned that gigantic earthquakes and tsunamis

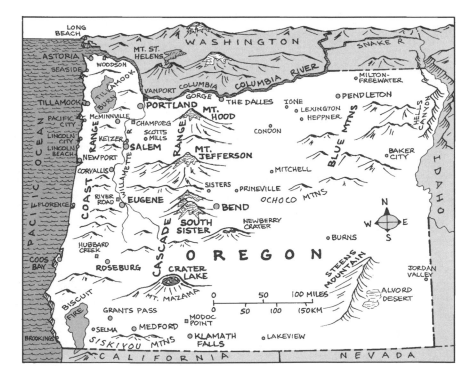

have in fact devastated the Oregon Coast every few centuries. The horrific headlines inside the front cover of this book are fictional, intended only to portray one conceivable scenario of the damage that could be caused by the next subduction earthquake.

If you find this fictional scenario shocking, consider that prehistoric Oregonians have seen much worse. In the 13,000 years that people have

lived here, unimaginable floods drowned everyone in the Willamette Valley and volcanic eruptions killed thousands across the state.

On this larger time scale, we see not only that Oregon is a land of turmoil, but also that these cataclysmic events recur with varying degrees of regularity. What at first appear to be random disasters are in fact part of larger natural cycles. Subduction earthquakes strike Oregon every 300 to 600 years. Rivers flood every ten to 100 years. Forests burn every 20 to 200 years. Even volcanoes erupt in cycles.

The largest Oregon forest fire in a century, the Biscuit Fire of 2002 sparked a controversy about fire recovery strategies.

Attempting to stop these cycles is hardly an answer. Dousing a forest fire, for example, can make the next fire bigger. Subduction earthquakes could only be stopped by freezing the liquid interior of the Earth itself—not really an option. Some disasters are simply the price we pay for inhabiting a living planet.

By understanding the rhythms, however, we may be able to sidestep disasters suffered in the past. If no one is standing in the way of a natural disaster, is it really a disaster at all?

Because this book focuses on natural phenomena that put lives at risk, I have omitted shipwrecks, city fires, and other man-made disasters. A different book will have to cover the stranding of the *New Carissa* in 1999, the blaze that destroyed Oregon's wooden State Capitol building in 1935, and the fertilizer truck explosion that leveled downtown Roseburg in 1959. I've also skipped the 15-million-year-old Columbia River lava floods and other cataclysms that preceded human colonization. Nor have I set out to recount every single ice storm and forest fire.

The 1964 Alaskan earthquake that destroyed much of downtown Anchorage may resemble a massive earthquake predicted for Oregon.

The story I have to tell is a special adventure, a guided tour through time, listening for the heartbeat of the land.

Many of the stories begin in prehistory—for example, when floods roared down the Columbia Gorge 800 feet deep, wiping out the heart of Northwest civilization. In these cases we'll rely on the geologic record, scientific research, and Indian legends as our vehicle.

Some of the stories recount cataclysms that have become defining moments in the lifetimes of modern Oregonians—the Columbus Day windstorm of 1962, the 1980 eruption of Mt. St. Helen, or the flood of 1996.

In the book's penultimate chapter, "Beyond the Cycles," we'll venture forward on an expedition into Oregon's future, admittedly a perilous landscape of projections and conjecture. If disasters occur in cycles, how reliably can we predict what will happen next? Have we already altered some cycles through development or global warming? What precautions might reasonably limit our risk of damage in the future?

The final chapter of this book is a fictional account of a major earthquake and tsunami on the Oregon Coast, set a dozen years in the future. The story is a companion piece to the fictional newspaper pages at the front of the book. Neither is intended as a specific prediction. No one can foresee the timing or effects of tectonic movement in the Cascadia subduction zone. All of the people and events described in the final chapter and in the foldout are entirely imaginary.

The other chapters of this book are non-fiction, backed by a lengthy bibliography of sources. But facts are not always enough. Because we are human, we relate to disasters in human terms.

It's all too easy to drive past the tsunami warning signs along the Oregon Coast's Highway 101 without giving them a second thought. They are merely highway signs. Would we react differently if we could actually see how a tsunami might change our lives?

The purpose of this book is not to provide definitive answers about the effects of future disasters. That is not possible. Instead the goal is to understand the past and provoke thought about the future.

We need to ask ourselves: What other warning signs are we driving past?

William L. Sullivan
Eugene, Oregon

CHAPTER I

Ice Age Floods

Many Oregonians recall the fearsome flood of 1996, when citizens frantically erected barricades along Portland's waterfront to save downtown. A few people still have nightmares about the 1949 flood that swept away Vanport, a city of 18,000 people.

But just try to imagine the horror of the first Oregonians, some 13,000 years ago, when a wall of water 800 feet tall thundered out of the Columbia Gorge at 80 miles per hour, churned across the site of present-day Portland, and flooded the Willamette Valley 400 feet deep.

Oregon's largest floods repeatedly turned the Willamette Valley into

Ice Age floods repeatedly roared through the Columbia Gorge, drowned the site of Portland, and flooded the Willamette Valley 400 feet deep, killing everyone in the area.

a lake. These Ice Age floods swept down the Columbia Gorge more than forty times between 12,700 and 15,300 years ago, unleashed by a giant ice sheet that covered most of Canada.

The toe of this continental glacier reached far enough south into the Idaho panhandle to dam the Clark Fork of the Columbia River. A 2000-foot-tall wall of ice backed up the river to create Lake Missoula, a 530-cubic-mile lake about the size of Lake Ontario. Of course ice floats, so it doesn't make a very permanent dam, especially for such a large river. Every 30 to 70 years, when the lake grew deep enough, the toe of the glacier would start to float. Then the ice dam would suddenly crumble, triggering a colossal flood that emptied the lake in a matter of days. A wall of water and icebergs surged across eastern Washington, roared through the Columbia Gorge, and backed up into the Willamette Valley as far as Eugene.

The Ice Age floods reamed out the Columbia Gorge, leaving waterfalls and scenic cliffs, as at Multnomah Falls.

It's hard to know how many people died in such incredibly large floods. Hundreds? Tens of thousands? We know that people lived in Oregon at the time. Campfire charcoal from caves in the high desert near Fort Rock has been dated at 13,200 years old. Perhaps these early inhabitants were cagey enough to avoid the Columbia and Willamette Rivers. With gigantic floods storming through every two or three generations, grandmothers might start warning their families not to camp near those nightmarish rivers, even if the fishing was great. Certainly no human artifacts have been found along the lower Columbia and Willamette that predate the Ice Age floods. Virtually everything and everyone was swept away.

The Controversial Theory of Dr. Bretz

An apocalyptic flood? A Biblical cataclysm? When J Harlen Bretz announced to a convention of geologists in 1923 that the scablands of eastern Washington apparently had been formed in an impossibly huge flood, his audience was appalled. Throughout America, geologists rejected his theory as a throwback to the dark ages of science, when religious scholars insisted that Noah's flood had shaped the Earth's landforms suddenly 4000 years ago.

It didn't help that Bretz pounded the podium with the passion of a tent-revival preacher. Worse, Bretz couldn't suggest a plausible source for such an enormous amount of water. The floodwaters had magically materialized in the midst of what is now a desert steppe. For decades Bretz was derided by his colleagues as a fool.

But Bretz had done his research correctly, and he was mostly right about his flood.

J Harlen Bretz grew up in Michigan, burdened with a first name that was a single letter—a "J" with no period. He earned a degree in biology from the University of Chicago in 1906, married a classmate, and accepted

A lobe of an Ice Age glacier from Canada intermittently dammed a branch of the Columbia River 12,700 to 15.300 years ago, backing up and releasing glacial Lake Missoula.

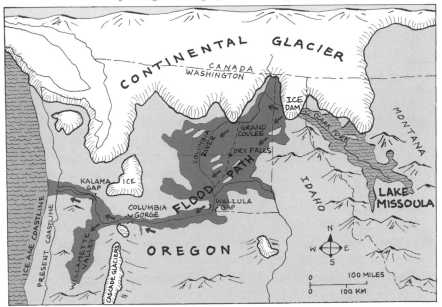

a job as a high school biology teacher in Seattle. There he began studying Ice Age glaciation as a hobby, in part because prominent geologists had just revealed the fascinating news that Puget Sound had been carved by a lobe of the Canadian ice shield. In his spare time after school and on summer vacations, Bretz mapped former glacial outwash lakes at Tacoma and Olympia.

After four years Bretz quit his high school job and returned to the University of Chicago to study geology full time. He earned his Ph.D. with high honors in 1913.

Now Bretz could focus knowledgeably on Washington glaciation. Perhaps because so much was already known about the Puget Sound area, he turned to eastern Washington. There he found a series of puzzles strewn across the desert landscape south of Grand Coulee Dam. In a vast region that he termed the "channeled scablands," he found gigantic, dry watercourses eroded to bedrock. As early as the 1830s, scientific-minded visitors had observed that these "coulees" must be old channels of the Columbia River. But Bretz determined that the dry channels were 600 feet higher than the Columbia River. Filling these channels would have required more water than all the rivers on Earth combined.

Bretz was particularly impressed by Dry Falls, where the Grand Coulee, a huge dry channel, leads to a 300-foot basalt cliff. Erosion on the bedrock lip of this dry waterfall shows that water once ran 200 feet deep along the rim of a cascade three and a half miles wide. Below the dry falls is a ten-mile splash pool. The hydraulics required to produce such landforms would dwarf Niagara Falls, a 165-foot cascade that is merely *one* mile wide.

Bretz knew Ice Age glaciation had to be involved. Although he couldn't pinpoint the source of the water, he recognized the footprints of a really big flood.

Unfortunately for Bretz, the announcement of his theory in 1923 came at a time when American geology was still struggling to disassociate itself from Biblical doctrine. As early as 1802, British geologists James Hutton and John Playfair had suggested that large canyons were not the result of Noah's flood after all, but rather had been created very slowly by the same gradual processes of erosion that are active today.

John Muir took up this banner in America in the late 1800s, daring to claim that Yosemite Valley's colossal cliffs were not the result of divine intervention, as was widely believed. Instead he suggested the canyon had been carved over the course of millennia by glaciers that moved just inches a day. In an attempt to convince skeptics, Muir trekked to the crest of the Sierra Nevada, found glaciers at the headwaters of Yosemite's creeks, drove rows of stakes into the ice, and measured the stakes' movement to prove the glaciers were alive.

What Bretz needed to convince his skeptics was a gigantic source of water. Because he suspected the water must have come from the Spokane area, although he couldn't imagine how, he used the term "Spokane Flood" for his theoretical deluge. Could the flood have been caused by a sudden glacial meltoff? Even Bretz admitted the idea didn't hold water—or at least, not nearly enough water.

What Bretz didn't realize was that the gigantic lake he was looking for had already been described in detail, years earlier, by Montana geologist Joseph T. Pardee. In 1910, Pardee had published a journal article about a vanished Ice Age lake that he termed Lake Missoula. Because Pardee's lake was two states and 100 miles to the east, Bretz didn't make the connection for years.

From Pardee's perspective in western Montana it was easy to visualize glacial Lake Missoula. Scores of perfectly level terraces line valley slopes for hundreds of miles, cut by the waves of the ancient reservoir. Early pioneers in the Bitterroot Valley mused that the terraces looked like staves on sheet music. The highest of these watermarks lies 4150 feet above sea level.

When Pardee traced the lakeshores to the west, he found that they all disappeared in Idaho, with no trace of a dam, at the mouth of the Purcell Valley near Lake Pend Oreille. Where was Lake Missoula's missing dam? Pardee postulated that it came from Canada and was made of ice. What happened to the lake's water when the dam failed? Pardee didn't say.

At Columbia Hills State Park near The Dalles, the Ice Age floods were 1000 feet deep. The current stripped soil from Horsethief Butte, leaving only bare cliffs. The rounded hills in the background were high enough that they stood above the flood and kept their soil.

Even when Pardee attended a geology conference orchestrated to discredit Bretz's theory in 1927, Pardee said nothing. Evidently he didn't want to get involved in the melee surrounding Bretz.

In 1942 Pardee published a second paper about vanished Lake Missoula. This time he described the strange series of mile-long ridges that had puzzled people in western Montana valleys for years. Pardee noticed that the

The floods denuded Columbia Gorge slopes, exposing cliffs and bare ridges such as Coyote Wall near Hood River.

ridges looked like gigantic ripple marks when viewed from an airplane. He theorized that the ripples formed when the monumental lake drained, but he still refused to speculate about where the water had gone.

In 1956 Bretz finally announced that he believed Pardee's glacial Lake Missoula was the source of his flood. By then he had also realized that the lake had launched many such floods, periodically filling, breaching its ice dam, and draining.

Some of Bretz's most vocal critics went to their graves believing that he was wrong. A new generation of geologists, however, began to accept the Ice Age floods.

In 2006 Congress designated the Ice Age Floods National Geographic Route. The National Park Service built interpretive sites along the path of the flood from Montana to Oregon. Highway pullouts and signs now describe Lake Missoula in Montana, Dry Falls in Washington, and the narrows of the Columbia Gorge in Oregon. The interpretive signs hail J Harlen Bretz as a visionary geologist.

More than three quarters of a century after Bretz first proposed his controversial theory, the story of his massive flood has at last won official recognition.

Anatomy of a Cataclysm

Just try to pronounce *jökulhlaup*. That's the scientific term for the kind of periodic glacial floods that drained Lake Missoula. The word *jökulhlaup* means "glacier run" in Icelandic. Icelanders have long understood the process that produces these glacial pulses. Compared to the Northwest's Ice Age floods, however, Iceland's floods are mere drops in the bucket.

The Northwest's *jökulhlaups* began when a tongue of the Canadian ice sheet extended down Idaho's Purcell Valley about 15,300 years ago, damming the Clark Fork and backing up Lake Missoula. Each time the lake rose to a level of 600 feet, the ice dam would start to float and water would begin squirting under the ice. Almost immediately, the immense pressure would break the dam apart, releasing the impounded lake at rates of up to a million cubic meters per second.

After the lake drained, the glacier would advance across the river and dam it again. In another 30 to 70 years, the lake would rise enough to break the ice dam again and release yet another flood. Perhaps a dozen of these floods pulsed into Oregon when people lived in the flood's path.

During those final 300 years before the glacier retreated for good, generations of Oregonians must have learned to fear the flood's warning signs. First the ground would shake, startling the birds from the trees. Then the hills would rumble, frightening the deer from their cover. Next a cold wind would roar by. A few moments later the water would loom up as a churning wall of ice, logs, mud, rocks, and trees.

Each of these gigantic floods met several major obstacles on the way to the ocean. The first roadblock was another lobe of the Canadian glacier. This tongue of ice dammed the Columbia River near present-day Grand Coulee Dam, creating glacial Lake Columbia. Although this reservoir didn't get deep enough to float its ice dam, it did divert the Columbia River south, forcing the current to spill through the Grand Coulee canyon over Dry Falls.

When the flood from Lake Missoula surged into Lake Columbia, water spread in all directions. The combined flood fanned out across eastern Washington, drowning the landscape from Wenatchee to Walla Walla.

The flood puddled up again at the Wallula Gap, a narrows south of Kennewick where the Horse Heaven Hills crowd the Columbia River. About 200 cubic miles of water arrived here on each of the first two days of each flood. The gap only had room for 40 cubic miles a day to get through, so the water backed up to create glacial Lake Lewis.

Beyond the Wallula Gap the flood spread out again to create glacial Lake Condon, a 1500-square-mile reservoir centered over the present-day city of Umatilla. Silt that settled in Lake Condon became the deep, rich soils now prized for growing Hermiston watermelons. Hat Rock, a hat-shaped basalt knoll that served as a Columbia River landmark for Lewis and Clark, is the remnant of a lava flow eroded by the flood.

Next came the slot-like canyon of the Columbia Gorge, the flood's only possible route through the Cascade Range. At the mouth of the Gorge the flood churned into a fury, stripping soil from The Dalles. To this day, low-lying areas near The Dalles remain a windy desert of exposed basalt bedrock. The loss of soil left stark, angular features such as Horsethief Butte and the barren plateau at Maryhill Museum's Stonehenge replica. Above the 1000-foot-elevation high water mark of the floods, however, the soil wasn't washed away. That's why the landscape at The Dalles suddenly

Ice Age Floods from the Great Basin

Lake Missoula has been gone for 12,700 years, but other Ice Age lakes continued to launch smaller, sporadic floods down the Columbia River. These less well-known floods came from the Great Basin, where the Ice Age had brought rain instead of snow.

Lake Bonneville, the largest of the Great Basin lakes, covered much of western Utah and eastern Nevada. Today all that remains of this inland sea is the Great Salt Lake. Prehistoric Lake Bonneville had no outlet until it grew so large that it lapped into southern Idaho and spilled out the Snake River drainage. The outlet quickly wore a canyon that drained a portion of the lake, sending a flood down through Hells Canyon to the Columbia River.

Similar floods drained prehistoric Lake Alvord, the current home of the Alvord Desert near Steens Mountain. Although the only surface water in this arid corner of southeast Oregon is now found at marshes and hot springs, Lake Alvord once filled a 30-mile-wide basin 200 feet deep. When the rainy climate at the end of the Ice Age allowed the lake to spill out

The Alvord Desert below Steens Mountain was once an Ice Age lake that spilled into the Snake River, sending a flood down the Columbia.

via Big Sand Gap to the Owyhee River, the lake level suddenly dropped almost 40 feet. The resulting flood down the Owyhee, Snake, and Columbia Rivers was 100 times smaller than a typical Lake Missoula flood. This would not have backed up the Columbia River into the Willamette Valley, but it could have obliterated human settlement along the Columbia itself.

The cliffs at Crown Point constricted the Ice Age floods so severely that Vista House (the view-point building at right) would have been 100 feet below water.

changes above the 1000 foot level, with wheat ranches and orchards on gently rounded hills.

The Columbia Gorge is so narrow that the flood backed up in a pool 150 miles long. Water waited as far away as Walla Walla, unable to clear the Wallula Gap until the Columbia Gorge could drain. Even the Deschutes River backed up 50 miles to Maupin.

Meanwhile the Gorge became a roaring pipeline, filled wall-to-wall with a maelstrom of mud, icebergs, rock, and water. The current reamed out the canyon like a gigantic ditch-digging machine, scouring talus from the cliffs on either side. The sheer rock faces that remain have created the waterfalls that define the area's beauty today.

The flood blasted out of the western end of the Gorge as if from a fire hose. Constricted by the cliffs at Crown Point, a wall of water jetted into the Portland basin at 80 miles an hour. The resulting erosion is now best seen from the air.

Ask for a window seat the next time you take off from Portland's airport. If you're facing south, look for Rocky Butte, the knoll where Interstate 84 and Interstate 205 join. Once this extinct volcano was a smooth-sided cone. The flood eroded its upstream side to a cliff. Downstream, the current left a low gravel ridge of sediment trailing behind it. Known as the Alameda Crest, this ridge of outwash debris is now traced by NE Alameda Drive.

If you look north as you take off from the Portland Airport, notice the long blue stripe of Lacamas Lake in the woods above Camas, Washington. This is an ancient flood channel, where the current took a shortcut across Clark County on its way to the sea. Although Lacamas Lake is 180 feet above the Columbia River, the Ice Age flood was so deep and swift at this point that it didn't matter.

For years geologists wondered why the flood backed up into the Willamette Valley when there was nothing obvious stopping it from going directly down the Columbia River to the sea. The only constriction in that direction is the Kalama Narrows, where the river is almost two miles wide. Apparently there was simply so much water, arriving so suddenly, that even the Kalama Narrows slowed the flood, backing up water 400 feet deep throughout the Portland basin. While the flood eddied here, about a third of the water found a different exit from this bowl, pouring south into the Willamette Valley so quickly that it left gigantic ripple marks in southeast Portland. The east edge of Reed College's campus is a "ripple" 100 feet tall and three miles long.

The flood actually found two routes south into the Willamette Valley — gaps cut by rivers through the Tualatin Hills. The largest gap was carved by the Willamette River at Oregon City. But the Tualatin River had also carved a gap at Lake Oswego.

Before the Ice Age floods, Lake Oswego was not a lake. It was the channel of the Tualatin River. The flood roared up backwards through this channel, gouging the lake's basin and dumping sediment in the valley beyond. After the flood, piles of sediment blocked the Tualatin River from returning to its old channel. Instead the Tualatin was forced to find a new route farther south, joining the Willamette south of Oregon City.

Although the muddy flood rushed into the Willamette Valley at freeway speeds, it left more slowly. The water lingered for perhaps a week, slowly settling out the fertile silt that has made farming here so successful. In some places near the Willamette River this foreign silt lies 100 feet deep. Excavations reveal stripes marking each of the valley's inundations. Time after time, the floods stripped topsoil from what are now the "scablands" of eastern Washington and delivered this bonanza to the giant settling pond of the Willamette Valley.

The final stretch of the floodwaters' journey to the sea was longer than one might guess because the coastline was farther west than it is now. At the peak of the Ice Age, glaciers had converted so much of the world's water to ice that sea level was 600 feet lower than it is today. Although sea level was rising by the time of the floods, it still would have been 300 feet below the present level, leaving the shoreline 30 miles west of Astoria. For 2600 years the Ice Age floods served as a giant conveyor belt, carrying immense amounts of mud and rock from the inland Northwest out this extended Columbia River valley to the sea. Samples retrieved by deep sea drilling show that the debris from Ice Age floods fanned out across the seafloor in layers with a combined thickness of 2000 feet.

The ancient floods sculpted the Northwest as we know it today. For those who know where to look, the scultpor's chisel marks are still fresh.

Relics of the Floods

Could people have survived the Ice Age floods? Several Indian tribes have legends of cataclysmic floods. A legend from eastern Washington recounts that the Columbia River flowed over Dry Falls until the trickster god Coyote changed its course. The Kalapuyans of the Willamette Valley credit Coyote with damming the Willamette River long ago to fill the entire valley with water. But because the geologic floods took place more than 12,000 years ago, and because they would have annhiliated most witnesses, it's hard to see the legends as history.

Glacial erratic rocks hitchhiked to Oregon on icebergs from the Rocky Mountains. An Ice Age flood rafted this boulder from British Columbia to a Willamette Valley hillside in what is now a small state park near McMinnville.

The most visual relics of the Ice Age floods in the Willamette Valley are glacial erratics, rocks that were rafted here on icebergs from the Rocky Mountains. The Erratic Rock Scenic Wayside preserves one of these stones on a hill near McMinnville. To see it, drive six miles west of McMinnville on Highway 18 toward the Oregon Coast. Watch closely for a small sign for the Erratic Rock State Wayside on the right, and follow a paved road north a mile or so to a tiny pullout with another sign.

A paved path climbs a quarter mile through a vineyard to the jagged, black, Cadillac-sized boulder. How do we know this rock floated here inside an iceberg? For one thing, the rock is made of argillite, a slate-like metamorphic stone that's unknown in western Oregon but common in British Columbia. For another, the boulder isn't rounded, proving that it wasn't rolled here by water.

When scientists first measured this boulder in 1950 it was even bigger. Public enthusiasm about the alien stone initially ran so high that visitors chipped souvenirs, reducing its bulk from an estimated 160 tons to just 90.

When you stand beside the McMinnville erratic rock and look out across vineyards and farmhouse rooftops into the hazy distance of the Willamette Valley, it's daunting to think this was all underwater. At an elevation of 306 feet, the rock is 150 feet above the valley floor, but was still 100 feet below the lake's maximum height. The site of Salem, for ex-ample, was under 200 feet of water. If Salem were in such a lake today, nothing would rise above the flood—not even the gold pioneer atop the State Capitol.

Geologists have identified 135 groups of erratic boulders in this former lake, strewn from Hillsboro to West Eugene. Each group presumably rep-resents one large iceberg that stranded and melted, releasing a variety of rocks.

The strangest of all these alien stones is the Willamette Meteorite, a 31,107-pound celestial traveler discovered in 1902 amid a cluster of small granite erratics on a West Linn hillside. Resembling a ten-foot peach pit, it is the largest meteorite in North America found in one piece, and the sixth largest in the world.

Most meteorites disintegrate upon impact. This one survived because it had a soft landing on the ice of the Canadian continental glacier. The glacier slowly shuttled the rock south, perhaps for thousands of years. Then Lake Missoula's ice dam broke, and the rock floated in an iceberg 400 miles to Oregon.

The strange shape of the Willamette Meteorite is partly due to Oregon's rainy climate. Because the meteorite is 92 percent iron and only eight percent nickel, the portion above ground rusted away, leaving a flat top with weird pits. Native Americans named the rock *Tomanowas*, and believed the rusty pools in the pits were sacred. They dipped arrowheads and tools ceremonially into the pools for power.

More than 12,000 years after the stone arrived in Oregon, its story became even more complicated. A West Linn farmer named Ellis Hughes noticed the stone in 1902 when he hit it with an ax and it rang like a bell. After he spent months digging it loose and dragging to his own property, it was displayed at the Lewis and Clark Exposition of 1905 in Portland. Hughes was sued, however, by the company that owned the land where he had found the meteorite. The company won the lawsuit and

The Willamette Meteorite is a glacial erratic left by Ice Age floods. A replica of the alien stone stands in front of the University of Oregon's Natural History Museum.

sold the rock to a New York collector for $20,600. Then the collector donated it to the American Museum of Natural History in New York City, where it has been a featured attraction since 1935.

In 1985 the New York museum cut a prominent 30-pound knob off the Willamette Meteorite and traded it for a meteorite from Mars. Dozens of smaller samples had already been sliced off by earlier collectors, but this latest cut was so unkind that Oregon's confederated tribes of Grande

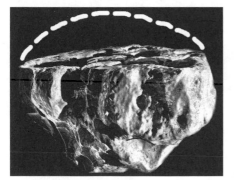

Because the Willamette Meteorite is 92 percent iron, the portion above ground had rusted away by the time the stone was moved in 1902.

Ronde lodged an official protest. They demanded that the sacred space rock be returned to Oregon. The museum responded by promising never to cut the rock again. They also agreed to "share custody" by letting the tribes perform ceremonies annually at the rock in New York.

The issue might have ended there, except that the anonymous owner of the missing 30-pound piece asked Bonhams Auctioneers to put the meteorite chunk up for auction in 2007. A full-page ad in *The Oregonian* touted "the rarest of collecting opportunities: the chance to acquire a prominently missing portion of a centerpiece exhibit at a world-renowned museum."

A tribal spokesman responded in an article for the Associated Press, "We are deeply saddened that any individual or organization would be so insensitive to Native American spirituality and culture as to traffic in the sale of a sacred and historic artifact. As a tribe, we do not participate in such sales and auctions. We view them with dismay."

The meteorite piece was expected to fetch more than $1 million, but it did not win its minimum bid and was withdrawn from sale.

Replicas of the entire, intact meteorite are on display outside the University of Oregon's Natural History Museum in Eugene and on the grounds of the United Methodist Church in West Linn. Considering that the original stone traveled through space to Canada and then floated to Oregon with a gigantic flood, it's perhaps not surprising that the rock has a hard time staying put.

The Ice Age floods that swept down the Columbia River may have killed thousands of people, but such floods are not threatening today. They won't recur until the next ice age. A different kind of flood, however, could kill just as many people, and it could strike any day. This more immediate threat is coming from the ocean, and its name is *tsunami*.

CHAPTER II

Tsunamis

Tsunamis—giant ocean waves—devastate Oregon's coastal communities every 300 to 600 years. As the fictional headlines inside the front cover of this book suggest, the next large tsunami could arrive any day. Tsunamis on the Oregon Coast must have killed thousands in the past, and undoubtedly will again.

Stumps on the Beach

When I was growing up, my family often spent weekends at a rustic cabin in Lincoln Beach, north of Newport. Of course summers on the beach were glorious, but I also looked forward to winter, when wild storms and high surf would strip away most of the sand, revealing the stumps of a mysterious cedar forest.

At high tide, waves wash over the old stumps, many of them three feet in diameter. The gnarled roots grip the gray mudstone like giant hands, broken at the wrists. If you pull off a long sliver of the wood, there's no mistaking the red color and pungent scent of cedar. The wood's aromatic oil acts as a natural preservative. The salt water has helped keep out rot as well. The stumps are especially easy to see at Lincoln Beach and

Stumps of cedar trees, exposed on Oregon beaches in winter, remain from a forest that could not have grown in salt water.

Neskowin, but similar ghost forests dot beaches for the length of Oregon and Washington.

Obviously a forest once grew on the beach, but how? Cedars cannot

grow in salt water. For years, even old timers just shook their heads in puzzlement.

Then in 1984 the U.S. government asked geologists at the California Institute of Technology to assess the earthquake danger at nuclear power plants along the Columbia River. The geologists reported that, although historic earthquakes in the area have been small, the entire Pacific Northwest has the potential for extremely large "subduction" earthquakes — temblors capable of destroying cities, changing the ground level, and launching gigantic tsunamis.

The beach stumps all date to 1700, when an earthquake dropped the Northwest's shore.

The Earth's crust is made of raft-like "plates" that shift around, grinding against each other atop currents in the liquid rock of the planet's interior. In their 1984 report, the CalTech geologists pointed out that Oregon is at the junction of two major plates, where the North American continent is ramming itself on top of the Juan de Fuca plate, a section of Pacific seafloor. In general, continental plates are granitic and are lighter than seafloor plates, which are mostly made of heavy basalt. When a continent collides with a piece of seafloor, the continent floats on top while the seafloor is "subducted" — pushed down into the Earth's molten mantle.

A giant fault line, called the Cascadia subduction zone, lies about 60 miles off the coast of Oregon, Washington, and British Columbia. All along this fault the North American continental plate is moving westward on top of the Juan de Fuca oceanic plate at the rate of three to four centimeters, or about an inch and a half, every year. But this contact zone is sticky, so the North American plate does not slide smoothly. Instead it jerks forward about 30 feet every 300 to 600 years.

The fact that the Pacific Northwest has not experienced a major earthquake in written history should not give us too much comfort, according to the CalTech geologists. If the two plates are really locked, then the coast may seem tranquil, but all the time it is slowly arching like a bow, storing energy to be released suddenly in a large quake.

Similar subduction earthquakes shook Chile in 1960, Alaska in 1964, Mexico in 1985, and Indonesia on December 26, 2004. The latter quake launched a tsunami that killed nearly a quarter million people on the Indian Ocean rim, some as far away as Africa.

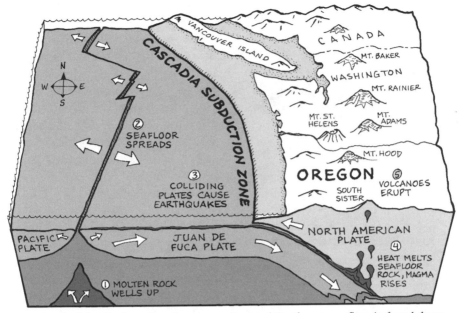

Massive "subduction" earthquakes occur when a plate of ocean seafloor is forced downward (subducted) by an advancing continental plate. If the slip zone is sticky, pressure can build for centuries. The resulting quakes are among the world's largest.

In 1984 a spokesperson for Portland General Electric, the owner of the Trojan nuclear power plant at Rainier, responded cautiously to the CalTech report, "It's a matter that ought to be studied" to see if evidence would prove or disprove the theory of major Northwest earthquakes and tsunamis.

In short: Where's the smoking gun?

One of the first scientists to look for proof of the killer earthquakes was Brian Atwater, a geologist at the University of Washington. When Atwater examined estuaries along the Washington Coast at Willapa Bay and Grays Harbor, he found the same ghost forests that line the Oregon Coast. In some estuaries, the snags of ancient cedar trees were still standing. These low-lying areas had evidently dropped to sea level hundreds of years ago, something only a massive earthquake could make happen.

Excavation revealed that thousands of additional tree stumps were hidden underneath the tidal marshes, buried by a layer of sea sand and marine shells. Although the debris was obviously from a tsunami, it was miles inland. Unimaginable waves must have washed the beach sand into the woods and killed the trees.

Now Atwater knew for certain—a catastrophe had indeed struck the coast. But when had it happened?

Radiocarbon dating of the ghost forests showed they were several centuries years old. The use of dendrochronology—counting the tree's growth rings and matching them against the pattern of rings in live

trees—proved that all of the trees along the beaches of Oregon and Washington had died in the same year. The Northwest's last great subduction earthquake and tsunami occurred in the winter between 1699 and 1700, more than a century before the arrival of Lewis and Clark. When it hit, the shore dropped as much as ten feet. Then the ocean flooded in, and salt water killed the trees.

Drowned estuaries along the Northwest shore remain as evidence that massive earthquakes have lowered the coast.

Ominously, Atwater discovered not just one layer of tsunami debris, but many, revealing that subduction earthquakes have launched tsunamis that ravage the Northwest coast every 300 to 600 years.

Since then, researchers at estuaries from Northern California to Vancouver Island have found similar "layer cakes" of strata. At the Coquille River in southern Oregon, subduction earthquakes have dropped tidal marshes and low-lying forests twelve times in the past 6700 years. At Bradley Lake in the coastal dunes just south of Bandon, ocean surges 15 to 25 feet deep have overtopped the dunes thirteen times in the past 7000 years, depositing layers of ocean sand and leaving the freshwater lake brackish for years. On the coastal plains near Long Beach, Washington, sheets of tsunami sand lie ten inches thick behind the beach's foredune. The debris sheets extend nearly a mile inland.

The debris layers also show that the Cascadia subduction zone doesn't always rupture along its entire length at once. In general, the southern end of the rift (off the shore of southern Oregon) seems to slip more frequently, causing slightly smaller earthquakes and more frequent tsunamis.

The date of Oregon's last tsunami has been pegged at 1700. The exact dates of earlier tsunamis are still debated, but they seem to fall around 1200 AD, 900 AD, 700 AD, and 300 AD, as well as 500 BC, 1050 BC, 1400 BC, 1800 BC, 2400 BC, and 2900 BC. Geologic evidence for tsunamis at similar intervals goes back as far as 5500 BC.

Clues in Japan

Brian Atwater was able to discover the precise date of the most recent subduction earthquake by turning to Japan, a country where historians have been recording earthquakes and tsunamis for many centuries. Working with researchers in Japan, he learned that the Japanese had recorded earthquakes accompanied by large tsunamis in 1611, 1677, 1896, 1933, 1968, 1983, and 1993.

The Japanese had also recorded three tsunamis that struck without the usual earthquake warning—presumably because the earthquake itself was too far away to be felt in Japan. Of these three "distant" tsunamis, researchers knew that a tsunami in 1960 had been caused when a quake in Chile sent a wave across the Pacific Ocean. The Japanese tsunami of 1952 had clearly been launched by an earthquake in Kamchatka. The tsunami that arrived on January 27, 1700, however, was called the "orphan" tsunami because it had never been connected with a known earthquake.

Atwater realized that the Japanese tsunami in 1700 must have traveled across the Pacific from an earthquake on the Cascadia subduction zone.

In Japan, records from seven shoreline sites report that the tsunami of 1700 reached heights of three to 15 feet, as measured on temple steps, in rice paddies, and on government buildings that are still standing.

"A tsunami struck Kuwagasaki village," according to one of the historic reports. "Villagers went to the hills. Fires broke out and twenty houses burned. In addition, thirteen houses were reported to have been destroyed by the tsunami. Because the tsunami and fires happened at the same time, villagers were unable to move anything, let alone furniture or tools."

In a different village 90 miles southwest of Tokyo the water came up as for a sudden high tide. A chronicler wrote that "the water also went into the pine trees of Ego. The receding water went out very fast, like a big river. It came in about seven times before 10 am of that day and gradually lost its power. It is said that when an earthquake happens, something like large swells result, but there was no earthquake in either the village or nearby."

The Japanese records enabled Atwater and his colleagues to pinpoint the time and size of the Cascadia subduction earthquake. Kenji Satake at the Active Fault Research Center in Japan ran a computer simulation of the tsunami. For a ten-foot wave to reach Japan, he deduced that the Cascadia quake must have been one of the largest in history. That meant the quake must have been caused by a rupture along the entire 1100-mile length of the Cascadia subduction zone. Calculating that tsunamis travel at speeds of up to 500 miles per hour across the open ocean, and that Japan is 5000 miles from Oregon, he concluded that the earthquake must have shaken Oregon at 9 pm on January 26, 1700. The devastating tsunami that hit the Oregon Coast would have arrived about half an hour after the quake.

More than three centuries have passed since a major earthquake released the pressure building along the Cascadia subduction zone. Already there is a ten to twenty percent chance that a great earthquake will occur here in the next fifty years. The odds are increasing all the time.

The stumps remaining on Oregon's beaches are not just a relic of a distant disaster. They are a reminder that a violent tsunami can and will devastate this coast again.

The Mechanics of Tsunamis

Tsunamis were once known as *tidal waves*, but this term lost favor because the waves are not caused by tides. Ironically, the replacement term doesn't fit all that well either. *Tsunami* means "harbor wave" in Japanese, and the waves aren't limited to harbors. Now scientists sometimes use the more accurate term *seismic sea wave*.

Call them what you will, the disasters can be caused by many things. Asteroid impacts are perhaps the least common cause, but their tsunamis may be the easiest to visualize. Just as a pebble tossed into a pond will send out rings, a large space rock hitting the ocean creates a series of concentric tsunami waves. A three-mile-wide asteroid landing in the Atlantic Ocean at 40,000 miles per hour, for example, would send a tsunami ten miles inland along the eastern seaboard of the United States, according to the Los Alamos National Laboratory. Impacts on this scale occur only once every ten million years, however, so the risk is relatively low.

Similar concentric tsunami "ripples" can be caused by volcanic eruptions, local earthquakes, and underwater landslides. A relatively small 7.0 earthquake near New Guinea in 1998, for example, surprised geologists by unleashing a 30-foot-tall tsunami that killed more than 2000 people. As it turned out, the earthquake triggered an underwater landslide that shifted a cubic mile of sediment, displacing enough water to launch a tsunami.

Underwater landslides like this often occur along the continental shelf, an underwater slope a mile or more tall. Off the southern Oregon Coast, where the continental shelf begins just 30 miles from shore, the slope is riddled with so many landslide slumps that some of them overlap. Two are so large that they almost certainly sent tsunamis ashore in southern Oregon, perhaps thousands of years ago.

The leading edge of a tsunami may resemble an ordinary breaker, but it is followed by a surge many miles long, raising the water level like a strange and sudden high tide.

The tsunamis we have discussed so far create concentric waves that become smaller and weaker as they spread out. Subduction earthquakes, however, are able to send large tsunamis across an entire ocean without losing much of their power. When the Cascadia subduction zone shakes, for example, it can raise or lower the seafloor along a fault 1100 miles long. The resulting tsunami waves aim their energy at right angles away from the line of the fault. Long lines of waves head west toward Japan and east toward Oregon at full force.

Tsunamis are so much broader than ordinary water ripples, and their pressure extends so much deeper, that they appear to behave quite differently. The breakers you normally see on the beach are created by wind. Depending on the wind and the shape of the beach, surf waves may be spaced about 300 feet apart. Waves that size affect only the top 150 feet of the ocean's surface. In contrast, each of the "ripples" generated by a large Cascadia earthquake is likely to be about a hundred *miles* wide. Tsunamis affect the ocean all the way to the seafloor.

Another obvious difference is speed. Ordinary waves are not particularly fast, but tsunamis are able to travel across deep oceans at seemingly impossible jet-plane speeds. The longer the distance between wave crests, the faster a wave will travel. Shallow water limits the speed. In the Pacific Ocean, where the average water depth is two and a half miles, tsunamis travel at an astonishing 440 miles per hour.

Of course no individual drop of water can move this fast. To understand how this works, consider a jellyfish floating in the open ocean. You don't see the jellyfish zoom along at the speed of each passing wave. Instead the jellyfish merely bobs in a gentle, circular motion as a wave goes by. Similarly, when a tsunami crosses an ocean, the water mostly stays put. What's moving at 440 miles per hour is the tsunami's *pressure*—the energy that stacks water into a wave.

Tsunamis are less than three feet tall in the open ocean, so ships at sea don't notice them. As each hundred-mile-wide wave approaches, a ship will rise very slowly for ten minutes. Then it gradually lowers as the wave passes.

When tsunamis reach shallow water they slow down. Because the front of the wave slows down first, the water piles up and the wave gets taller. By the time the wave nears the beach it may be traveling at 20 miles per hour—about the same speed as an ordinary surf wave. Unlike an ordinary breaker, however, the front of a tsunami wave is backed by a sheet-like surge of water many miles long. Depending on the slope of the beach, the front of this surge may well curl into a towering crest thirty to fifty feet high. This dramatic "wall of water" generally curls and collapses offshore. The frothing, churning wave that actually hits the beach may not look particularly frightening, but it is actually the front of a long surge of water that grows, rises, and stays high for ten minutes or more.

People on the beach are often fooled by tsunamis, partly because the level of the sea may drop several feet before the first wave arrives. Videos taken by tourists at resort beaches in Thailand during the 2004 Indian Ocean tsunami show unconcerned beachcombers poking around on the

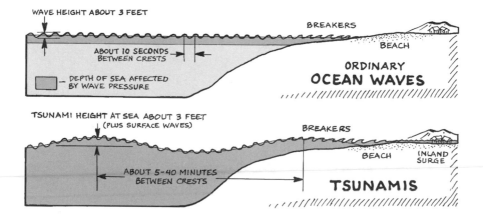

oddly exposed mudflats and tide pools. The people don't even seem alarmed by the large wave on the horizon, particularly if they're on a shallow beach where the wave has already crested and broken far from shore. The frothy breaker coming toward them doesn't look fast enough or large enough to be a threat. A wave that size looks as if it will splash on the beach and quickly retreat.

But when the wave finally reaches the beach the water doesn't stop. In the tourist videos of the 2004 tsunami, people begin to run only when the wave is at their feet. Bystanders just a few yards further up the sandy slope watch with concern, but don't turn to run until the water reaches them too. The onlookers obviously cannot believe that this strange rogue wave will keep coming. What they are seeing, of course, is merely the leading edge of a seismic sea wave many miles wide.

A cubic yard of water weighs almost a ton, so when the tsunami surges inland beyond the beach, it packs enough wallop to shove aside cars, fences, and wooden buildings. The faster the surge, the more power it packs. The front of the surge is made even more dangerous by the logs, cars, and other debris it soon carries. Low-lying areas near the beach quickly become muddy lakes littered with flotsam. After the waters swirl and eddy for a few minutes, the tsunami's first long wave finally retreats, sucking everything it can out to sea. This is often the most dangerous part of a tsunami. Loaded with debris, the rapidly retreating floodwaters batter buildings and carry away people, sweeping them a mile or more to sea.

People who survive the first wave are still often fooled. Because the "ripples" of a tsunami arrive as separate surges five to forty minutes apart, it is not safe to return to the beach when the water retreats. If you've survived the flood on a third-floor hotel balcony, for example, resist the temptation to climb down for a look around. Additional wave surges—some of them possibly larger than the first—may arrive as much as eight to ten hours later, depending on the tsunami and the shape of the coastline.

Tales from 1700

Lewis and Clark were inquisitive explorers, but they did not discover one shocking fact about western Oregon: Most of the land they visited here—including Cannon Beach, Fort Clatsop, Long Beach, and the banks of the lower Columbia River—had been overswept by tsunami waters 105 years earlier. Thousands of Indian villagers must have died at these sites just five generations before the Corps of Discovery arrived in 1805. Perhaps the explorers weren't able to communicate well enough with local tribes to ask such questions. Perhaps the subject never came up. Or perhaps the legends they heard seemed too fanciful to be true.

Later visitors who learned the local languages recorded startling stories. James Swan lived with the Makah tribe in 1864, near the tip of the Olympic Peninsula in what was then the Washington Territory. He wrote in his diary that a tribal leader told of a sea flood in the "not very remote" past that covered all but the highest ground. The flood left canoes in trees, killed many people, and dispersed canoes full of survivors—some of whom later founded new tribes elsewhere. During the flood, ocean waves took a five-mile shortcut across the tip of the Olympic Peninsula, from the Pacific Ocean to Neah Bay on the Strait of Juan de Fuca, leaving Cape Flattery temporarily as an island.

A plank longhouse at the Ridgefield Wildlife Refuge 20 miles north of Portland resembles Chinook buildings seen by Lewis and Clark.

Forty miles south on Washington's Pacific coast, a story told for generations by the Quileute and Hoh tribes recounts that "there was a shaking, jumping up, and trembling of the earth beneath, and a rolling up of the great waters."

Such stories were widely considered legend, rather than history, until the early 1990s, when Brian Atwater's discovery of tsunami evidence from 1700 spurred researchers to take a second look at the old tales. Ruth Ludwin, a seismologist at the University of Washington, was particularly intrigued by the legend of Thunderbird and Whale, a story told in slightly varying forms by tribes from Vancouver Island to Tillamook.

In the legend, Whale is an evil god who eats other whales, leaving coastal tribes without meat or oil. Meanwhile a good god named Thunderbird notices that the people are starving. Thunderbird lifts Whale out of the ocean and flies with him to his mountain aerie, where they battle. Unfortunately the struggle launches a devastating storm that includes "a shaking, jumping up and trembling of the earth beneath, and a rolling up of the great waters," according to a Quileute version of the story recorded in 1934. A Tillamook version, recorded in Oregon 1898, says the battle ended up "violently shaking the mountain, so that it was impossible to stand upon it."

It's easy to see such tales as cultural memories of a great earthquake and tsunami. In one tribe's version of the story, Thunderbird has to return to the ocean to battle Whale's son, Subbus. That struggle creates what seismologists today would call an earthquake aftershock and a secondary seismic sea wave.

Some of the old stories include surprisingly vivid details. On Vancouver Island, the Cowichan tribe says the earth shook so long that people cowered on the ground and felt sick. Plank longhouses collapsed and hillsides slid loose. Old people pounded the ground with stone axes, trying to make the shaking stop. When the water started rising, people ran for their canoes. Some families laid planks between two canoes so they could pile their belongings on board. Those who survived anchored their canoes to a large stone.

A few of the tales blame the whole disaster on disobedient or disrespectful tribal members. In one version, elders warn that misbehavior could cause the ground to shake from east to west. The shaking would make beach sand so loose that people would have trouble walking.

The central hearth of a longhouse was a stage for retelling history and legend.

In a Makah story, a violent earthquake strikes at night. The elders urge young people to flee to high ground. Those who heed the advice spend a cold night shivering in the woods. They return in the morning to find their villages swept away, including all the young people who didn't take the elders' advice.

One of the tales attributes a positive side effect to the tsunami. The Yuroks on the northern California coast rely on estuaries and tidal marshes for clamming and fishing. A tribal legend says the coastal lowlands were originally dry land. One day Thunder and Earthquake were strolling this prairie, musing that the ocean really ought to come farther inland. Earthquake said, "It will be easy for me to do that, to sink this prairie." He stomped the ground as they walked along, pushing down the land. "The earth would quake and quake again and quake again," according to the legend, "and the water was flowing all over."

The closer researchers looked at the Northwest Coast, the more evidence they found of tragedy: Abandoned villages. Campfire pits buried by tsunami debris. Fishing weirs dropped below the waves by earth-

A tsunami launched by the Alaskan earthquake in 1964 proved deadly in Oregon.

quakes. Tales of death and destruction.

The ghost forest of stumps on the beach was just one of many overlooked clues to the Northwest Coast's violent past.

True Stories from a Dark Night in 1964

At first Monte McKenzie was glad he had brought his wife and four kids to the Oregon Coast for spring vacation. It was March 29, 1964, and the family from Tacoma, Washington had spent a wonderful day building forts in the driftwood at Beverly Beach State Park, a few miles north of Newport.

The day had been so sunny and warm, and the kids had been so excited about the driftwood lean-to they had built in the dry sand far above the high-tide mark, that the boys begged to be allowed to spend the night in their "beach cabin." Louie, Bobbie, and Rickie, age eight to six, jumped up and down when Monte gave in to their pleading and agreed. His wife and Tammy, their three year old, were less enthused.

The sun had set by the time Monte actually brought the family's sleeping bags down to the beach. A cold wind came out of the twilight. The campfire they built sent sparks and smoke into their log shelter, but failed to chase the chill. Even the "beds" they had scooped out in the soft-looking sand turned out to be rock hard.

Finally they fell asleep to the roar of the ocean, unaware that a massive earthquake had rattled Alaska, four thousand miles away, at 7:37 that evening. For four hours a silent sea wave rolled toward them across the Pacific Ocean.

Just before midnight, Monte awoke to the sound of rain. He wished they had camped in their waterproof tent. He knew the driftwood roof of their lean-to would leak like a sieve. The rain got louder. Surprised that he still couldn't feel any drips, Monte propped himself up on one elbow and peered into the blackness. Then the sound of rain began changing to a weird, growling roar.

Suddenly a wave churned into the shelter, soaking the sleeping bags with cold water. Before Monte could cry out, the foamy wave filled his mouth, lifted him, and slammed him against the log wall. He gasped for air, struggling to get his arms out of the wet sleeping bag.

Trapped in the bag, suffocating in the seawater, lost in the darkness, Monte had never experienced such a hellish nightmare. For five interminable minutes the cold, sandy water roiled about the shelter, bumping logs, debris, and bodies in a maelstrom that rose to within a foot of the log roof. Monte and his wife managed to prop themselves against the walls, barely standing tall enough to breathe.

And then, as suddenly as it had come, the water drained away.

Still gagging, Monte stripped away his sleeping bag. He felt about the dark shelter and found a single wet form. "Honey?"

"The kids," she managed to say. "Find the kids."

Monte ran outside, barefoot in his pajamas. By starlight, he could make out a limp shape on the wet, smooth sand. It was Ricky, their six year old.

The boy was dead.

Monte searched for Bobbie, Louie, and little Tammy, but the ocean had taken the rest of the children away without a trace.

Oregon had little warning of the 1964 tsunami. No one in Oregon had felt this particular earthquake, although a few Portland houseboat owners noticed their boats bobbing oddly. Besides, no perceptible tsunami had struck Oregon in all of recorded history. It also made sense that a tsunami from an earthquake in Alaska would hit British Columbia first. Coastal communities in Canada had not reported any unusual waves.

Clatsop County Sheriff Carl Bondietti must have sighed when federal officials issued a routine alert at 10 pm, saying a tsunami might follow the Alaska quake. The feds had cried wolf before, with two false alarms

The Necanicum River in Seaside in 1917. Because this inland part of the city is actually lower than the oceanfront Promenade, the surge of a tsunami is strongest here, cutting off escape routes to Highway 101.

in the past six months. Still, Carl eventually headed his patrol car toward Cannon Beach, just in case. By 11:15 pm he was almost there when his car radio crackled to life with alarming news that a wave really *was* coming. Somehow the tsunami had had little effect in Canada, but it had already swamped Neah Bay in Washington—the same bay where James Swan had recorded the Makahs' tsunami legend in 1864.

Carl had fifteen minutes to evacuate more than a thousand people from Cannon Beach!

Carl hit the gas. He squealed into the driveway of Cannon Beach fire chief Del McCoy, jumped out, and pounded on the front door. Del stepped outside, and in Carl's words, "all hell broke loose."

Seaside's oceanfront Promenade in 1917.

A wall of water and debris surged down the street toward them. By the time the two men managed to reach the downtown fire station, water stood three feet deep and the city's power was out, rendering the sirens useless. Telephones were dead. Logs had smashed the Elk Creek bridge, closing the Beach Loop road.

Meanwhile in Seaside, the wave smacked against the Promenade's seawall at 11:30 pm, but failed to crest over the Turnaround. As if frustrated by this rebuff, the seismic wave surged up the Necanicum River to attack the city from behind. Rising eight feet atop a high tide, the Necanicum swept over the bridges between downtown and Highway 101, destroying the Fourth Avenue bridge, closing the Avenue G Bridge, and damaging three others.

Adjacent Neawanna Creek went berserk. The normally sluggish slough surged backwards, smashing the windows of a nine-bedroom house owned by retired Navy captain Charles Jackson. Water poured in six feet deep, overturning a piano. The captain's two teenage sons fled upstairs. Outside, the family's car tumbled into the creek. When the backwards Neeawanna reached the Venice Trailer Park it floated an empty 50-foot mobile home, ramming it against other trailers. Neighbors startled by the collision awoke to find six inches of water in their bedrooms.

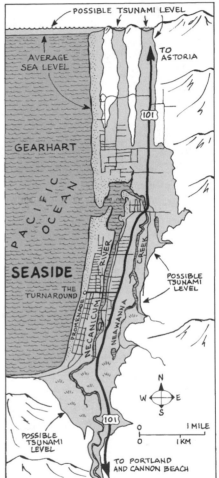

A major tsunami would submerge virtually all of Seaside and Gearhart, according to tsunami hazard maps from 1995.

At the same time the seismic wave was slowly spreading south down the Oregon Coast. In Lincoln City, the wave rolled into the D River (billed as the world's shortest river) and surged across Devils Lake, wrecking boats at the state park docks.

At Depoe Bay (the world's smallest harbor), the wave poured in over the breakwater and raised the entire bay 14 feet, scattering docks and boats.

At Beverly Beach, the McKenzie children drowned in their sleeping bags. Despite an extensive search, only one would be found.

At Florence the wave backed up the Siuslaw River 16 feet high, knocking out power and telephone lines, floating riverside trailers, and tearing boats loose from their moorings.

At Sunset Bay State Park west of Coos Bay, Mrs. Leland Stanley of Eugene was in her pickup camper when she heard what sounded like thunder outside. The wave picked up her camper and dropped it onto a picnic table, leaving her rattled but unharmed.

The 1964 tsunami tossed cars against homes in Seaside.

Even with a death toll of five—the four McKenzie children and a Seaside woman who died of a heart attack—the disaster in Oregon couldn't match the devastation in Crescent City, a city of 3000 just south of the Oregon border. There the wedge-shaped coastline funneled the tsunami into a low-lying business district, killing eleven people and battering 29 downtown blocks with more than $25 million in damage. The water scattered cars like toys, swept wooden buildings off their foundations, and hurled logs through the city.

Two of the dead in Crescent City were children. One unidentified woman was found dead in the wreckage of a motel. Eight people tried to escape their swamped house in a rowboat, but it capsized and all but one of them drowned.

Peggy Sullivan, a pregnant 31-year-old woman living in a south Crescent City motel with her 9-year-old son and 3-year-old daughter, heard from the television news at midnight that the danger was past. She was wary, though, so she went to bed with her clothes on. A roar awakened her an hour later. She looked out the window and saw water. By the time she could grab her two children and get outside, the water was two feet deep. She ran with her kids across Highway 101. "I looked back and saw cabins floating right behind us, turning and crashing together," she later told a reporter.

Twice the waves knocked Peggy underwater. She lost her grip on the older boy. Finally a wave washed her against a car. Surrounded by floating logs, she managed to cling to the car's door handle.

"I was screaming for help. I just knew my son was gone." Miraculously, Peggy and her two children were reunited without serious injury when the water retreated.

The tsunami's first wave had passed. But three more major surges followed, spaced roughly half an hour apart. Because the tide was falling, the additional waves didn't cause much trouble in Oregon. In Crescent, City, however, the fourth tsunami wave was the biggest.

"When it came, buildings just seemed to disappear," mayor William Peepe recalled. Boats from the harbor wound up on the shore, and cars wound up in the harbor.

The wave snapped powerlines, starting an electrical fire at a car dealership. The fire spread next door to a Texaco storage yard with five 10,000-gallon oil tanks. At 3:30 am, the tanks exploded.

"Several fires started and came together, burning out six or seven blocks," the mayor said. Black smoke curled into the sky for days. "South of Crescent City on Highway 101, nothing is left at all—not that you could recognize."

In 1964 the Northwest coast learned what a tsunami can do. But people still didn't understand that a much, much larger tsunami was coming.

When the Sea Returns

Daniel Cox makes waves at Oregon State University. Not only does he generate miniature tsunamis in a swimming pool-sized tank, but as director of the Hinsdale Wave Research Laboratory, his research is also making waves in the scientific world and the popular media.

When Cox unleashed a replica of a major tsunami on a scale model of Seaside in his 50-yard-long tank in 2007, thousands of Oregonians watched on television as the flood roared house-deep through the streets. It didn't take much imagination to picture the cars and people that would be swept away. For a virtual tour of the tsunami lab and the Seaside model, click on *www.nacse.org/%7emoorchr/vwrl/*.

Wave research at OSU dates from 1972, when the Hinsdale lab opened a Large Wave Flume to study the effects of waves on jetties, oil drilling platforms, and the like. That tank is twelve feet wide, 15 feet deep, and as long as a football field. When the lab added the $5.4 million tsunami tank in 2003, skeptics grumbled that a high-tech swimming pool full of sensors must be part of some government boondoggle.

Two authentic disasters silenced the doubters. A December, 2004 earthquake off the coast of Indonesia launched a tsunami that killed nearly a quarter million people on the Indian Ocean rim. Then in August of 2005 a tsunami-like storm surge from Hurricane Katrina inundated New Orleans, killing 1700 people on America's Gulf Coast.

"We no longer had to justify our existence," Cox recalls. In 2008, an additional $1.1 million grant from the National Science Foundation funded a piston-driven wave maker for the tank. The largest such device in the nation, the new piston more accurately reproduces the very long, sheet-like waves of storm surges and large tsunamis.

The goal of Cox's research is simple — to save lives. The process is more complicated. Cox creates precise, repeatable waves that help with computer simulations of tsunamis. Planners then use the results to improve building designs and adjust evacuation plans.

Like many Oregon researchers in his field, Cox worries specifically about the gigantic earthquake and tsunami that will hit our shore when the Cascadia subduction zone ruptures. Modeling the tsunami's impact is only the first step. An even bigger challenge is spreading the word. Many people still don't understand the scale of the danger. Even more don't know what to do.

What should you do if you're at the coast when the Big One hits?

If you're at the coast, you should expect a tsunami after you feel an earthquake with 20 seconds or more of strong ground shaking, according to the State of Oregon Department of Geology and Mineral Industries. The threat is particularly serious if the shaking is so strong that it's hard to stand up.

Even if there are no sirens, you should immediately head inland to high ground — on foot. If there is no high ground nearby, climb the stairs of a large, well-built steel or concrete building. Cars are not likely to be useful for your escape because bridges will be damaged and people will be crowding the roads. Cars caught in the tsunami are likely to be crushed by debris and submerged in the flood. In short, an automobile is one of the worst possible places to be when the tsunami arrives.

At first the ocean may rise somewhat, especially if the quake has lowered the ground level. Then the water will briefly withdraw. The first tsunami wave crest should strike the Oregon Coast 14 to 30 minutes after the earthquake. Additional wave surges can arrive every five to 40 minutes for as much as eight or ten hours. In some places, waves arriving during the second or third hour after the earthquake may be the largest.

In Seaside, Long Beach, and other low-lying areas where there is no high ground nearby, the safest place to evacuate is to the second or third story of a solid building. Wood-frame buildings will splinter, collapse, or float. Well-engineered, reinforced concrete or steel buildings should withstand the wave but will quickly fill with water. If you are on a lower floor, you may find yourself trapped against a ceiling.

Those who are swept away, particularly as the tsunami surge withdraws, might cling to floating objects. But because the retreating wave is likely to suck them far out to sea, and because the water along the Oregon Coast is so cold, people hanging onto floating debris may well die of

---

The 2004 Tsunami that Circled the Globe

The Indonesian quake of December 26, 2004 measured 9.3 on the Richter scale. In moments the quake released more energy than the United States uses in a month. It launched the deadliest tsunami since 1883, when Indonesia's volcanic island of Krakatau exploded, creating a sea wave that killed 36,000.

Like the subduction earthquakes that rock Oregon, the Indonesian temblor was caused by shifting plates of the earth's crust. Along the west shore of Indonesia, the Indian seafloor plate lurched beneath the Burmese continental plate supporting Thailand and Malaysia. The quake lifted a 740-mile stretch of seafloor 42 feet. The resulting tsunami killed a total of 230,000 people in eleven coun-

The 2004 tsunami surged ashore at Ao Nang, Thailand.

tries. Tourist videos of the tsunami's effects can be viewed at *www.asian-tsunami-videos.com.*

Satellite measurements show the tsunami waves stood only 20 inches above the average sea level in the open ocean, followed by a trough 16 inches below the norm. When the wave reached shore, it slowed from 500 to 20 miles per hour and crested briefly in breakers 33 feet tall.

Some of the waves circled the globe. Stations in Antarctica, Brazil, and Mexico recorded waves up to 3 feet high. A full day after the earthquake, waves from the tsunami arrived at Canada's Atlantic shore. More than 15,000 miles from their epicenter, the waves were no longer obvious to casual observers, but gauges in Halifax showed the sea level slowly rose and fell 18 inches at one-hour intervals as each crest passed.

hypothermia before they are rescued.

A 1995 study found that public buildings on the Oregon Coast were woefully unprepared for this scale of disaster. Of the 117 schools examined, 64 were likely to collapse in a major earthquake. An additional 22 schools would probably be hit by the ensuing tsunami. Ten of the coast's 13 hospitals would be damaged or flooded beyond use. In many communities, all of the emergency response resources would be wiped out, including police, fire, and communications centers. Although oil tanks and chemical dumps might survive the initial earthquake, 48 of 56 hazardous sites examined in the study were in tsunami inundation zones. Flood damage at these sites could contaminate the coast's ground and water for years.

Tsunami warning signs are a visible part of the Oregon Coast's disaster preparations.

After this alarming report, tsunami warning signs were put up along the Oregon Coast, identifying evacuation routes to high ground. Communities began gradually retrofitting or moving schools, fire stations, and 9-1-1 call centers away from the danger zone.

Tsunami warning alert systems have also been improving. The country's first Tsunami Warning Center was established after a 1946 earthquake off the Aleutian island of Unimak. That quake launched a wave that destroyed an Alaskan lighthouse an hour later, killing the lighthouse's entire staff. Scientists realized that a warning system could have saved lives. The government built a warning center in Alaska, and another later in Hawaii. For years the warning system was slow. From 1980 to 2000, the average time it took to issue a tsunami alert was eleven minutes. Since then, improvements have reduced that time to just two minutes.

One of the improvements has been to mount pressure sensors on the ocean floor. The pressure of an ordinary surf wave dissipates in the ocean a few hundred feet down. But the waves of a tsunami are so long that they increase pressure all the way to the seafloor. The National Oceanic and Atmospheric Administration (NOAA) has installed six sensors in the Pacific Ocean, from two and a half to four miles deep. Called *tsunameters,* the sensors are not affected by ordinary waves, but when they register a tsunami they send signals to a surface buoy that relays the information by satellite to the stations in Alaska and Hawaii. The tsunameters allowed scientists to call off a November, 2003 alert issued after an undersea quake measuring 7.8 on the Richter scale struck near the Aleutian Islands. The seafloor sensors showed the resulting sea pressure was so small that tsunamis would not be a threat.

The Indian Ocean tsunami of 2004, with its shocking death toll of nearly a quarter million, prompted Congress to authorize an additional $125 million in 2006 to strengthen the tsunami warning system. Representative Jay Inslee of Bainbridge Island introduced the bill, noting, "The Cascadia subduction zone is the evil twin of the Indonesian fault zone." The extra funding paid for coastal alert systems, evacuation plans, and additional buoys along the Atlantic and Pacific coasts. The new buoys are capable of measuring a rise in ocean level as small as a tenth of an inch.

A 1960 tsunami surprised many in Hilo, Hawaii, despite warning sirens.

Will people evacuate when they hear the tsunami alert sirens? A survey after the May 23, 1960 tsunami in Hilo, Hawaii found that only 41 percent of the adults in the hazard zone who heard the sirens actually moved to high ground. Most of those who stayed behind said they thought the sirens were a preliminary signal (35 percent). A few didn't know what the sirens meant (4 percent). Others thought the sirens were warning about some different danger (17 percent), or else they knew what the sirens meant and simply ignored them (3 percent).

Consider that these disturbing survey results are from Hawaii, an area frequently hit by tsunamis. Also consider that the 1960 Hawaiian tsunami was caused by an earthquake in Chile, so the people of Hilo had *ten hours* of warning. Four hours before the wave struck, the sirens blared for 20 minutes. Despite all this advance notice, when the tsunami finally arrived in Hilo, 61 people died and hundreds were injured.

Will people on the Oregon Coast take tsunami warnings more seriously? The modern siren station in Cannon Beach has 16 loudspeakers with a range of nearly half a mile. Solar-charged batteries power the installation, so it won't be out of service when commercial power fails, as happened in the 1964 tsunami. Nonetheless, if the results from Hilo are any measure, about 59 percent of the population of Cannon Beach may ignore or misinterpret the warning. In Cannon Beach alone, nearly 4000 people might stay in the hazard zone. Hundreds would die.

There are other hints that some Oregonians may ignore the warning. The siren signal for a tsunami is a steady three-minute blast. Complaints about frequent, noisy drills on the Oregon Coast have caused some communities to turn off the wailing sirens. Instead the speakers broadcast pleasant-sounding doorbell chimes, emitting the mellow gongs of Westminster bells during tsunami evacuation drills.

Although the Emergency Alert System (formerly the Emergency Broadcast System) regularly tests radio coverage, the actual warnings during these drills are sent only to officials, mostly via pagers, fax, and email. In short, the drills don't practice public evacuation so much as they check that the message could get through when the time comes.

"It doesn't fully test the system," a meteorologist for the National Weather Service admits, "but it's as good as we can get without causing panic."

In Japan, a country with a thousand-year tradition of dealing with tsunamis, evacuations are practiced in order to *reduce* panic. The alerts use multiple warning systems. Sirens wail in cities, ancient bells ring in villages, sound trucks blare warnings in rural areas, radios relay bulletins, and television stations run subtitles or windows on TV screens. During

Hundreds of homes surround Siletz Bay. But like all Oregon estuaries, it is a drowned river mouth, repeatedly lowered by earthquakes and filled with tsunami debris.

Despite warnings and tsunami hazard maps, prices remain high for homes in endangered areas, as here on Salishan's low sand peninsula near Lincoln City.

Japanese tsunami alerts, more than half of the at-risk population evacuates to safe ground within five minutes, even when the warning comes in the middle of the night.

When tsunamis strike Japan, less than 20 percent of the population in hazard zones dies. In western Indonesia, where evacuation drills were not practiced, up to 60 percent of the coastal population died in the 2004 tsunami. Obviously, public awareness matters.

Oregon geologists prepared the first tentative maps to show the extent of the tsunami hazard on Oregon's Coast in 1995, responding to a new Oregon law limiting construction of police and fire stations in tsunami zones. These early maps mainly identified areas below an elevation of about 20 feet. Even this quick appraisal drew alarming conclusions. Virtually all of Seaside, with a population of 5860, would be underwater. Most of Gearhart, Rockaway Beach, and Pacific City lie in harm's way, as do huge swaths of Lincoln City, Waldport, Coos Bay, and other coastal towns.

Since then, researchers have calculated that high tides, storm winds, channeling, and ground shifts could push the tsunami's surge much higher than first predicted. As we learn more, the hazard maps are being redrawn. A worst-case scenario map released for Cannon Beach in 2008, for example, doubled the danger zone, putting the city's recently built fire station at risk after all. The state Department of Geology and Mineral Industry's Web site at *www.oregongeology.com* provides the latest maps, precaution tips, and evacuation brochures.

The model of Seaside that Daniel Cox built in his tsunami tank looked a lot like a giant Monopoly game board. Stylized yellow houses and boxy blue hotels lined the streets like toys. But the model is not intended for play. When Cox's wave machine sent water splashing through the model town in 2007, real, live officials from the city of Seaside asked to be on hand to see the results for themselves.

Increasingly, those who love the Oregon Coast are realizing that this is not a game where a bad throw of the dice could send a car-shaped token to Jail. When the tsunami comes, thousands of lives will be in peril.

CHAPTER III

Earthquakes

"RISK OF EARTHQUAKES IN OREGON VERY LOW," a headline reassured readers of the *Oregonian's* Science section in 1983. The state seemed marvelously immune to the calamities that regularly rattle our

neighbors in California. But just six months later, after geologists realized the danger posed by the Cascadia subduction zone, a sobering *Oregonian* headline admitted, "Research finds powerful earthquake possible in NW."

Since then we've jolted to the top of the list of the country's earthquake hazard zones. We've even been slapped by a few disturbing temblors, including one that very nearly felled the State Capitol's dome. Despite all of this, most Oregonians still haven't taken basic precautions to make their homes safer, and only schoolchildren seem to know what steps to take when the floor starts dancing.

Earthquake damage to highway surfaces is typically not as severe as to bridges.

The Big Ones

The biggest quakes to rock the planet occur when continents crunch forward across the ocean floor. As we saw in the previous chapter, the problem with these subduction zones is that the contact line is often

Once thought immune to major earthquakes, Oregon is now high on the hazard list. Loose sand and fill dirt amplify an earthquake's motion. This can be particularly damaging for older brick or concrete structures like Newport's 1936 Yaquina Bay Bridge, built on sand.

sticky, so the continent jerks forward with a big earthquake every 300 to 600 years.

How big are subduction earthquakes? The handiest measuring stick is a scale named for American seismologist Charles Richter. Each higher number on the Richter scale represents a 32-fold increase in the energy released. This means that the 9.3 subduction earthquake off Indonesia in 2004, for example, was 32 times more powerful than the famous San Francisco earthquake of 1906, a local slip of the San Andreas fault that rated 8.3. Quakes measuring 2.0 are the smallest that can normally be felt by humans. Quakes of 4.0 can cause moderate damage in populated areas, while 6.0 quakes can cause severe damage and 8.0 quakes can cause tremendous damage in populated areas.

The next subduction earthquake to strike Oregon is likely to measure about 9.0 on the Richter scale. That would make it about *half a million times* more powerful than the 5.6 Spring Break Quake that nearly destroyed the State Capitol dome in Salem in 1993.

Although the Richter scale has no upper limit, the largest earthquake in recorded history is the 9.5 subduction quake that struck Chile in 1960.

How big was that? If you add up all the earthquakes on the planet for the entire century after San Francisco's 1906 quake, the Chilean quake accounts for nearly a quarter of the total energy released. That's a lot.

Strange things happen when the earth shakes this hard. One of the oddest things is that the ground can liquefy. If you vibrate sand or loose soil hard enough it becomes quicksand. Beaches, fill dirt, and river sediment turn to goo. Concrete bridge pillars sink like torpedoed ships. Buried sewer pipes bob up like emerging submarines. Gas pipelines bend and burst. The ground itself puddles up or squirts out in fountains.

Brian Atwater, the geologist who realized that the ghost forests on the Northwest's coast had been dropped into the sea by a giant earthquake, also went looking for places where earthquakes had liquefied the soil. All along the lower Columbia River he found deposits of sand and mud that had squirted out on January 26, 1700.

Giant earthquakes have another side effect that is just as strange. For years scientists puzzled about the low mounds of dirt that dot valley floors of western Oregon and Washington. Spaced about 50 feet apart and perhaps a foot tall, the mounds cover the prairie near Centralia like giant goosebumps. Similar mounds cover the plateau of the Tom McCall nature preserve along the old Columbia River Highway west of Hood River.

Scientists speculated that these bizarre mounds might have been created by ancient civilizations, by gigantic extinct gophers, or by hexagonal cracks in melting glaciers. Now it appears that subduction earthquakes

Geologists believe giant earthquakes shook the ground rhythmically, creating strange mounds that pimple the plateau of the Tom McCall Preserve west of Hood River.

made the mounds. The ground shook so violently that it rippled the soil together into polka dots, just as flour on a cookie sheet dances into patterns if you vibrate the pan.

Yet another feature of large earthquakes is that they reverberate strongest through loose soils—the same dangerous areas that can turn to quicksand. Fill dirt on estuaries and flood plains wiggles like Jell-O, amplifying the shaking.

For an example of this kind of amplification, look at San Francisco. In the late 1800s, buildable real estate in hilly San Francisco was so costly that developers cut down hills, dumped them into the bay, and built entire city districts on loose fill dirt. Most of the buildings in these areas collapsed in 1906 because the fill amplified the earthquake. That same part of San Francisco suffered major damage in the 1989 Loma Prieta earthquake when the Marina District turned to quicksand once again. Newscasts showed apartment buildings that had sunk to their third story.

Many of the Northwest's buildings, highways, bridges, and airports have been built on similarly unstable fill. Geologists have been busy mapping the danger zones. The results show that entire districts of our cities have been built on land resembling trampolines. Still, the cost of moving or retrofitting old structures is so high that little has been done.

For a sample of what might happen when the Big One hits Oregon, let's take a look at other subduction earthquakes that have struck the Americas recently—Chile in 1960, Alaska in 1964, and Mexico City in 1985.

Valdivia, Chile: May 22, 1960. The biggest earthquake in recorded history, tipping the Richter scale at 9.5, followed the same pattern as our own Cascadia subduction quakes. Like Oregon, Chile is also crunching westward into the Pacific, gulping chunks of seafloor every few centuries. Along the way the continent's edge rumbles into a mountain range—the Andes between Chile and Argentina. As in Oregon, the seafloor rock eventually is dragged down deep enough that it melts. Then it burps back up as a string of volcanoes about a hundred miles inland.

Fewer than 6000 people died in the Chilean quake of 1960, partly because it struck on a Sunday afternoon when most people were outside their homes. It also helped that some traditions had survived from previous subduction earthquakes. Although the previous event struck Chile 385 years earlier in 1575, people were still cautious about building on low land near the sea, a hunch that proved wise.

The 1960 earthquake shattered Valdivia, a city of 113,000. Valdivia is near the coast about 450 miles south of Chile's capital, Santiago. Moments after the quake struck, the ocean at Valdivia's port of Corral rose twelve feet. Then the water receded. An hour later a tsunami 25 feet deep surged inland, followed ten minutes later by a wave 30 feet tall. A few miles north, the coastal town of Tolten disappeared. The waves washed ships in

the Valdivia River a mile back and forth, and then sank them. Houses that were swept into the river sometimes stayed afloat longer . than the ships.

The quake crumbled Spanish colonial forts that had stood for centuries. The entire coastline dropped, flooding low land permanently, creating estuaries, and deepening rivers. Water and liquefied soil squirted out of the

The 1964 Alaska earthquake crumbled land at Turnagain Heights, Anchorage.

earth. Thousands of people cowered in churches, which seemed to withstand the wrath of nature better than the military forts. Two days later the nearby Cordon Caulle volcano erupted, shaken awake by the jolt.

Prince William Sound, Alaska: March 27, 1964. Just before dinnertime on Good Friday, a subduction earthquake measuring 9.2 shook Anchorage. During the next three minutes, a piece of Alaska the size of Oregon jerked upwards as much as 35 feet, permanently stranding docks and beaches. Meanwhile, a similar-sized area in the western part of the state dropped as much as eight feet.

Most schools and many commercial buildings in downtown Anchorage were ruined. Cracks opened in the snowy streets. The entire residential district of Turnagain Heights crumbled like a broken cookie, wrecking 75 houses. The loose soil under the luxury subdivision fragmented into a seething jumble of chunks, pitch-

A slump opened up past L Street in Anchorage during the 1964 earthquake.

ing wood-frame houses around like peach crates.

The quake's epicenter was in Prince William Sound, 75 miles east of Anchorage and about 55 miles west of Valdez. After the quake, the people of Valdez evacuated their damaged city, which then caught fire and burned to the ground.

In Seward, the quake launched a landslide that dropped half a mile of shoreline into Resurrection Bay. Water sloshed hundreds of feet up the bay's opposite shore. Then, a few minutes later, the tsunami from the main earthquake arrived to further devastate the waterfront.

Tilted house in Anchorage near L Street after the 1964 earthquake.

Fifteen people died in the Good Friday earthquake. Another 110 Alaskans died in the tsunami, with an additional five victims in Oregon and eleven in California.

Mexico City, Mexico: September 19, 1985. This subduction earthquake shouldn't have killed 9000 people. It certainly shouldn't have left 100,000 homeless in Mexico City. After all, the quake measured 8.1 on the Richter scale, substantially less than the quakes in Chile and Alaska. What's more, this epicenter was out in the Pacific Ocean, more than 200 miles from the Mexican capital.

Toppled control tower at Anchorage airport after the 1964 earthquake.

But Mexico City is built on a drained lake. The Aztecs had originally founded their capital on a swampy island in Lake Texcoco, partly for defensive reasons and partly because they had seen an eagle eating a snake on a cactus there—an omen that seemed promising at the time. After the Spanish conquered the city by marching up a causeway with cannons, the lake was eventually filled in and covered with a metropolis of 20 million people.

The 1985 earthquake made the ancient lakebed reverberate like the skin of a timpani drum. The shaking lasted three or four minutes, amplified by the loose soil. The ground liquefied in places, sinking foundations and tipping buildings. Three 28-story skyscrapers and the Continental Hilton crumbled. All three of the city's largest hospitals collapsed, crushing 1200 people. Downed powerlines sparked fires. Broken sewer lines

Earthquake Dancers of the Northwest

Native Northwest tribes have traditions that show how important earthquakes have been in their history. At traditional ceremonies of coastal tribes, earthquake dancers don masks and whirl bull-roarers to imitate the sound of a quake. The audience watches from a tippy plank bench that allows dancers to dump them on the ground.

For the Nuu-chah-nulth (Nootka) of Vancouver Island, the dance tells the story of supernatural mountain dwarfs who live in caves. The dwarfs lure the unwary into their caves and encourage them to join in a dance around a big wooden drum. If the visitor is

Tsunamis and earthquakes play important roles in native Northwest culture.

clumsy enough to touch the drum with his foot, he contracts a dread affliction known as "earthquake foot." Every time the victim steps on the ground, he causes an earthquake.

According to the legend, no one who suffers from the earthquake disease lives very long.

created a public health disaster for months.

Since then, stricter building codes have made new buildings in Mexico City more likely to withstand a major quake. Nonetheless, two basic problems remain—the city is near a subduction zone, and it's built on a lakefloor that ripples like a waterbed.

The Deep Earthquakes

Subduction earthquakes are the largest temblors on the planet, but two other, smaller types of earthquakes also shake Oregon—deep quakes and local quakes. All three varieties are caused by the collision of North America with the Pacific Ocean's seafloor plates. That collision creates a lot of stress, and the stress works itself out in different ways.

Deep "intraplate" earthquakes can be almost as large as the gigantic subduction temblors. Two of these deep quakes have rocked the Pacific Northwest in living memory—in 1949 and 2001. Centered 32 miles beneath Puget Sound, the quakes ranked 7.1 and 6.8 on the Richter scale. The 1949 quake was the deadliest in the Northwest's recorded history,

An April 13, 1949 earthquake shook bricks loose in Seattle.

and the 2001 quake was the costliest. Both did most of their damage in Washington, but shook Oregon too.

Intraplate earthquakes earn their name because they occur underneath the North American plate, and not out in the ocean where separate plates are colliding. As we've seen, the Juan de Fuca seafloor plate is being overridden by the continent, ramming all that oceanic rock deep down underneath North America. By the time this slab of Pacific seafloor gets underneath Puget Sound it starts breaking up, cooked by the Earth's inner fires. The resulting intraplate or "slab" earthquakes aren't as big as subduction quakes, and they aren't as sharp as local earthquakes in faults nearer to the surface, but their distinctive rolling motion can be felt at great distances.

Our two most recent intraplate earthquakes were centered just north of Olympia, Washington. They could just as easily have been centered under the Willamette Valley. Geologists cannot map these troublesome fault zones with precision because they are simply too far underground.

Let's take a look at the results of Washington's two intraplate quakes to get an idea of what they can do.

Puget Sound, Washington: April 13, 1949. Measuring 7.1 on the Richter scale, this quake set Seattle's 42-story Smith tower swaying "like a pendulum," according to panicked office workers. Chimneys collapsed in Oregon beach cottages, elevators jammed in Portland, and brick buildings crumbled in Olympia. The next morning, the *Oregonian* declared the earthquake "by far the worst in the recorded annals of the Northwest."

Centered 90 miles southwest of Seattle, the quake killed eight people and caused $15 million of damage. A 23-ton section of the uncompleted Tacoma Narrows bridge fell from a construction tower and smashed through a barge. At the Boeing aircraft factory, where 15,000 workers were busy assembling $100 million worth of B-50 bombers for the Cold War, one man said the giant planes were "flapping their wings like seagulls."

A brick wall collapsed in downtown Centralia, burying 70-year-old Mark Kuveric. When workers uncovered him that afternoon, they found his constant companion—a small dog—had died by his side. Only a few bricks fell from the facade of Castle Rock High School, 50 miles north of Portland, but one of them killed the school's 18-year-old student body president, Jack Roller, as he ran out the door.

Injuries in Oregon were minor, and mostly caused by panic. The rumble of what seemed to be an invisible freight train sent Roland Latford rushing out his own front door, where he tripped and broke his arm. Bertha Twing wrenched her left knee when she became frightened and leapt off the loading dock of a sawdust company.

Elsewhere in Oregon, thousands of glass bottles smashed to the floor of the chemistry laboratory at Reed College's Eliot Hall. Maryetta Devereaux of Gearhart was dismayed to find that the quake had shaken the molded Jell-O out of her kitchen ice box and splattered it on her floor. Mrs. James Somerville marveled that an unseen hand was helping with her chores, mysteriously moving a heavy metal iron back and forth on her ironing board. All across Portland, old-fashioned pendulum clocks stopped short at 11:56 am. At Salem High School, on the other hand, the old tower clock that hadn't worked for months suddenly started up.

Puget Sound, Washington: February 28, 2001. When the most expensive earthquake in Pacific Northwest history rolled into downtown Olympia, Steve Cooper was standing in the doorway of his 1915 building. A three-foot-tall swell rippled toward him, lifting sidewalks and buildings as it came. The swell hit Steve's building with a cracking, booming sound. Tons of decorative stucco rained onto the sidewalk from the building's facade. "You could see everything heave," Steve later told a reporter. "It was like a bomb going off."

When the rumbling hit the Washington State Capitol building, governor Gary Locke halted a meeting and fled outside. Pillars supporting the Capitol dome developed frightening cracks. Government offices later looked as if they had been trashed by vandals.

In Seattle, Bill Gates calmly decided he wasn't really going to give his prepared speech in the Westin Hotel's grand ballroom, where chandeliers were swaying and falling. Gates' audience ran for the exits.

Elsewhere in Seattle, 30 people were trapped in the Space Needle for two and a half hours. The 1962 landmark had been designed to survive an earthquake by swaying, so it gave the visitors a wild ride.

Meanwhile, officials evacuated the corporate headquarters of Starbucks after its brick facade collapsed onto the street. Starbucks had bought the four-story 1916 building in 1993 and had spent millions on a remodel, including an earthquake retrofit in 1996.

The main runway at the Sea-Tac airport dropped a foot, forcing planes to an auxiliary strip.

Power failed for 300,000 homes in Washington.

In Oregon, people felt the quake from The Dalles to Coos Bay. Portland's 43-story Bancorp Building swayed 20 inches to either side.

The 6.8-magnitude earthquake injured a total of 400 people — most of them in Washington — and caused a staggering $2 billion in damage. The toll would have been higher if the epicenter hadn't been so deep. Intraplate quakes release a lot of power, but because they're 30 miles or more beneath the surface, the damage is spread out.

The third kind of earthquake in Oregon — after massive subduction quakes and deep intraplate earthquakes — are local quakes. Although local quakes are smaller and much closer to the surface, they're much sharper and just as dangerous.

Oregon's Other Faults

A map of Oregon's earthquake-prone fault lines looks like a broken windsheld. The collision of the North American plate with the Pacific's Juan de Fuca plate has shattered the continent's rock. The entire state is being stretched diagonally as North America strains toward the southwest.

Although subduction earthquakes and intraplate quakes score higher on the Richter scale, these smaller fractures are also building up stress.

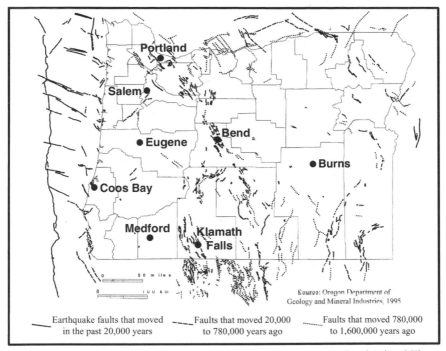

Earthquake faults that moved in the past 20,000 years	Faults that moved 20,000 to 780,000 years ago	Faults that moved 780,000 to 1,600,000 years ago

Source: Oregon Department of Geology and Mineral Industries, 1995

Some of the most recently active earthquake zones in Oregon are near Portland and Klamath Falls. The large fault line in the Pacific Ocean is the Cascadia subduction zone.

Because some of the shallow faults lie directly beneath cities, they can cause a lot of damage when they let loose.

Portland is on some of the shakiest ground. The Portland Hills rise above the city as straight and steep as a wall. During excavations for the MAX light rail tunnels in 1996, geologists found that the hills are not merely rising along a fault line—they're sliding to the northwest. We've long known that Southern California is slipping northwest along the San Andreas fault. Now it seems our Coast Range is heading in the same direction. A quick glance at the map shows that the Columbia River jogs north around the Portland Hills. The river once ran due west to the sea. The Coast Range has been migrating north, and the Portland Hills have shoved the river north along the way.

You're likely to find a local earthquake hot spot wherever you see an abrupt, straight-edged ridge like the Portland Hills. Look around and you'll see that Oregon has a lot of these ominous, fresh-looking hills, notably at Klamath Falls, Silverton, Bend, La Grande, Baker City, Steens Mountain, and Lakeview.

Historic quakes of the Pacific Northwest

Every day Oregon shivers with earthquakes. Most are so small that they can be registered only by seismographs. About once a year, however, a temblor is jarring enough that a lot of people feel it. Here are some of the largest in the region's history.

January 26, **1700**: off Pacitic Northwest coast, magnitude **9.0**
1872: North Cascades, Washington, magnitude **7.4**
November 23, **1873**: off Southern Oregon coast, magnitude **6.8**
October 12, **1877**: Portland, magnitude **6.7**
February 4, **1892**: Portland, magnitude **5.6**
March 7, **1893**: Umatilla, magnitude **5.7**
April 18, **1906**: San Francisco, magnitude **8.3** (3000 dead, $374 million damage)
May 13, **1916**: Richland, Washington, magnitude **5.7**
July 16, **1936**: Milton-Freewater, magnitude **5.8** ($100,000 damage)
December 29, **1941**: Portland, magnitude **5.6**
May 12, **1942**: Corvallis, magnitude **5.0**
April 13, **1949**: Olympia, Washington, magnitude **7.1** (8 dead, $15 million damage)
December 16, **1953**: Portland, magnitude **5.6**
August 18, **1961**: northwest Oregon, magnitude **4.5**
November 5, **1962**: Portland, magnitude **5.2**
March 7, **1963**: Salem, magnitude **4.6**
March 28, **1964**: Alaska, magnitude **9.2** (140 dead, $311 million damage)
April 29, **1965**: Renton, Washington, magnitude **6.5** (7 dead, $50 million damage)
May-July, **1968**: Adel, east of Lakeview, up to magnitude **5.1**
April 12, **1976**: Maupin, south of The Dalles, magnitude **4.8**
May 18, **1980**: Mt. St. Helens, magnitude **5.1** (triggered eruption)
November 8, **1980**: off Oregon Coast, magnitude **7.0**
February 13, **1981**: Mt. St. Helens, magnitude **5.5**
November 3, **1981**: off Oregon Coast, magnitude **6.2**
November 22, **1981**: off Oregon Coast, magnitude **5.7**
March 13, **1985**: off Oregon Coast, magnitude **6.1**
July 12, **1991**: off Oregon Coast, magnitude **6.6**
March 25, **1993**: Scotts Mills, east of Woodburn, magnitude **5.6** ($30 million damage)
September 20, **1993**: Klamath Falls, magnitude **5.9** and **6.0** (2 dead, $10 million damage)
December 4, **1993**: Klamath Falls, magnitude **5.1** (aftershock)
January 28, **1995**: Seattle, magnitude **5.0**
May 2, **1996**: Duvall, Washington, magnitude **5.4**
July 2, **1999**: Satsop, Washington, magnitude **5.9**
February 28, **2001**: Puget Sound, magnitude **6.8** (400 injured, $2 billion damage

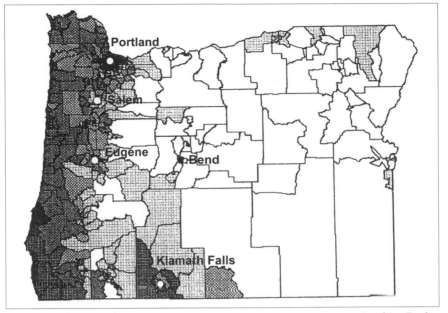

An earthquake probability map of Oregon shows the least dangerous areas in white. Darker shading represents increasingly dangerous parts of the state. (Source: Oregon Department of Geology and Mineral Industries)

For the first century of Oregon's recorded history the quakes from these local faults were fairly small, lulling Oregonians into a false sense of security. A jarring wake-up call came in 1993. Here's the chronology:

Portland: November 5, 1962. When the earth shook in the Portland area, one indignant woman called the *Oregonian* to ask why they hadn't printed an advance warning. With a magnitude of just 5.2, the temblor lasted only a few seconds, but it managed to knock groceries from shelves in the Cedar Hills shopping center. Plate glass windows shattered in downtown Vancouver. No one was hurt. Everyone agreed that earthquakes weren't much of a problem in Oregon.

Off the southern Oregon Coast: November 8, 1980. Elizabeth Kempin wondered, "Am I dreaming?" She sat up in bed in her Grants Pass area home. It was 2:28 in the morning, and the glass lid of her candy dish was rattling.

A hundred miles to the south the earthquake was hitting much harder. A family driving Highway 101 near Eureka, California, sailed into a black void where an overpass had collapsed. A pickup truck behind them sailed off too, smashed into their car, and sent all five to the hospital. The pickup driver was treated and released. The quake did not cause any other injuries.

Although this 7.0 earthquake was the most powerful to strike the lower 48 states since 1959, it did relatively little damage because it was centered offshore and impacted a mostly rural stretch of coastline.

Scotts Mills, east of Woodburn: March 5, 1993. Ricky Bowers balanced a cup of coffee on the dashboard of his 1989 Hyundai. It was 5:34 in the morning and he was on his usual red-eye commute from the Willamette Valley village of Amity to his construction job in Portland, just keeping pace with the cars ahead at 55 miles per hour.

Ricky thought he knew the Highway 18 bypass around McMinnville by heart. But then he saw something he didn't recognize. An odd, thin shadow had suddenly appeared across the road in the middle of the Yamhill River bridge.

Before Ricky could hit the brakes a tremendous jolt sent him flying forward out of his seat. The seat belt strained across his chest, stopping his head just short of the windshield. Hot coffee flew everywhere.

What had he hit?

His car was airborne, arcing upwards. When the Hyundai slammed back onto the pavement, all four tires blew out. The chassis screeched and spewed sparks. The car slewed out of control, leaving black smoke and the stench of burning rubber. A hundred yards later, the car finally stopped.

The oil pan had been sheared off onto the pavement. The frame had been dragged six inches out of shape.

Ricky banged open his door, shaken and still unclear what had happened. The drivers behind must have wondered too. The first two cars managed to slow enough that they only blew out one tire apiece when they hit the mysterious gray line on the bridge.

By then Ricky was flagging down traffic. A heavy truck was coming, and if it weighed down the bridge, he was afraid everything might collapse into the river. Locking up the brakes, the truck screeched to a stop just 20 feet short of the bridge.

The truck driver got out, as bewildered as everyone else, and joined the others examining the strange gray line. Somehow an entire section of the bridge had dropped six and a half inches, exposing the end of a concrete slab.

Ricky had hit the speed bump from hell.

Only when the state police arrived did Ricky learn that he had driven through an earthquake. A rocking motion had shaken one of the bridge's spans off its mounts. The span's girders had fallen onto a concrete pier. Ricky's car had plowed into a low concrete wall. Miraculously, he had walked away with just a sore shoulder.

The "Spring Break Quake" of 1993 shook a million Oregonians awake that Thursday morning. Most people felt the shaking for 15 seconds, but seismograph needles wobbled three times that long. The local Mount Angel fault line that slipped is not marked by a sharp ridge like the Portland Hills fault. Instead it runs beneath the floor of the Willamette Valley from Woodburn southeast to the little village of Scotts Mills, the quake's epicenter.

Ruth Schnider of Silverton told the *Oregonian*, "It woke me with a big roar. My grandson and I popped out of bed at the same time. We watched the walls. The walls looked like big ribbons. All four of them were tilting into the room."

Although the quake rated just 5.3 on the Richter scale, it rattled a heavily populated area, so it racked up an impressive $30 million in damage.

The rotunda of the 1937 State Capitol cracked. The impressive, marble-faced dome would have collapsed entirely if the quake had lasted another eight to ten seconds, according to a subsequent computer simulation. The 23-foot, 10-ton gold Oregon Pioneer statue atop the dome wobbled, twisted an eighth of an inch and cracked its base. Multi-million-dollar repairs later patched cracks in the rotunda murals, anchored the gold pioneer statue, and reinforced the brick inner structure of the dome with steel bands.

Built of brick with a marble veneer, the Capitol rotunda in Salem cracked and nearly collapsed in the 1993 quake.

In Mount Angel the earthquake nearly tipped over the 200-foot-tall bell tower of St. Mary's Catholic church. The 1912 church's brick walls were so badly cracked that engineers initially thought they would have to be razed. Stained glass windows shattered, organ pipes jackstrawed, plaster rained from the ceiling, and a statue of St. Benedict turned in place, facing left instead of right.

Damage from the 1993 quake was lighter in Portland. At Washington Park a zookeeper reported that the chimpanzees began barking in alarm seconds before the quake. "It's a very loud, shrill, 'Wah.' It means something's wrong." The attendant said an adult male orangutan also seemed distressed, but added, "We gave him some Maalox, and that seemed to help."

After the 1993 quake, the Highway 18 bridge over the Yamhill River required repair, but inspections revealed that the state's 7000 other bridges were undamaged. Other than Ricky Bowers' sore shoulder, the only injuries to people were minor cuts from broken glass.

Two weeks before the Spring Break Quake, geologists had announced that faults in the Portland Hills were capable of generating earthquakes measuring 7.0 on Richter scale. If those faults had ruptured instead of the

---

Did you feel the Spring Break Quake?

More than a million people in northwest Oregon felt the March 5, 1993 earthquake. Damage reports poured in from a wide area between Portland and Salem:

• The brick facade of the 68-year-old Molalla High School collapsed. The school's 600 students were never allowed to return to the building after spring vacation. Officials decided to tear it down and rebuild from scratch.

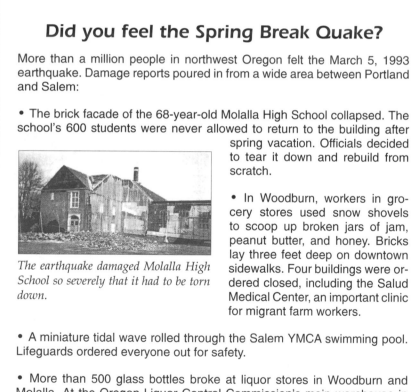

The earthquake damaged Molalla High School so severely that it had to be torn down.

• In Woodburn, workers in grocery stores used snow shovels to scoop up broken jars of jam, peanut butter, and honey. Bricks lay three feet deep on downtown sidewalks. Four buildings were ordered closed, including the Salud Medical Center, an important clinic for migrant farm workers.

• A miniature tidal wave rolled through the Salem YMCA swimming pool. Lifeguards ordered everyone out for safety.

• More than 500 glass bottles broke at liquor stores in Woodburn and Molalla. At the Oregon Liquor Control Commission's main warehouse in Milwaukie, however, officials reassured the public that all 2,498,944 bottles stored there were safe.

Mount Angel fault, the earthquake would have been centered directly under Portland, and could have been a thousand times more powerful.

Klamath Falls: September 20, 1993. Phyllis Campbell had first met her husband Ken when they were growing up in Lebanon, Oregon. Now they lived in Phoenix, Arizona, but they liked to vacation in Oregon each summer to visit old friends and to escape Arizona's hottest weather. At 59, Ken was already planning his retirement. He figured he would have time to restore classic cars and make wooden toys for their grandchildren.

The Campbells' 1993 summer vacation started out terrific. They had joined some high school chums on a cruise up the Inside Passage to Alaska. Then they had driven to Newport to see the Oregon Coast Aquarium, and they had stopped in Sisters to visit more friends. It was Monday by the time they left Sisters. They decided there wasn't time to swing through Crater Lake National Park on the way home. Besides, they had done that last year. So they steered their pickup straight south on Highway 97, looking forward to the room they had reserved at a bed & breakfast in Klamath Falls.

Night was falling by the time they got their first view of Upper Klamath Lake — a vast, dark blue sheet, speckled with the silhouettes of ducks and pelicans. It was just that time of evening when Phyllis worried about hitting a deer. The danger seemed especially high at Modoc Point, where the highway squeezes between the lake and the steep face of sharp ridge.

Suddenly, at 8:29 pm, there was a flash of light. A moment later another flash lit up the whole sky. Phyllis assumed it must be lightning. In fact an earthquake had struck, disrupting Klamath County's power supply. An electrical surge was blowing up transformer fuses on power poles beside the road.

Next a loud *crack!* startled them both. Ken just had time to shout "No!" before the windshield smashed inward. His side of the pickup cab crumpled, and the truck spun out of control.

When the truck stopped, Phyllis still didn't know what had hit them. Ken had been killed instantly, but she had been miraculously spared. Her only injury was a scratch on her thumb.

Phyllis unbuckled her seat belt and tried for a while to unbuckle Ken's. Then she realized the engine was still racing. The whole truck could go up in flames at any moment. She tried to get out, but the door was jammed and the power windows wouldn't work. Next she tried to turn off the car, but when she turned the key the whole ignition unit came out in her hand.

The engine was still running when a man pried open the door and helped her outside.

Phyllis stood on the road, dazed and disoriented. A 14-foot boulder had broken loose from the cliffs of Modoc Point and crushed her husband. She had lived. Why?

"We don't understand God's reasoning," Phyllis later told an Associated Press reporter. "We just have to trust what he puts in our way."

Meanwhile, 15 miles south in Klamath Falls, the magnitude 5.9 earthquake had toppled brick facades, shattered storefront windows, and sent dinner guests stampeding out of restaurants. At the office of the Klamath Falls *Herald and News*, the news staff held an emergency conference at 9 pm. The police radio was saying there'd been a fatality at Modoc Point. A man named Kenneth Campbell had been killed by a falling rock. Reporters Ashley Conklin and Todd Kepple were sent north on Highway 97 to check it out.

As a sports reporter, Ashley Conklin wasn't used to covering stories about dead people. She worried about what they might find. When a police roadblock stopped them short of the accident scene at Modoc Point, she had to admit she was a little relieved. She could simply interview the men at the roadblock to get the story. She was still taking notes at 10:46 pm when a second, equally large earthquake rocked the ground.

A few minutes later a pickup squealed up to the roadblock. A man jumped out and asked if anyone knew CPR. His 82-year-old grandmother was terrified of earthquakes. She had moved here from California to escape them. He thought she might have suffered a heart attack.

Both Ashley and Todd had taken first aid courses in resuscitation. They quickly took down the address and drove out to help. They found Anna Horton slumped on the porch of her small rural home, with her distraught son Ray by her side.

Ray had been trying to calm his elderly mother ever since the first earthquake hit at 8:29 pm. She had no history of heart illness, but when the second quake struck, panic had simply stopped her heart.

Todd took the lead, restarting her heart by thumping her chest. He continued for ten minutes, trying to keep her alive. Ashley had never been so scared. She kept track of a feeble pulse in the elderly woman's wrist. But when Ashley looked into the woman's cold blue eyes, she knew the emptiness of death was taking hold. The earthquake had claimed its second victim.

The two earthquakes Monday evening ranked 5.9 and 6.0 on the Richter scale. The quakes destroyed eight houses and damaged 85. Property losses totaled $10 million.

Sixty refugees in Klamath Falls spent the night in the Mazama High School cafeteria. Despite freezing weather, another 40 refugees were so afraid of buildings that they camped in a tent city erected by the National Guard on the school football field. Dozens of aftershocks were powerful enough to be felt, and seismographs recorded hundreds more.

Out-of-town media crews began arriving in Klamath Falls within hours. A KGW-TV team flew in from Portland at midnight. By Tuesday morning, camera crews from Medford, Seattle, San Francisco, and Los Angeles were prowling through downtown, obviously disappointed by the shortage of debris. They interviewed passersby. They interviewed each other. One cameraman even objected when workers began cleaning bricks off the sidewalk before he could film the damage.

Aftershocks continued to rattle Klamath Falls for months, including a 5.0 quake on December 4.

Although the initial Klamath Falls earthquakes came just six months after the Spring Break Quake in the Willamette Valley, geologists believe the timing was coincidental. Oregon is riddled with local fault lines. These shallow faults mostly slip on their own schedules, with 500 years or more between major quakes. The problem is that our recorded history only goes back two centuries, so we have no idea which fault will let loose next.

Are You Ready to Rock?

Once Oregon was thought to be immune to earthquakes. Today we know that we have them in three different flavors—devastating subduction earthquakes like the 1700 catastrophe, deep intraplate earthquakes like the Puget Sound temblors of 1949 and 2001, and sharp local jolts like the Spring Break Quake of 1993.

Despite all of this knowledge, we're not much better at predicting earthquakes than before. Mystics who foresee ground movement from the bubbles in hot springs or the antics of animals do not have a reliable track record. Scientific papers have suggested that land may sink slightly in the decades before a great subduction earthquake, but even this is vague and controversial.

To date, the best we can do is to map probabilities. The probability maps drawn by geologists show that the closer you live to the Oregon Coast, the more likely you are to experience a big earthquake. Portland and Klamath Falls also fall into the high risk category. Parts of eastern

Oregon look pretty good, but no place is completely safe.

How prepared are we?

Not very. Consider Oregon's school buildings. More than half of them could collapse in a major earthquake, according to a 2007 report by the Oregon Department of Geology and Mineral Industries. The 190 schools that are most likely to crumble enroll fifteen percent of Oregon's students. Rural schools in Vale, Monument, Scio, Prairie City, and Myrtle Creek were rated as "100 percent likely" to collapse in a big quake. Age is part of the problem. The median age of Oregon school buildings is 46 years.

In other words, if the nostalgic brick schoolhouse in your neighbor-hood has not been reinforced, it could be a death trap for children. To make schools safe, districts have been adding reinforced concrete walls inside, bolting metal bars that hold the ceiling to the walls, and bracing hallways so students can get out when the shaking begins.

If our schools are shaky, what about our other buildings? Most of the high-rise buildings in downtown Portland and Seattle were built after earthquake codes took effect in 1976, but even these buildings remain vul-nerable to sustained earthquakes. Subduction earthquakes often continue for three minutes. That could make tall buildings sway until they fail.

In Eugene, a 1999 engineering study examined 40 downtown build-ings considered at risk. The study assumed that a subduction earthquake

Newport's 1936 Yaquina Bay Bridge is one of many coastal bridges unlikely to survive a subduction earthquake, complicating relief efforts for victims of the ensuing tsunami.

measuring 9 on the Richter scale might have an effect in Eugene measuring about 7. At that scale, the report concluded that of the 28 commercial buildings studied, five would have extensive damage and an additional two—both made of unreinforced brick—would be completely destroyed. Even steel buildings are at risk. Of the 14 steel buildings studied in downtown Eugene, two would suffer extensive damage. One of Eugene's most dangerous buildings is City Hall, built in 1964 atop concrete pillars. In an earthquake, the entire structure would tilt off its pillars onto the parking level beneath it, crushing the city's police car fleet.

The good news is that most houses in Oregon are framed with wood, and wood-frame houses hold up well in earthquakes.

Brick buildings are dangerous unless reinforced. Falling bricks cause most earthquake-related deaths in the Northwest.

Imagine a wooden crate on a waterbed. Even if you jump on the bed, the crate rolls with the waves. So your wood-frame house may be OK. What you're more likely to lose are chimneys, foundations, windows, concrete block walls, and brick facades.

Almost every year, building codes are toughened to keep pace with what we are learning about Oregon's earthquake dangers. Unfortunately, insurance companies are changing their earthquake policies just as fast. Many companies no longer offer earthquake insurance in Oregon at all. Those that do generally exclude anything built before 1976—unless you hire independent earthquake consultants and pay for the retrofits they

Built in 1964 before earthquake building codes were introduced in Oregon, Eugene's City Hall is one of many public buildings vulnerable to collapse.

recommend. Expect massive retrofits and high premiums if you've built with brick.

Even if you succeed in getting an earthquake policy, the deductible will be a staggering ten to twenty percent of the building's value. In other

What to do when the ground shakes

Before the quake

Brace freestanding chimneys. Secure bookcases to the wall. Use sticky putty or fishing line to secure china, glassware, and other objects on high shelves. Make sure you have fire extinguishers. Collect emergency supplies, including canned foods, flashlights, bottled water, a first aid kit, and a portable radio with extra batteries. Know where the shutoff valves are for gas, electricity, and water. Plan where the family should reunite in case you're separated.

When the quake hits

If you're indoors, get under a desk or table, but stay clear of windows. Don't stand in a doorway, a dangerous strategy that was endorsed years ago. If you're outside, stay away from power lines, brick walls, trees, and buildings. School-children in Oregon have been taught to "drop, cover, and hold" when they feel an earthquake. It's good advice.

Afterwards

Salem's First Methodist Church may be one of many historic brick structures to collapse.

Check people for injuries and stay indoors. Check for the smell of leaking gas or the sound of running water. Turn off the stove and don't use the fireplace. Listen to radio reports and be prepared for aftershocks.

words, if your house is worth $300,000, you can expect to pay for the first $30,000 to 60,000 in earthquake damage out of your own pocket, no matter what. Not surprisingly, most Oregonians don't have earthquake insurance.

With or without insurance, it's important to take some basic precautions to keep people safe and reduce damage. This is particularly true if you live or work in a building atop sand, fill dirt, or valley floor sediment, all of which amplify the shaking of an earthquake.

Most of the people who have died recently in Northwest earthquakes have been struck by falling brick. If you have a freestanding chimney, brace it to the roof by bolting two pipes at angles to the top. If your building has walls or facades made of brick or concrete block, consider reinforcing them with steel. Ask an engineer for advice.

Most injuries inside buildings result when heavy objects or glassware are thrown off shelves. Walk around your house, looking at your shelves. Televisions, china, books, vases, clocks, statues—all of these can become projectiles during an earthquake. If you're going to leave such potential weapons on high shelves, tie them in place with fishing line. If you like to have china or glassware on display, simply get some sticky craft putty (available at craft stores), put a dab on the bottom of each piece, and stick them to the shelf. For a couple of dollars and ten minutes' work, you will have prevented your heirloom stemware from turning into dangerous, flying shards.

Bookcases are particularly hazardous because they can tip over in an earthquake, crushing children and pets. Secure the tops of bookcases to the wall with wire. Another good method is to screw a piece of plumber's strap (a metal strip with holes) from the top shelf to the wall.

Meanwhile, don't underestimate the risk of fire. In San Francisco's 1906 quake, fire caused far more damage than the earthquake itself. This is often true with large earthquakes because gas and water lines can rupture. Then a single spark will ignite the gas and there won't be any water to put out the resulting blaze. Don't expect fire insurance to help, either. If the blaze that burns down your home was caused by an earthquake, ordinary fire insurance won't pay you a dime for the loss. So keep fire extinguishers handy, and make sure everyone in your building knows where the extinguishers are.

Most of these earthquake safety rules, along with the additional tips in the boxed insert on page 70, are already well known to Californians. People in that state know about the San Andreas Fault and expect earthquakes. Oregonians, however, are not yet as aware of our earthquake history. We have a lot of catching up to do if we hope to be prepared when the ground starts shaking.

CHAPTER IV

Volcanoes

Even casual visitors to Oregon are told that Mt. Mazama blew up long ago to create Crater Lake. But most descriptions of Mt. Mazama overlook the human cost of that eruption—the hundreds of people who were incinerated when a blast of hot gas and ash roared through Indian villages 7700 years ago.

It's easy to dismiss Mt. Mazama as ancient history because Oregon has not had a single volcanic eruption since becoming a state.

Neither had Washington until 1980.

Perhaps it's no wonder that so many people ignored warnings in order to get a close look at Mt. St. Helens on May 18 of that year. To be sure, sensors revealed that the mountain's north face was bulging a meter a day. But geologist David Johnston saw no reason to leave his observation post just seven miles away.

Oregon's deadliest eruption destroyed Mt. Mazama and killed hundreds of people. The caldera is now filled by Crater Lake.

And then the top third of Mt. St. Helens suddenly slumped toward David's outpost. The peak looked as if it were casually shrugging off its entire head. A superheated cloud of ash billowed toward him at a seemingly impossible speed.

Today, with data from satellites, we know that two of Oregon's volcanoes—South Sister and Newberry Crater—are bulging. Magma is rising beneath Oregon. Swarms of earthquakes are stirring under Mt. Hood.

Our volcanoes are very much alive.

Mount Mazama

When humans first arrived in Oregon, Mt. Hood was not our tallest peak. At 12,000 feet, Mt. Mazama in southern Oregon stood half a head higher than Hood. Mt. Mazama was about the size of Mt. Adams, but a little broader. Like other major Cascade summits, Mazama was a composite volcano — a mishmash of jumbled lava and cinder layers. Handsomely bedecked with glaciers, Mazama didn't look like a killer.

Even the best-looking volcanoes get cranky when silica turns their magma stiff and sticky. Silica is the same stuff you'll find in window glass or beach sand. Given half a chance, silica rises to the top of a magma reservoir, stiffening the lava and making it more likely to clog volcanic vents. This happens a lot because silica is relatively light.

Not all silica-rich magma is violent. Sometimes it squeezes out in toothpaste fashion. Then, if it cools fast enough, it becomes obsidian, a shiny black glass. But when a vent gets clogged and pressure builds, the silica fills with gas bubbles. Then the silica blasts out as volcanic ash — tiny, abrasive shards of glass that darken the sky. Larger chunks of silica become pumice, a rock so madly frothed that it floats.

According to a Klamath legend, Crater Lake was the home of an evil god named Llao.

Mt. Mazama had been pumping out the usual lava and cinders for about 100,000 years before it started showing signs of more dangerous behavior. About 12,000 years ago, massive flows of a stiff, silica-rich lava called dacite oozed out of its flanks. The gooey flows filled glacial valleys with 1000 feet of gray rock, draining magma from the volcano's interior. By the time of the dacite eruptions, fireworks probably weren't shooting from the summit anymore. Instead, cinder cones began erupting from a broad arc of vents on the mountain's northern slope — the same circular crack that later became the caldera rim.

These volcanic tantrums may well have inspired a legend told by the Klamath tribe. According to the legend, Mt. Mazama was inhabited by an evil god named Llao. This demon demanded that he be allowed to marry the tribe's most beautiful maiden. When she gave him the cold shoulder, Llao blew his top. Quite literally, he detonated his mountain in a fit of revenge, hoping to kill every Klamath man, woman, and child with a rain of fiery rock.

The ensuing holocaust nearly succeeded in wiping out the tribe.

Imagine that you had been near Mt. Mazama on that dreadful day, picking huckleberries on Union Peak. From that one particularly lucky vantage point, a dozen miles southwest and upwind of the volcano, you might have survived to watch the whole show.

Judging from the similarly earth-shaking performance of Krakatau, a volcano that erased an entire Indonesian island from the map in 1883, we suspect that Mt. Mazama's destruction was a drama in three acts.

Settle into your seat at Union Peak. Here's Mazama's playscript.

In **Act One,** a clogged vent on Mt. Mazama's northeastern flank suddenly explodes, uncorking the volcano with a deafening boom. A

Union Peak, an extinct volcanic plug twelve miles southwest of Crater Lake, had a front-row seat for Mt. Mazama's blast.

mushroom cloud of pumice, ash, and rock boils 45,000 feet into the sky. Lightning crackles from hellish black clouds.

This act goes on all day, blasting twelve cubic miles of rock out of the mountain. You're pretty badly shaken on Union Peak, and probably running low on huckleberries, but things are much worse downwind.

From the summit of Union Peak, Crater Lake's rim now appears as a jagged horizon.

Ten feet of fiery rock is falling on Klamath Marsh, twenty miles to the east. Each projectile hits the lake with a sizzle. According to the Klamath legend, the only people to survive jump into the water and breathe through reeds.

Because of the northeast wind, the future sites of Seattle and Reno escape with just a few inches of ash, but Pendleton is buried by a full foot of grit. Even Saskatchewan is dusted with half an inch. Directly upwind on Union Peak, however, you're miraculously OK.

Act Two begins when the mountain starts to run out of steam. The initial blast has not only hollowed out the volcano, but has also fractured the surface with a gigantic, five-mile-wide spiderweb of cracks. The biggest crack circles the mountain, tracing the arc of vents on the northern flank.

Then the entire summit of Mt. Mazama slowly crumbles straight down into the emptied magma chamber.

The ground shakes and the earth roars as the mountain falls. At the same time, a fiery ring of ash starts jetting up from the perimeter of the five-mile-wide chasm. For a breathtaking moment

Mt. Mazama emptied its magma chamber from a side vent (1), emitted lahars as it collapsed (2), widened and flattened the caldera floor with steam explosions (3), filled with water, and then erupted Wizard Island (4).

this colossal crown is beautiful beyond words — as red as the glow of an exploding star, as symmetrical as the splash of a rock in a pond.

Next the superheated ash spills down the mountain's flanks. From where you are standing, it looks as if a witch's cauldron has overflowed. In all directions, glowing avalanches are racing down the slopes at 70 miles an hour, incinerating trees and animals in their path.

What you are watching is a lahar, a volcano's deadliest weapon. *Lahar* is the Indonesian word for lava, but geologists use the term for the glowing avalanches unleashed by volcanic blasts. A famous lahar from Italy's Mt. Ve-

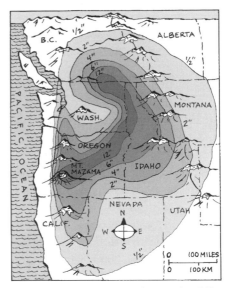

Ashfall from Mt. Mazama's eruption fell a foot deep in Pendleton and half an inch deep as far away as Saskatchewan.

suvius destroyed the Roman city of Pompeii in 79 AD, killing thousands of people. Hot ash buried the inhabitants of Pompei so quickly that they were caught forever in their final poses. Now excavated, the casts left by bodies reveal men clutching togas to their mouths, women sheltering children, and surprised people cowering against walls.

Because you are cowering on top of Union Peak, however, you have some time to watch the lahar's fiery tongue streak toward you. The deadly avalanche is roaring along at more than a mile a minute, swallowing everything in its path. It's still three miles away when it splits in two. One branch curves to the west, careening down the Rogue River canyon twenty miles to engulf Indian

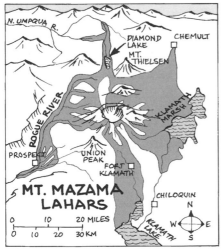

Deadly avalanches of glowing ash (lahars) raced down Mt. Mazama's slopes to Diamond Lake and the future sites of Prospect, Chemult, and Fort Klamath.

hunting camps near Prospect. The lahar's other branch turns southeast, toward the villages at Klamath Lake.

Elsewhere around the ruin of Mt. Mazama, similar lahars are fanning eastward to Klamath Marsh and Chemult. A lahar to the north has rolled across Diamond Lake and is rampaging ten miles down the North Umpqua River canyon.

When the curtain falls on Act Two, the only life visible from your lookout is a dusty stand of trees below and behind Union Peak.

In comparison, **Act Three** is so long and dull that you leave. The exhausted volcano steams for years. Occasionally there's a rumble as rockslides widen the caldera from five miles to six. Ground water seeping into the caldera sets off minor explosions, each with a boom and a plume. Eventually you discover that other people have survived too. One of them explains the eruption as the revenge of Llao—a story that will be remembered more than 7000 years.

The taboos surrounding this spirit-infested mountain became so strict that only shamans and power seekers dared to visit it. No one in the Klamath tribe spoke idly of such a place, and they certainly didn't tell white explorers. Maps of Oregon failed to show Crater Lake until 1853, when John Hillman and a group of gold prospectors stumbled upon the brilliant blue pool. The report of their astonishment spread the lake's fame and led to the establishment of Crater Lake National Park in 1902.

Mt. Mazama's climactic blast spewed 12.2 cubic miles of rock, pumice, and ash into the atmosphere. Ice cores from Greenland glaciers show the ash layer distinctly, and narrow the date to about 5677 BC. The blast darkened the skies for up to three years and lowered the average temperature of the northern hemisphere one degree Fahrenheit.

The deadliest part of Mt. Mazama's eruption were the lahars—the glowing ash avalanches. That's pretty typical. Worldwide, lahars are responsible for sixty percent of the fatalities related to volcanic events. The remaining forty percent of volcano victims succumb to disease or starvation long after the eruption. The diseases are caused by the lingering effects of breathing ash and noxious fumes. Volcanic ash particles are sharp shards, like asbestos, and get caught in the lungs. The starvation results when arable regions are laid waste. Excavations show that Mt. Mazama ashfall forced people to abandon parts of Central Oregon for thousands of years.

Ironically, volcanic ash gives a critical boost to soil fertility in the long run. The minerals supplied by volcanic ash are a key reason that Oregon

How long did Crater Lake take to fill?

With a volume of more than four cubic miles, Crater Lake contains more water than all of Oregon's other lakes and reservoirs combined. The 1943-foot-deep lake has no inlet creeks, so how could it possibly have filled?

Wizard Island from The Watchman.

Surprisingly, enough rain and snow fall on Crater Lake that scientists estimate it took less than 740 years to fill. The only reason the caldera doesn't overflow is that the low, northern rim has a layer of permeable rock where water leaks out. The water probably percolates through the ground to Boundary Springs at the head of the Rogue River, although attempts to prove this have failed.

In any case, a 120-foot-wide shelf eroded by waves around Crater Lake's shore shows that the surface level has been pretty much constant for a long time.

has become an agricultural powerhouse. Places without volcanoes, such as Australia, often have such poor soil that they have to import food.

During the first 500 years after Mt. Mazama's collapse, a cubic mile of lava oozed onto the caldera floor, covering the rubble there. Wizard Island popped up during these early years as well, erupting sporadically while the caldera filled with water. The other symmetrial volcanic cone on Crater Lake's floor, 1500-foot-tall Merriam Cone, never saw the light of day. It erupted entirely underwater, and remains 486 feet below the surface. Imagine the boiling water and the vast clouds of steam that must have accompanied that submarine eruption!

There have been no eruptions at Crater Lake for 4800 years. To be sure, hot springs on the lake bottom show there's still fire in the old mountain. But if you're nominating an Oregon peak for the honor of Most Likely To Erupt, you need to look farther north.

Newberry Crater

The Newberry volcano has bulged four inches in the past 70 years — a fact that doesn't seem all that alarming by itself. The 7984-foot volcano is not a showy Cascade snowpeak like Mt. Hood or even Mt. Mazama. It's just a humble-looking, low silhouette on the horizon southeast of Bend. But the swelling suggests a blip of liquid rock is slowly bubbling up from beneath. Although the rate of swelling isn't speedy, it's fast enough to have accounted for the creation of the entire 200-cubic-mile mountain over the past half million years.

On average, the Newberry volcano erupts every 1500 years. It has been 1200 years since the last eruption, so we're about due for a little excitement. Speculators drilled a 3000-foot-deep well on the volcano in 1981. testing the potential for geothermal energy. They hit such hot rock that the drill bit melted. Something hot is down there, and it's coming our way.

Pumice from the Newberry Volcano landed as far away as Idaho. The frothy rock lies deep on the caldera's Pumice Desert.

What's on tap ? It's hard to tell, because Newberry has tried a little of everything.

Most of Newberry's eruptions have been runny lava flows of black basalt. Layer upon layer, they built up the bulk of the 25-mile-wide mountain. By volume, this is Oregon's largest peak, but it's so broad that it's easy to overlook, even when you're driving right by on Highway 97. One of the runny lava rivers spread north to form the Badlands, a jumbled

From Paulina Peak's viewpoint of Newberry Crater, it's easy to visualize how the Big Obsidian Flow oozed down from the caldera rim (at right) toward Paulina Lake (at left).

lava landscape east of Bend. The flow looks very fresh, not much older than the 7700-year-old Mazama ash that dusted the top of it. Even more recent basalt flows from Mt. Newberry's flanks surged about 7000 years ago through the Lava Cast Forest, created Lava River Cave, and briefly dammed the Deschutes River at Benham Falls. At the Lava Cast Forest east of Sunriver, soupy lava flooded a stand of big trees, coating tree trunks. Then the wood burned away, leaving a grove of weird rock tubes.

Violent explosions were once a big part of Mt. Newberry's repertoire. Repeated mega-blasts *a la* Crater Lake blew out a six-mile-wide caldera. Geologists have traced Newberry ash from fifty eruptions across five different states. Chunks of pumice from the most violent blasts landed as far away as Idaho.

Because Mt. Newberry has not collapsed lately, its caldera looks a little more shopworn than Crater Lake's. The rim is forested and less cliffy. A single large lake once filled the hole, but recent cinder cones and obsidian flows have parted the waters, leaving two separate lakes—Paulina Lake and East Lake. Today both have hot springs on their shores, a reminder that Newberry's volcanic coffeepot is still percolating.

Cinder Hill, one of the Newberry volcano's many parasitic cinder cones, overlooks the caldera and East Lake.

Excavations reveal that the popular Paulina Lake Campground, in the midst of this cauldron, has been occupied for at least 9000 years. Some of the first people in Oregon left campfire charcoal, animal bones, and traces of tent poles near the lakeshore here. Interestingly, these summer campers might well be the same folks who wintered 30 miles to the southeast in Fort Rock's cave. That cave yielded the oldest dated artifacts in Oregon— 70 pairs of sagebrush sandals with a radiocarbon age of 9053 years, plus or minus 350 years. Summers are hot at Fort Rock. Like modern Oregonians, the Fort Rock sandal weavers probably headed for the hills when the heat of August hit. And every thousand years or so, the campers who happened to be at Paulina Lake would have been surprised by an eruption.

The latest Newberry eruption, and quite possibly the most recent in all of Oregon, is the Big Obsidian Flow, dating from about 800 AD. The fifth largest obsidian flow in North America, it is now one of the most popular attractions in the Newberry Crater National Volcanic Monument. If you

The Central Pumice Cone (on the horizon behind Paulina Lake) erupted in the middle of Newberry's caldera, dividing its original lake in two.

hike an easy 0.8-mile loop trail, you can climb a metal staircase onto the Big Obisidian Flow, read interpretive signs, and marvel at the banded, glassy rock beside the path.

At the same time that the Big Obsidian Flow was oozing out, Vikings were sailing the Atlantic. Charlemagne was annexing Italy to his empire. And people were camping at Paulina Lake.

The most daring of those campers might have stayed to watch the eruption. After all, the volcano wasn't spewing cinder bombs, darkening the sky with ash, or even shaking the ground very much. Instead, glowing lava was simply squeezing up out of a vent near the caldera rim. The lava kept coming for several months, creeping downhill two miles toward the lakeshore. Today when you drive to the viewpoint atop nearby Paulina Peak, the flow looks like a puddle of chocolate cake batter spilled into the caldera by a clumsy giant.

During the actual eruption, people close enough to the Big Obsidian Flow would have seen a 120-foot wall of rock advancing through the woods. The wall moved at the ponderous pace of about six feet an hour. Cracks in the steaming rock face glowed a dull red. Boulders broke loose from the cliff and tumbled through the forest, smashing trunks. Along the front of the wall, trees bent forward and burst into flame.

The eruption of the Big Obsidian Flow must have been quite a show. Judging from the bulge beneath the Newberry volcano, a sequel is in the works.

What causes Oregon's volcanoes?

Among Oregon volcanoes, Newberry Crater is an outsider. It isn't lined up with the main string of the Cascades and is unlike those lofty snowpeaks in many ways.

The Newberry volcano is fueled by the Brothers fault zone, a collection of east-west cracks that runs across Oregon from Bend to Brothers to Burns. This rift zone has been leaking lava for ten million years. Relatively fresh eruptions dot the map in a long line from east to west. Some of the most visible mementoes include the Jordan Craters lava beds northwest of Jordan Valley, the Diamond Craters lava fields southeast of Burns, Glass Buttes on Highway 20 east of Hampton, and the flows at Newberry Crater.

The Brothers fault zone is yet another result of North America's collision with the seafloor plate underlying the Pacific Ocean. Because that collision is not quite head-on, Oregon is being stretched diagonally. The Brothers fault zone allows the southern half of the state to slide westward

A fresh-looking spatter cone in front of Coffeepot Crater marks one of the lava vents that form a line across Eastern Oregon on the Brothers fault zone from Jordan Valley to Bend.

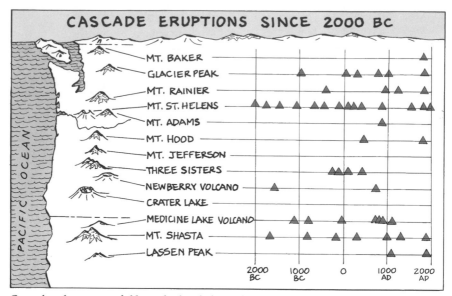

Cascade volcanoes are fed by melted rock that bubbles up as a result of the collision between North America and the Pacific seafloor plates. It's hard to know exactly when or where the next bubble will appear.

faster than the rest. The fault zone also marks the northern limit of the Great Basin. Crustal stretching in the Great Basin is so severe that it has shattered Nevada into a checkerboard of sudden valleys and fault-block mountains. The lava that leaks through cracks like the Brothers fault zone comes mostly from the earth's mantle.

The Cascade Range, on the other hand, is a byproduct of the Cascadia subduction zone off Oregon's shore. Remember how the seafloor plates are being rammed underground as North America crunches westward? All of that seafloor mud, sand, and rock winds up thirty miles or more underneath western Oregon. When the seafloor debris gets deep enough, it melts. Then, because it's lighter and hotter than the crust above it, great blobs of this seafloor material start bubbling upwards. These bubbles reach the surface in a long string about 100 miles inland, where they pop up as the volcanoes of the Cascade Range.

As long as Oregon keeps moving westward, lava will keep bubbling up beneath the Cascades. The range is like a giant pot of porridge, with its burner on simmer. Even geologists can't predict exactly where the next bubble will rise, or when it will pop.

Mount Saint Helens

Although this violent volcano is based in Washington, its fallout has hit Oregon too. Mt. St. Helens awoke with a murmur on March 20, 1980. Only volcanologists were alarmed on that Thursday. The peak shivered with a swarm of minor earthquakes that topped out at 4.8 on the Richter scale. Scientists flocked to the 9677-foot mountain and listened carefully to its pulse. Seismographs revealed that the tremors were coming faster and faster. Finally the shaking merged into one continuous rumble.

The volcano scientists warned that this was not a good symptom. Magma must be moving inside the mountain. Then after six days, the quakes stopped. The volcanologists warned: Watch out.

The symmetrical cone Mt. St. Helens sported before 1980 was actually a recent creation, built entirely since 400 BC.

Many people found it hard to take the warning seriously. Only one person had ever been injured by a volcano in the entire history of the United States. The most recent eruption in the lower 48 was ages ago, when Mt. Lassen burped in 1917.

No one evacuated. No danger zone was designated.

People began paying more attention a day later on March 27, when Mt. St. Helens actually began erupting. A series of explosions blackened snow atop the mountain's scenic, symmetrical cone. A plume of ash rose 11,000 feet from a new summit crater 1700 feet wide and 500 feet deep.

There were no injuries, but Washington Governor Dixie Lee Ray declared a state of emergency. She ordered the evacuation of everyone within ten miles of the mountain, including 50 Forest Service personnel, 320 Weyerhauser forest workers, and everyone in the Spirit Lake area. Highways within 20 miles were closed. The U.S. Army Corps of Engineers began draining nearby reservoirs in case lava flows threatened dams.

One of the volcanologists, David Johnston from the Geological Survey in Menlo Park, California, had been monitoring the mountain at timberline when he heard a boom and saw a cloud rise from the summit. He later told the *Oregonian* that he realized "this is an extremely dangerous place to be. If it were to erupt right now, we would die." Volcanoes are unpredictable, Johnston said. Glowing avalanches could roar down the slopes at 100 miles per hour. "We're standing next to a dynamite keg, and the fuse is lit. We just don't know how long the fuse is."

The Toutle River was still cutting through 1980 avalanche debris in 1991.

Most locals watched this hullabaloo with skepticism. Only one family out of 150 actually evacuated from the Cougar area south of Mt. St. Helens. "We're not going anywhere," Lois Livingston at the Cougar Store told a reporter. "People around here are taking it like a joke."

Moving vans began shuttling the belongings of some Spirit Lake residents out of the danger zone. Meanwhile Harry Truman, the owner of the Spirit Lake Lodge, announced he wasn't leaving. A cantankerous elderly man with 40 cats, Truman told TV camera crews that the whole shebang was a farce. The mountain wasn't dangerous, and he certainly wasn't packing up.

For a few weeks Truman became a national celebrity, a defiant symbol of independence, standing up to denounce yet another government scare.

Meanwhile the mountain simmered and attention flagged. A month later, after warm weather had melted the snowpack, more and more sightseers sneaked past the roadblocks for a close-up look at the volcano.

Mike and Lu Moore of Castle Rock, Washington thought it would be fun to backpack to Fawn Lake, twelve miles north of the volcano. They took along four-year-old Bonnie Lu and baby Terra Dawn, who was still breastfeeding.

In Newberg, motel owner Joyce Kirpatrick was so excited about the volcano that she decided to slip into the restricted zone with her cousin

Harold for a camping trip.

At the same time geologists were mounting metal tripods with little mirrors on the mountain's slopes. By bouncing laser beams off the mirrors, they determined that the volcano's north face was bulging more than three feet a day. David Johnston staffed an observation post directly in front of the bulge to keep an eye on things.

Even for a peak in the geologically youthful Cascade Range, Mt. St. Helens is amazingly young. No rock near the mountain is more than 37,600 years old. When people first arrived in the Oregon Country 13,000 years ago, the mountain may not have been here at all. Everything above timberline is less than 2400 years old. Ash layers excavated throughout eastern Washington prove that this peak has erupted violently at least a dozen times. An eruption in 1400 BC probably destroyed the entire peak, blasting two and a half cubic miles of rock into the air. A map of the volcano's relatively recent mudflows and lahars looks like a tomato hurled against a wall.

The lava flows that created Ape Cave pulsed down Mt. St. Helens' southern slopes in about 100 AD. Mudflows and lahars flooded the slopes from 200 to 350 AD. Ash blew out around 850 AD. A more massive eruption in 1550 AD dammed Spirit Lake and created a Fuji-shaped summit with a big lava dome intrusion.

With this volatile history, it's no wonder that the Klickitat tribe named Mt. St. Helens *Tah-one-lat-clah* ("fire mountain"). The peak's violent past may also have launched the Klickitat legend of Loowit, the demon goddess of Mt. St. Helens.

Loowit was the evil spirit who turned herself into a beautiful maiden and set up camp on the Bridge of the Gods, a dam created across the Columbia River by the Great Spirit to encourage peaceful commerce. Loowit drove the chiefs of the Multnomah and Klickitat tribes mad with jealousy. The ensuing war destroyed the Bridge of the Gods and made the Great Spirit so angry that he turned all the principal characters into mountains. Wy'East, chief of the Multnomahs, became Mt. Hood. The Klickitat chief became Mt. Adams. And the

Ape Cave, North America's longest lava tube at 2.3 miles, was created by lava flows on Mt. St. Helens' south flank in 100 AD.

beautiful but evil Loowit became Mt. St. Helens. The legend suggests that Loowit's beauty is merely a facade. Her violent nature would not stay concealed forever.

When the first white explorers arrived, Indians were still talking about a big eruption of Mt. St. Helens in 1800. A vent on the northwest slope (the location of the later bulge in 1980) had spewed ash twelve feet deep and launched a lava flow below the Toutle Glacier.

Spectacular eruptions from 1835 to 1857 amazed early missionaries and settlers. Mt. St. Helens' white snows turned black. At Fort Vancouver, the ash clouds were so dark that candles had to be lit at midday. Glowing fountains of cinders and lava illuminated the nights. Ash covered the ground as far away as The Dalles. Sources agree that the fireworks weren't coming from the summit itself, but rather from a vent on the northern slope—again, the location of the 1980 bulge.

Spirit Lake in 1991. Indians claimed an evil spirit lived in the lake because small, unfelt earthquakes would send out mysterious waves on still days.

Then nothing happened for 132 years. Although Mt. St. Helens is the most violent volcano in the Cascades, it has routinely been quiet for as much as 500 years at a stretch, waiting for another bubble of magma to surface.

In 1980 the next bubble of magma finally surfaced. A 5.1-magnitude earthquake at 8:32 am on Sunday, May 18, 1980 cracked the bulging volcano along fractures left by earlier vents on the north face, slumping 1314 feet of the summit toward David Johnston's viewpoint. Uncorked by this gigantic landslide, the volcano exploded, suddenly blasting out superheated gas.

David just had time to radio five words to his central office: "Vancouver! Vancouver! This is it!"

A wave of 1300-degree-Fahrenheit gas roared across the hills, incinerating everyhing in its path. In a moment, David and 56 other people near the mountain were dead.

The shock wave from Mt. St. Helens' explosion flattened forests for 17 miles, toppling four billion feet of timber.

Meanwhile the summit landslide rumbled northward and divided into halves.

The eastern half of the avalanche slid into Spirit Lake at 150 miles per hour, burying Harry Truman, his lodge, and his 40 cats under more than 100 feet of debris. The hot avalanche plowed into Spirit Lake. Water sloshed 800 feet up the far shore, leaving a "bathtub ring" that's visible even today. As the water washed back it swept thousands of trees into the boiling lake, creating a logjam of driftwood that still covers much of the surface.

Drift logs from the 1980 eruption may float in Spirit Lake for a century.

Within moments, all life was extinguished in Spirit Lake. Debris raised the lakefloor 295 feet and left a dam that later raised the lake's surface 200 feet.

Meanwhile, the western half of Mt. St. Helens' massive landslide was racing down the Toutle River. On the ridge where David Johnston had just died, the avalanche hit so hard that it surged 600 feet high and slopped over a pass. Nearby, hundreds of feet of debris dammed side valleys that would later fill to form Castle and Coldwater Lakes. Downstream, dozens

Mt. St. Helens in 2005, with its second lava dome steaming.

Who heard Mt. St. Helens?

One of the most puzzling things about Mt. St. Helens' eruption on May 18, 1980, was the sound of its catastrophic blast. People as far as 400 miles away in Montana, Ashland, Newport, Bend, Spokane, and Vancouver B.C. heard earth-shaking booms so clearly that callers jammed emergency phone lines trying to ask what had happened.

Meanwhile, people in Portland heard nothing. Why?

Clara Fairfield, a curator for the Oregon Museum of Science and Industry, was puzzled too. She surveyed people to find out who had heard the blast. Of 1200 respondents, most of those within 100 miles of the volcano had missed the boom altogether. A mysterious zone of silence extended from Albany north to Olympia and from Astoria east to Hood River.

May 18, 1980.

Just beyond that quiet zone, however, the blast was so loud that it shook the ground. On the Oregon Coast and in Central Oregon, people reported three to five booms so loud that birds flew from the trees and cattle stampeded.

Clara later discovered that volcanologists are familiar with this odd phenomenon from other big eruptions. Evidently the blast mostly projected its sound waves upwards. The waves bounced off layers in the atmosphere and then echoed back to earth 150 to 400 miles away. But the sound waves skipped the area near the volcano itself. Because several different layers of the atmosphere reflected the shock wave, people hundreds of miles away heard several loud booms.

of people died when torrents of mud and logs destroyed 200 homes, 27 bridges, and 200 miles of roads and railways. With bridges out, traffic on Interstate 5 was diverted west to Astoria. When mudflows reached the Columbia River, they reduced the channel depth from 40 feet to 14, stranding 31 ocean-going ships in upstream ports.

At the same time, the volcano's gigantic ash plume was drifting east, dumping four inches of white grit on Yakima. The noon sky darkened as if it were night. When a crop-dusting airplane was caught in the ash cloud near Ellensburg, the pilot lost visibility, crashed, and died. Forest fires raged, but fire crews didn't dare fight them. The Portland International Airport canceled flights due to ash. The plume crossed the United States in three days, and circled the earth in 15.

Within hours, 20 helicopters from the Washington National Guard began searching for survivors. Ash was so thick the first day that the choppers couldn't land in the restricted zone. The crews mostly counted bodies. On the second day, an airman spotted a young couple who had miraculously survived. Mike and Lu Moore were struggling with their two small children through a dead forest choked with ash.

The Moores had awakened Sunday morning to a low rumble that shook the ground. Moments later the air pressure fluctuated wildly, popping their ears. Then the sky turned black. Terrified, they fled their tent and broke into an abandoned mining shack. Pumice pummeled the roof. Hot gas roared outside. Ash filled the air. That afternoon they emerged to a moonscape. Unable to reach their car in the deep ash, they spent Sunday night in their tent. On Monday they were trying again to reach their car when a helicopter landed nearby. Three crewmen stayed behind so there would be room in the helicopter for the frightened family.

Mt. St. Helens' 1980 eruption killed 57 people, twelve million fish, and 7000 deer, elk, and bear. Economic damage and cleanup cost $1.1 billion.

In the years since 1980, wildflowers and tree seedlings have reclaimed the pumice plains. Spirit Lake still has a mat of drift logs, but the water

An October 2004 eruption heralded the birth of a second lava dome in Mt. St. Helens' crater. Although that dome-building phase ended in 2007, similar eruptions are likely in the future. (Photo by Randy Wilson)

itself is clearer than ever. Trout were surreptitiously introduced to the lake in the 1990s and have grown to giant size. A National Volcanic Monument protects the volcano and most of its blast zone.

But the public's attention span isn't very long. Tourist enthusiasm has waned. Twenty-seven years after the blast, the park closed two of its interpretive centers for lack of use.

An unstaffed geologic survey camera captured an ash eruption on March 8, 2005.

The shortage of visitors is particularly frustrating for park rangers because the volcano is likely to erupt again soon. A blob of magma rose inside the ruined mountain's crater from 1980 to 1986 to form a 876-foot-tall lava dome. A second lava dome emerged just inside the crater's south wall between 2004 and 2007, quickly pushing up 1400 feet. On March 8, 2005, it sent up a plume of ash and steam 36,000 feet.

Lupine wildflowers pioneered the pumice plains, fixing nitrogen that allowed other plants to grow.

These dome-building eruptions added the equivalent of a pickup truckload of rock to the mountain every few seconds. Although the eruption paused in 2007, it's almost certain to resume before long. Mt. St. Helens may well rebuild its entire Fuji-shaped cone within two centuries.

The threat of another deadly explosion may not be imminent, but Mt. St. Helens is definitely reloading. In the meantime, we ought to be paying attention because Mt. St. Helens is giving us an idea of what might happen to other Cascade volcanoes where trouble is brewing.

Mount Hood

Oregon's tallest peak seems serenely symmetrical from Portland, but the gap-toothed crater visible from Timberline Lodge looks more threatening. In fact, Mt. Hood shares many of the violent traits of its sister, Mt. St. Helens.

Mt. Hood exploded southwards about 1500 years ago, blasting several hundred feet off its summit. As at Mt. St. Helens, lahars of glowing ash raced down the slopes, undoubtedly killing people along the way. Mudflows filled river valleys and clogged the Columbia River channel. On the mountain itself, a massive landslide left a debris fan below a gaping new crater.

One difference between the two volcanoes is that Mt. St. Helens' debris fan is now a restricted area, while the debris fan at Mt. Hood is the site of Timberline Lodge, a ski area packed with tourists year round.

Admittedly, the two volcanoes are not exactly twins. Mt. Hood is much older than Mt. St. Helens, dating back at least half a million years. It's also been a little less violent. The lava at Mt. Hood has never contained enough silica to make it blast out as pumice or ooze out as obsidian.

Lava domes are part of the two mountains' family resemblance. About 13,000 years ago a big lava dome rose high on Mt. Hood's summit. That eruption left a fan of avalanche debris that created the flats at Elk Meadows and the smooth ski slopes at Mt. Hood Meadows. The dome itself remains as Steel Cliff, sliced open by the White River Glacier.

Around 500 AD, an explosion ripped off the mountain's summit and created Timberline Lodge's debris fan. Then a lava dome emerged in the newly formed crater. In 1781 another eruption demolished the old lava dome, blanketed the mountain's slopes with half a foot of ash, and created a new lava dome, now known as Crater Rock.

The 1781 eruption also launched lahars and mudflows. Because there was already a thick debris flow at Timberline Lodge, the new flows were shunted west. They swept down through Paradise Park, creating that area's open, treeless slopes. Then the flows split into two forks. One branch buried Lost Creek. At Lost Creek Campground, a mile-long hiking trail

An explosive eruption blew out Mt. St. Helens' north flank in 1980. Lava domes emerged in 1980 and 1994. *An explosive eruption blew out Mt. Hood's south flank in about 500 AD. The Crater Rock lava dome emerged in 1781.*

Could Mt. Hood explode like Mt. St. Helens? Between 50,000 and 100,000 years ago the peak sent a blast northward that buried the Hood River Valley with 120 feet of avalanche debris and dammed the Columbia River 100 feet deep.

now visits cedar snags that were killed by mud and later exposed by the creek. By counting the rings of similar trees, scientists have pinpointed the date of the eruption to the fall of 1781 or the early winter of 1782.

The other fork of the mudflow filled the Sandy River valley from Ramona Falls to Zigzag. Trees are still struggling back on Old Maid Flat, where a layer of cobbles and mud lies 30 feet deep. The lodgepole pine woods are so sparse at McNeil Campground and along the Ramona Falls trail that hikers can glimpse Mt. Hood between trees.

The eruption's mud flows caught the attention of early explorers. British Captain George Vancouver sent Lieutenant W.E. Broughton up the Columbia River in 1792 to scout the Oregon territory. After naming Mt. Hood for a British naval hero, Broughton marveled that the Sandy River had nearly dammed the Columbia with a sand bar. When Lewis and Clark paddled past in November 1805 they named the present-day Sandy River the Quicksand River. Its valley, they said, was a braided wasteland of debris and dead trees, although they couldn't imagine why.

Native legends could have given Lewis and Clark an explanation for the devastation. The Multnomah tribe said a jealous chief named Wy'east had been turned into Mt. Hood by the Great Spirit. Even as a mountain, Wy'East kept fighting with Mt. Adams over the lovely but treacherous Mt. St. Helens. In his rage, Wy'east hurled hot rocks, poured fire down slopes, filled valleys with debris, and occasionally blew up his own summit.

Geologists today say that accurately summarizes Mt. Hood's arsenal of natural disasters.

The crater area between Mt. Hood's two lava domes (Crater Rock and Steel Cliff) has never completely cooled. A series of fiery eruptions between 1853 and 1865 alarmed pioneer settlers. Newspapers reported that smoke, flames, hot cinders, and blackened snow were visible from Portland. Today, gas fumaroles in the crater still remain hot enough to boil water. Climbers often remark on the smell of sulfur. A curious climber who ventured too close in the 1930s succumbed to the noxious fumes and died.

Mt. Hood might erupt again tomorrow, or it might be quiet for a century. A recent warning came on June 29, 2002, when an earthquake beneath Timberline Lodge measured 4.5 on the Richter scale. Swarms of lesser earthquakes in the past few decades have centered one to three miles beneath Mt. Hood's summit. Other tremors have clustered under the

Mt. Hood from the Timberline Trail just west of Timberline Lodge.

White River Canyon just east of Timberline Lodge. The earthquakes may be caused by rising magma, although geologists aren't sure.

It's difficult to predict what Mt. Hood's next eruption will look like. Given the mountain's history, however, odds are that the next blast will aim south again, blanketing Timberline Lodge and Government Camp with ash. A lahar might singe forests and spark fires. All but the least cautious skiers and tourists would probably have time to evacuate.

The greatest damage is likely to be done by mudflows—Mt. Hood's specialty. If the 1781 eruption is any guide, these torrents of rock, ash, and melted ice might actually miss Timberline Lodge. Instead they'll careen east down the White River to the Deschutes River, and west down the Zigzag and Sandy Rivers to the Columbia. Along these routes, highway drivers, riverfront homeowners, and campers could well be in serious danger when Mt. Hood reawakens.

An Italian perspective on volcanoes

One reason Oregon's volcanoes seem quiet is that our recorded history is so short. To help visualize eruptions here, you might look to Italy, a country with a long and well-documented history of volcanism.

The cone of Mt. Vesuvius towers over central Italy, much as South Sister towers overs Central Oregon. A violent eruption of Mt. Vesuvius in 79 AD

buried the walled Roman city of Pompeii (population 15,000) with about ten feet of hot ash and other pyroclastic debris. Rediscovered in 1748, Pompeii has been exca-vated to reveal Roman buildings, streets, frescos, crosswalks, snack bars, and even political graffiti. The body casts of men, women, and children have been found cowering by a garden wall where they fled while trying to escape.

A roaring avalanche of hot gas and ash left body casts in Pompeii, Italy.

No doubt similar body casts exist in Oregon, where pyroclastic flows of Mt. Mazama entombed early Oregonians 7700 years ago. But because we don't know exactly where these early people lived we don't know where to search.

Violent, Mazama-style eruptions are rare. To see a less violent type of eruption, take a four-hour hydrofoil boat ride from Naples to the small Ital-ian island of Stromboli. A short trail on this island leads to a piz-zeria patio where you can watch the volcano erupt every three to twelve minutes. During the day the volcano rumbles and belches clouds of white steam. By night, when the pizzeria is lit only by candles, you can see that the eruptions also include fountains of glowing red cinders.

Italy's Stromboli volcano spews cinders every three to twelve minutes.

Cinder cone eruptions have been so common in Central Oregon over the past few thousand years that it's surprising we haven't experienced one lately. At first these eruptions look a lot like Stromboli. After a few months, however, the fireworks typically die out and lava oozes from the cone's base. Stromboli is unusual because it has been spewing cinders every few minutes for 2000 years.

A bulge 3 miles west of South Sister indicates that magma is rising.

South Sister

When you drive across McKenzie Pass, you can't help but marvel at the vast barrens of jagged lava flows, where the rock is so fresh that trees have yet to get a foothold. In fact the Three Sisters, to the south of McKenzie Pass, may be the site of Oregon's next volcanic eruption.

An area three miles west of South Sister began bulging in late 1997 or early 1998, tilting the entire mountain a few inches to the east. The bulge is about ten miles wide. The ground in the center rose an inch a year until 2004, and then slowed to about half that rate. This growth suggests that magma is rising beneath the mountain, pushing up the landscape along the way.

A swarm of 300 very small earthquakes in 2004, the first quakes measured near the mountain for decades, point to a lava reservoir that's still about four miles deep. The fact that the largest

North and Middle Sister. Surrounded by recent lava flows and cinder cones, the Three Sisters are in a very active volcanic area.

South Sister's summit is a broad volcanic crater. Each summer melting snow in the crater creates the state's highest lake, Teardrop Pool.

quake measured a mere 1.9 on the Richter scale suggests that the rock is so hot and liquid that it can flow upward without major earthquakes. Most likely, the lava is runny basalt. But the most recent eruptions in the area have been gooier rock, high in silica and hence more explosive.

The bulge is growing so slowly that it was discovered only by satellites with radar. In comparison, recall that Mt. St. Helens was bulging at the rate of more than three feet a day before it blew up in 1980. This indicates that South Sister is not likely to erupt in the next year or two—but the odds of an eruption in the next 50 to 100 years are relatively high. A chronology of Cascade eruptions shows that Mt. St. Helens erupts at least once a century, while the Three Sisters area has a cluster of eruptions every 1000 to 2000 years. It's been a little over 1200 years since South Sister's last outburst.

Predictions are difficult because the Three Sisters are in one of the least documented volcanic areas in the country. Historically, Central Oregon has been sparsely populated. Laws forbade white pioneers from settling east of the Cascades until the 1860s. The area's largest city, Bend, is one of the youngest in Oregon—platted by a land developer in 1903 and incorporated in 1905. South Sister and Mt. Bachelor may have puffed out ash and steam repeatedly in the 1800s without attracting media attention. Fumaroles that melt holes in the snow on the north side of Mt. Bachelor's summit certainly suggest a recently active past.

An eruption today would be a very different story. More than 100,000 people now live downwind of the Three Sisters, drawn to subdivisions of new homes with spectacular, close-up views of sunny, snow-capped volcanoes. The houses, of course, are built atop relatively recent lava, pyroclastic flows, and ashfall from those same volcanoes.

Broken Top is extinct, and it's a good thing. In the past, its explosive eruptions have buried Central Oregon with fiery debris.

The natives who lived here in past millennia seemed to have understood that Central Oregon was a dangerous place. Red petroglyphs mark the end of a 1200-year-old lava flow at the foot of South Sister, where the chunky lava dammed Hells Creek to create Devils Lake. The petroglyphs and demonic names suggest this was recognized as a place of violent power.

The volcanoes here may have been threatening, but they also provided early Oregonians with an incredibly valuable commodity — obsidian. In a culture that relied on stone tools, easily shaped volcanic glass was far more prized than gold. Artisans lugged finished arrowheads and raw blocks of

Blobs of liquid rock that are blasted out of cinder cones often cool in flight and land as teardrop-shaped "lava bombs."

obsidian north to the great trading center at the Columbia River's Celilo Falls, near what is now The Dalles. From there, canoes carried Central Oregon obsidian throughout the Northwest and as far north as Alaska.

The Three Sisters' best obsidian was also the riskiest to collect. Hikers today still marvel at the glittering black rock along the Obsidian Trail, three miles west of North Sister. A series of eruptions that began 3000 years ago besieged the area's prized Obsidian Cliffs. Obsidian collectors trekking to the area would have found themselves barraged by lava bombs, choked with poison gas, and cut off by rivers of lava. Over the years at least 125 vents have erupted here.

Lava flows from the McKenzie Pass area dammed the McKenzie River 3000 years ago, creating Clear Lake.

If you would like to tour this battlefield by car, you might start by driving Highway 126 to the headwaters of the McKenzie River at Clear Lake. A string of cinder cones three miles east at Sand Mountain fired the opening shots of the eruptive series. The cones blew cinders into the sky. Then they poured out a stream of lava that dammed the McKenzie River, creating Clear Lake. The water rose so quickly and it was so cold that it preserved a drowned forest. If you rent a rowboat at the Clear Lake Resort, you can look down through the amazingly clear water at the eerie snags rising from the lake bottom. Scuba divers, protected from the nearly freezing water by insulated suits, sometimes swim amidst the ghostly trunks like giant birds in an alien jungle. The wood is not fossilized, merely refrigerated, so scientists have been able to carbon-date samples to about 1000 BC.

At the same time, a different lava vent opened closer to McKenzie Pass. Basalt poured out of Belknap Crater, forming a 6-mile-wide mound on the south side of the pass. In 900 BC, Yapoah Crater erupted on the slopes of North Sister, building a cinder cone and blanketing the entire area with ash. Just 20 years later, Belknap Crater oozed yet more lava. Meanwhile, a new vent opened at Little Belknap Crater, pouring basalt all the way down to what is now the Dee Wright Observatory, the stone lookout building beside the crest of Highway 242. Because this flow had to detour around two small hills along the way, it left "lava islands" where trees survived. The Pacific Crest Trail now hugs those islands before sallying out across the barren rock.

So many eruptions rocked the area between 700 BC and 600 BC that the outbursts started to overlap. Like a row of Roman candles, Four-In-One Cone spewed fire from a line of four vents. Collier Cone blew up North Sister's Collier Glacier, triggering mudflows that swelled and muddied rivers all the way to Astoria. Yapoah Crater sent out two massive basalt floods that lapped against Belknap Crater's rock. Then Four-In-One Cone and Collier Cone poured out lava flows of their own. The longest of these caromed off Obsidian Cliffs, buried ten miles of the White Branch, dammed Linton Lake, and puddled up at Proxy Falls.

At McKenzie Pass the Pacific Crest Trail crosses recent Belknap Crater lava, with the spire of Mt. Washington in the background.

Yes, you say, but all this havoc happened more than 2000 years ago.

Not quite. The largest lava flow of all welled up from Belknap Crater in about 500 AD. Ash darkened the sky. Cinder bombs fell miles away. More and more basalt oozed out of the volcano, flooding nearly a third of what is now the Mt. Washington Wilderness. To the south the rock stopped just short of what is now Highway 242, damming Hand Lake. To

North and Middle Sister from Four-In-One Cone, a fresh string of cinder cones.

the west, however, the basalt flood cascaded eight miles to the McKenzie River canyon.

The long-suffering McKenzie River had been bedeviled by lava before. This time the rock created thunderous cataracts at Sahalie Falls and Koosah Falls. Downstream, basalt buried the river so thoroughly that the water now percolates underground through lava tubes for three miles to Tamolitch Dry Falls. Only in extreme floods does the river manage to emerge atop the lava and pour over this 100-foot falls. Otherwise the mighty McKenzie is forced to bubble humbly out of a turquoise pool at the base of a dry lava cliff.

Sooner or later, the McKenzie Pass area will definitely host more fireworks. In the meantime, attention has shifted to the south side of the Three Sisters.

Half a dozen big puddles of chunky, silica-rich lava squeezed out from the base of South Sister in about 800 AD. One of them dammed Devils Lake. Another created the mile-long Rock Mesa flow above Wickiup Plain. Other, similar flows line the Fall Creek Trail to the Green Lakes basin. Ash from those eruptions still chokes the slopes of Broken Top.

Now a bulge is growing just a few miles to the west.

What should we do to prepare for South Sister's next eruption?

The simple answer is to watch and wait.

The most likely scenario is that we'll get yet another relatively harmless little cinder cone. First there might be a surprising initial blast that powders Bend with a half inch of ash. Schools might close for a day. After that, however, people will be setting up their lawn chairs on Sunriver patios each evening to watch the red glow on the skyline with binoculars. The Forest Service will already have closed the Three Sisters Wilderness and limited traffic on the Cascade Lakes Highway to official vehicles. Camera crews will be buzzing the area with helicopters. A small forest fire may burn the James Creek Shelter, three miles west of South Sister. If it's winter, enough snow might melt to send a mudflow down

Like most cinder cones, Four-In-One Cone's eruption ended with a lava flow. The basalt tore out a cone's wall and streamed 4 miles toward the McKenzie River.

Separation Creek to the McKenzie River, but it's unlikely to cause much flooding. After a few months, a lava flow might leak from the base of the new cinder cone, ooze a mile or so through the woods, and stop. Then mapmakers will redraw the Three Sisters Wilderness maps, and everything will return to normal.

That's one possible scenario. How about the worst case?

In the unlikely event of a major explosive eruption, sensors will almost certainly give geologists time to order evacuation of the area within a dozen miles of South Sister. That would close the Cascade Lakes Highway and McKenzie Pass. When the blast comes, only a few backpackers and thrill seekers might die, but forests and buildings could be destroyed as far as Elk Lake and Mt. Bachelor. South Sister's glaciers could melt, launching a gigantic mudflow that races west, sweeping away bridges and riverfront homes along the McKenzie River all the way to Springfield. Another mudflow might churn north down Whychus Creek, flooding the city of Sisters. Meanwhile, a gigantic ash plume would turn the sky black. A foot of ash could fall in Bend, cutting power and stopping traffic for a day. Hospitals would slowly fill with victims of respiratory ailments.

But within a week, golfers would be back on the courses and Bend's traffic would be as bad as ever.

Does it get any worse than this? Probably not. The minor-cinder-cone

A winter eruption of South Sister could melt glaciers and launch mudflows.

scenario is something we might expect every few centuries in Central Oregon. Mostly, it calls for ordinary caution. The devastating-blast scenario might happen once in 10,000 years. Even then, we'll have at least a few days of warning.

Oregon's volcanoes are very much alive, but they're not necessarily impossible neighbors.

CHAPTER V

Flash Floods

If you drive halfway across eastern Oregon to visit Heppner, 60 miles southwest of Pendleton, you'll find an Old West village by a dribbly creek in a dusty world of sagebrush hills. The first thought that springs to your mind is not likely to be flood danger. Heppner is a tiny oasis, lost in a lonely landscape marked by a desperate *lack* of water.

But this is in fact the site of Oregon's deadliest deluge, where 259 people lost their lives on June 14, 1903.

A Dark Day in Heppner

Heppner lies along Willow Creek, at the bottom of a natural funnel where four watersheds converge, draining 150 square miles of Blue Mountain foothills. Of course this is why settlers chose the location in the first place, to make the most of what little water there was. The downside is that the town has been ravaged by 19 flash floods in a century.

Henry Heppner and Jackson Morrow opened the first store here in 1873. That led to the city of Heppner, seat of Morrow County. A few years later when a railroad spur arrived to haul out the county's production of sheep, cattle, and wheat, Heppner had blossomed to a city of 1200, with a half dozen saloons, a bordello, two churches, a blacksmith shop, a jewelry store, plank sidewalks, and plenty of hitching racks for the cowboys who rode its dirt Main Street.

The summer of 1903 began so dry that everyone worried about the wheat crop. Only two inches of rain had fallen in four months. When black clouds rolled across the hills, farmers looked to the sky with relief.

But the clouds were unusually black. Lightning crackled. Thunder boomed. Hailstones the size of marbles pelted the ground until they lay inches deep. Then the rain let loose—a downpour that dumped an inch and and a half of water on the hills above town within a few minutes.

The 1903 flash flood tore a swath through Heppner two blocks wide.

With no forest and little soil, the uplands shrugged this bounty into Willow Creek's canyon. The water surged to the edge of town, where it backed up against Fred Krug's steam laundry, a stout two-story building that spanned the creek.

Most families were at home that Sunday evening at 5:16 pm. It hadn't rained much in town, but the thunderstorm had been spectacular. No one was alarmed by the roar of what they assumed was yet more thunder. As a result, there was no warning when the waters of Willow Creek broke through the steam laundry and raged across the city as a six-foot wall of debris.

For most people, the first sign of trouble was when buildings jerked off their foundations and began spinning down the streets.

When the flood smashed into the front of Alexander Gunn's home, he grabbed the baby and kicked open the back door. His wife Elizabeth and their daughter Mary followed him out the back, running for their lives toward the Methodist church. Behind them, a roaring wall of water and debris 600 feet wide was demolishing the town. Houses skidded down Main Street and splintered.

Alexander and his daughter Mary reached the church steps first. Elizabeth was almost to the steps when she tripped on her long dress. With the baby in his arms, Alexander stepped back down to help his wife. As Mary watched in horror from the church doorway, the flood rolled over her family. In a moment, her parents and her baby brother were gone.

On Chase Street, the Consers and the Minors lived side by side in two of the area's nicest homes—elegant two-story buildings with carpenter Gothic gingerbread woodwork on the gables. Their backyards extended down to the grassy bank of little Willow Creek. The park-like yards separated them from the shacks on the far bank where Chinese laborers lived.

On that Sunday afternoon banker George Conser, his wife, and their Japanese servant were sitting in the backyard with two family friends, Johnnie Ayers and Dr. Buell McSword. The group had been amused by the play of lightning on the hills. After the thunder grew particularly loud, Mrs. Conser noticed floodwater coming down the creek. "Let's go inside," she suggested. Johnnie and the doctor scoffed that they were perfectly safe. Nonetheless, she took her husband George by the arm and hurried inside.

Seconds later the flood flattened the shacks upstream, killing eight Chinese men. Then the wall of water swept through the Conser's backyard, carrying away Johnnie, the doctor, and the servant. A surge of mud, rocks, trees, and debris smashed the Consers' home off its foundation. Water poured through the windows and doors. The walls pitched and groaned.

Scenes from the Heppner flood of 1903.

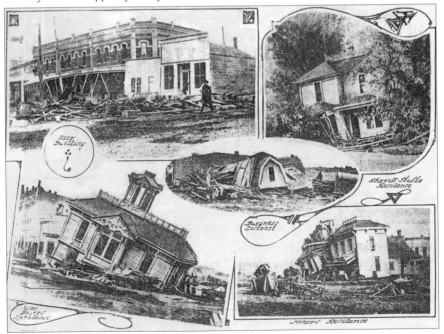

The upper story of the Minor family's home came to rest against a Methodist church.

George Conser and his wife struggled up the stairs. They had barely reached the upstairs bedroom when the walls of the first floor collapsed. The town spun past the bedroom windows as if they were on a merry-go-round. George clung to his wife. When the muddy water rose to their necks, they kissed each other goodbye.

But then the Consers' house lurched to a halt. The water sloshed to one side and drained. George kicked out the window. To their astonishment, they were able to step out onto dry ground. Even more surprising, their neighbors' house had followed them through the streets. Two gables of the Minors' second story had landed cockeyed against the Methodist church. Only one room of that house remained intact. Inside it, the entire Minor family had survived.

Others were less fortunate. Downstream, farmers heard the cries of people clinging to wreckage in the maelstrom, but could do nothing to save them. When the flood swept away the home of 70-year-old Julius Keithly, his house cracked in half along the ridgeline. Julius managed to crawl up onto the roof. He floated for two miles in a torrent of debris. Along the way he spotted his wife Amanda clinging to some lumber. Julius held out his hand to help her onto the roof. Their fingers touched. But he didn't have the strength to pull her up, and she floated onward to her doom.

Half an hour before the flood hit, the lightning storm had awakened Leslie Matlock from his Sunday afternoon nap in the posh Palace Hotel. Les had lived for several years in Room 48 of the turreted three-story brick hotel on the corner of Main and May Streets. His parents lived only a few blocks away—his father had once been Morrow County sheriff—but Les himself had drifted into the life of a professional gambler, playing cards with the salesmen and cowboys who frequented the town's saloons. Earlier that day, Les had stopped by his uncle's house for supper. Dr. McSword and Johnnie Ayers had been there too, talking about plans to travel to Uruguay. After dinner Johnnie and the doctor had invited Les over to the Conser home. Les had declined, saying he needed some rest. His line of work often kept him up late at the saloons.

When the thunder kept booming outside his hotel, Les got out of bed, pulled on his boots, and went downstairs to take a look. The clouds were dark, but the only people who seemed frightened were the hotel waitresses. Les shrugged and joined a salesman for a drink in a nearby saloon. They had downed two shots and were about to order a third when a group of women came running up, warning everyone to leave.

"Leave? Because of a storm?" the barkeeper asked. "I'm staying till hell freezes over."

Les took the warning more seriously. The thunder outside had become a continuous roar. He headed back toward his hotel. Along the way a crowd of people shouted for him to join them on a hill behind the First National Bank. Only when he had climbed the hill did he realize what was happening to the town below.

From his higher vantage point, Les saw with horror that a sea of muddy water was sweeping away half of Heppner. A block behind the Palace Hotel, wooden buildings were floating past like rudderless ships. The houses of his parents and his uncle were already gone! And the Consers and the Minors and the Ayers—all of them gone. Because there had been so little warning, most of his family and friends had almost certainly drowned.

Up on that hill above Heppner, Les met his old schoolmate and lifelong friend, Bruce Kelley, a 31-year-old cattleman from a nearby ranch.

Bruce said, "Les, every person in Heppner is going to be swept away and drowned."

Les replied bitterly that he thought so, too.

Bruce weighed this for a moment. "Les, I think if we get our horses and start right away, maybe we can save the people at Lexington and the valley below."

The city of Lexington, only slightly smaller than Heppner, lay nine miles downstream. Beyond that, the town of Ione was another eight miles. The road down Willow Creek would be washed out, and night was falling. They would have to ride cross-country over the hills in the dark, trying to outrace a flash flood. Even for a gambler, the odds seemed impossibly high. But hundreds of lives might be at stake.

"Let's try," Les said. "Get our horses from the livery. I'll get wirecutters for the fences."

Les ran down Main Street to the Gilliam & Bisbee hardware store. It was locked for Sunday, but he kicked the door open. Inside it was so dark he could hardly see. Finally he found a pair of wood-handled pruning shears — good enough to cut wire, he hoped — and rushed outside. Bruce was already riding up the street with the first two horses he had found.

Les swung into the saddle. Then the two riders were off, galloping across the hills northwest of Heppner.

Lightning blazed in the night sky. At the first barbed wire fence, sparks raced along the wires. The metal strands sang with electricity from the storm. Les braced himself and chopped with the shears. A little surprised that he had not been electrocuted, Les got back in the saddle. Then on they rode.

Minutes later Les' horse stepped in a badger hole and stumbled in the dark. Les was thrown so hard onto the ground that his head reeled. But he

The 1903 flood tore through Heppner one block behind the Palace Hotel.

managed to catch the horse, remount, and gallop on.

Just outside of Lexington they met a one-legged man and a small girl staggering up from the town.

"Has the flood hit yet?" Les called out.

The man nodded. "It just went through."

Bruce looked to Les. "Ione. That's eight more miles, but we might still warn them in time."

The two horsemen rode through the debris that had been Lexington. The flood had swept through only a few minutes earlier, at seven o'clock. The water had backed up behind a railroad bridge above the town. Then it had burst through with such a colossal roar that everyone in town had fled. No one had died, and although many buildings were destroyed, the damage was less severe than in Heppner.

Les's horse was about to give out, so they stopped at a farm and quickly traded for a fresh mount. Then they set off across the hills, faster than ever. A few miles later they could tell from the roar in the canyon that they had finally passed the flood. They cut down to the valley floor just ahead of the muddy waters and raced along the dark road toward Ione.

Now they cried out at each of the farmhouses along the way, "Flood! Get to the hills!"

Windows opened and heads poked out in amazement. "What?"

"Heppner's washed away!" Les shouted.

When they finally galloped into Ione, Bruce and Les split up to spread the alarm. Minutes later they gathered the townsfolk on a hill. Even after the flood rumbled past at 10 pm, no one wanted to return to their homes. Would another surge come? Les and Bruce helped pile fenceposts for a bonfire on the hill. They huddled there through the night.

In the morning they realized the flood damage was much less severe than in Heppner. Only one house had washed away. But mud lay thick in the streets and yards. The threat had been real, and everyone in Ione had survived. Bruce Kelley and Les Matlock were hailed as heroes.

Back in Heppner, people wandered all night through the ruins of the city, searching for survivors. A salesman who had been staying at the Palace Hotel explored the wreckage of the Matlock family home. Although Les's father was dead, he found Elizabeth Matlock alive, shivering under a pile of boards.

The next day, the orphaned Mary Gunn was able to identify the corpse of her mother Elizabeth only from her engagement ring, inscribed to "Libbie."

The body of Julius Keithly's wife Amanda was found in a drift pile eleven miles downstream.

George Conser, who survived the flood, told a reporter, "I was as sure that we were going to die as I am that I am now alive. But the mental panorama of my life was not spread out before me to the extent of recalling a single deed, good or bad."

A few days later relief brigades began arriving from Portland and Pendleton. Trains brought volunteers and supplies as far as Ione, where the rails ended, twisted like corkscrews. From Ione to Heppner, strings of searchers walked 17 miles up Willow Creek's valley, pulling corpses from piles of mud and debris. Sometimes deposits of hailstones had preserved the bodies in ice, despite daytime temperatures of 100 degrees. More often, the corpses had putrified. Flies and a horrible stench filled the air.

On the fifth day after the flood a dog stopped at the corner of the wrecked Matlock building, sniffed, wagged his tail, and started to dig. Puzzled workers came to help. Soon they uncovered a muddy, groggy German shepherd that had been buried for most of a week. The dog shook itself, wagged its tail a little, and limped down the street with the dog who had found it.

The flood killed nearly a quarter of the city's population. Today as you walk through Heppner's cemetery, you'll see grave after grave with the same dread date — **June 14, 1903.**

In 1983 the town's long history of flash floods convinced the U.S. Army Corps of Engineers to build the $37 million Willow Creek Dam. The 160-foot-tall concrete wall spans the valley above Heppner, backing up a 268-acre reservoir. The dam is credited with stopping flash floods in 1996 and 1997.

Flash Floods in Mitchell

Summer thundershowers have triggered flash floods through many other eastern Oregon settlements, including Arlington, Weston, and Imnaha. But only Mitchell, with a population of 180, can compete with Heppner for the sheer frequency of damage.

Life in Mitchell has always been a struggle. Near the geographic center of Oregon, the town began in the 1860s as a stagecoach stop on the rugged military road between The Dalles and the Canyon City gold fields. Today Mitchell is a ranching center and a stop for travelers on Highway 26 between Prineville and John Day. In summer, bicyclists intent on crossing the state sometimes pitch tents on the lawn of the city park along Bridge

With a population of 180, Mitchell today is about the same size as it was in 1904.

Creek. Tourists in motorhomes occasionally detour off the highway, gape out their windows at the mostly abandoned plank storefronts on Main Street, and then drive on to the John Day Fossil Beds National Monument. In fall, a few elk hunters from the nearby Ochoco Mountains stop to warm up at the cafe with a breakfast of pancakes and eggs.

Because Bridge Creek's canyon floor is hardly 200 feet wide, Mitchell's Main Street has little choice but to squeeze awkwardly near the stream. Flash floods in 1889, 1904, and 1956 wiped out most of the buildings on the lower side of the street. Fires in 1899 and 1937 destroyed buildings on the opposite side. The people of Mitchell don't give up easily.

Four lives were lost in Mitchell's **June 1889 flood,** but not because Bridge Creek tore out most of town. The trouble came four miles downstream at the Carroll ranch.

It was election day and Sam Carroll had gone into town to cast his ballot. Women couldn't vote, so his wife Nancy was left behind in the ranch house with their five children—Autie, Julia, Clyde, Maggie, and baby George.

Julia was ten years old. She later recalled that the weather was so stormy her mother spent the day indoors, whitewashing walls. The roar of the rainstorm was frightening. When Nancy finally had to go outside to get another tub of water from the creek, she stopped short in the doorway and exclaimed, "Oh look, children!"

The creek had jumped its bank on one side of the house. An irrigation ditch was overflowing on the other. The only remaining route to high ground was hundreds of yards away, on a bridge across the ditch. Nancy grabbed two quilts and the baby. Then she herded the family out into the storm. They were struggling toward the bridge when Julia saw the flash flood churning down the valley, pushing ahead a wall of debris from the ruins of Mitchell.

Nancy began praying out loud. The baby began crying.

Her eldest son Autie said, "If we can get to the hill we'll be all right."

Nancy shook her head. "We can't get there in time."

"Oh!" little Maggie cried. "We can't live any longer, can we?"

Autie grabbed Clyde and waded into the ditch. They fell down, but Autie found his footing and dragged Clyde up the far shore. Then he waded back and took Julia across.

Autie had gone back for a third trip when the flood hit.

Julia was caught waist-deep in the muddy water. Somehow she managed to wade up to the hillside. When she looked back, everything was gone—the ranch house, her mother, her siblings, everything.

Julia huddled on that slope a long time, shivering as she stared at the floodwaters that had stolen her world. Finally she walked over the hills to a neighboring ranch. Only the next day did she learn that her brother Clyde had also survived.

Nancy Carroll is buried with her children Autie and Maggie in the Carroll cemetery along Bridge Creek. Her baby, George, was never found.

On Friday the 13th in **July of 1904** another colossal thunder and lightning storm swept through Mitchell, killing two elderly residents. People throughout eastern Oregon were still on edge from the Heppner disaster that had claimed 259 lives the previous summer.

Torrential rains pelted the hills about Mitchell all that afternoon. When a roar issued from Bridge Creek's canyon, all but two of the town's

A newspaper account of the 1956 flood is framed on the wall of a Mitchell cafe.

Mud and Debris Mitchell's Memento of Flash Flood

citizens hurried to high ground.

Accounts vary as to why Mrs. Becham, age 86, and Martin Smith, age 90, remained behind. Perhaps they couldn't hear the roar. Were they too infirm to escape? Or did they scoff at the danger?

A 25-foot wall of water rolled into Mitchell with a tremendous crash, tearing away 28 buildings on the north side of Main Street. Two livery barns collapsed in splinters. Forty horses drowned.

Four hours later, at ten o'clock that night, the same thunderstorm reached Heppner, sparking panic there. Willow Creek washed out the bridges and railroad grades that had been rebuilt after the previous year's flood. This time, however, damage was greater in Mitchell than in Heppner, because the people of Heppner had not rebuilt their houses near Willow Creek.

A broken ankle was the most serious injury of Mitchell's **1956 flash flood.** But there is a lot more to the story of that ankle than you might first suspect.

The story begins when two boys from Beaverton, barely old enough to drive, got their hands on a decrepit old car and took off on a road trip to eastern Oregon. Eldon Thom, age 16, had just acquired his driver's license and a sputtering 1941 sedan. Brent Berg, age 15, broke his piggy bank for gas money. Then the two of them lit out to see the country and find adventure.

All went well until the morning they hit the road east from Bend. They had motored 83 miles through increasingly barren terrain when the car suddenly died at a bridge just outside of Mitchell. It was 11 am. What a dusty, nowhereville place to get stuck, Eldon thought.

The boys left their car beside a creek bridge and thumbed a short ride to the town's garage. Clarence Jones, mechanic and owner of the garage, was not particularly pleased to see them. Even a brief description of the car's ailments convinced Clarence that the boys could never afford the necessary repairs. Still, his heart was not made of stone. He let them use his telephone.

It must have been tough for Eldon, calling his mother to confess how far afield he had strayed. Relieved to hear him, his mother agreed to drive to his rescue. Eldon, too, felt relieved.

The day was still sunny and hot as the boys marched back to their car to wait. But the longer they sat in the car that afternoon, the weirder the weather became. Giant black thunderheads boiled overhead. At four o'clock the sky opened up with a torrential rainfall. The boys had never seen it rain so hard.

When the rain didn't let up for a full hour, the entire population of the town started running across the bridge toward a hillside.

Eldon looked up the canyon. "I think there's some water coming. We should get out of here fast." He opened the driver's side door and joined the crowd heading for the hill.

Brent didn't want to go outside in a pouring rainstorm, and besides, the windshield was so blurry he couldn't see what Eldon was talking about. When Brent finally made out the churning wall of water in the canyon, he just had time to open his door. Suddenly he was neck deep in the flood. He let go of the door handle and was swept away.

After bobbing downstream for awhile Brent managed to hang onto the top of a fenceline. By pulling himself up, hand over hand, he dragged himself to a house on the bank. Brent didn't know it, but this was the six-room home of Clarence Jones, the owner of Mitchell's garage. Brent tried in vain to open the door. Then the flood surged, broke open the door, and swept him inside.

Brent climbed onto a bed that was floating around inside. A moment later the flood ripped the house off its foundations and sent it swirling downstream. The house caromed off boulders, disintegrating to wreckage. Brent sailed off a waterfall to shallower water. Finally he managed to crawl out onto the shore.

Brent sat on the bank of the raging stream a minute or two, disoriented and shivering. The town of Mitchell, he decided, was probably on the other side of the creek. The quickest way to reach help might be to swim across. Convinced of this logic, he waded back into the flood. Of course the current swept him away. Another mile downstream he managed once again to pull himself out, this time by grabbing onto some brush. Now his ankle was hurting and night was falling.

Fifteen year olds can make poor decisions, but they can also be amazingly resilient. Brent limped painfully up along the creekbank for two miles on his broken ankle. Finally he found a house that had survived the flood. This time it turned out to be the home of the local sheriff. No one was home.

Brent broke open the door. The power was out. The phone didn't work. He changed into dry clothes from the sheriff's bedroom closet. Brent was still cold, and the house was dark. So he went outside, hot-wired the sheriff's car, and turned up the heat.

When the sheriff returned home that night at 10 pm, Brent had a lot of explaining to do. At first the sheriff had a hard time believing the tale. He

Mitchell's Oregon Hotel survived the flash floods, although buildings across the street did not. Originally built in the 1860s, the hotel burned in 1937 and was rebuilt in 1938. After the 1956 flood the hotel offered free rooms to refugees, including Eldon Thom and Brent Berg.

knew the flood had swept away a boy five hours earlier. Half the town had witnessed the tragedy, and everyone agreed the poor child could not possibly have survived. The sheriff had expected a search party to find the boy's body the next day, miles downstream. What was the kid doing in his car, wearing his clothes?

Brent and Eldon spent the night in the Oregon Hotel, a historic Mitchell inn that had opened its doors to refugees. The next day, Eldon went looking for his 1941 sedan. He found the car wrapped around a concrete abutment a mile and a half below the bridge. The flood had torn off the doors and ripped the engine loose from the chassis. If he and Brent had stayed in the car, they would have been crushed.

Four bridges, eleven houses, three trailers, a garage, a service station, and dozens of cars were destroyed in Mitchell's 1956 flash flood. The town's post office was gutted so severely that its heavy steel safe was found seven years later, ten miles downstream near the John Day Fossil Beds' Painted Hills.

The only personal injury, however, was a broken ankle.

CHAPTER VI

River Floods

In Ken Kesey's classic Oregon novel, *Sometimes a Great Notion*, generations of the Stamper family battle floods that threaten their riverfront home. Under the motto, "Never Give A Inch," the Stampers see themselves as heroes. But by the end of the book, readers are left wondering if stubbornness hasn't been their doom.

River floods seem to be Oregon's most reliable natural disasters. Planners draw maps of 20-year, 100-year, and 500-year floods, as if these were scheduled events. Why, then, are we surprised almost every winter by inundated homes and washed out highways? Are the rivers really wilder and higher than in the past?

As scientists learn more about how rivers work, we're starting to reevaluate the flood control measures we've taken for granted in the past. Western Oregon is a rainy place. Fighting our rivers as enemies may not be a long-term solution.

Champoeg in about 1905. After disastrous Willamette River floods in 1861 and 1890, the emptied townsite became a destination for picnics and historical pageants.

To understand the problem, it helps to look back to see the different ways Oregonians have dealt with devastating floods. It's a story full of tragedy, heroism — and yes, foolishness.

The Flood of 1861

The largest Willamette River flood in recorded history hit in 1861, when the river spread as wide as eleven miles across the valley floor. In

Eugene the flood crested twice, on December 1 and December 8, 1861. Water remained in downtown for nearly two weeks, standing four feet deep in the newly constructed Lane County Courthouse, in the middle of what is now 8th Avenue at the downtown Park Blocks. Skinners Butte was an island in a sea stretching across the city from College Hill in the south to Coburg in the north.

As the 1861 flood moved downstream, it obliterated several towns along the way. In the Corvallis area, two rival settlements had been platted on opposite sides of the Willamette River, with Marysville taking the high ground to the west and Orleans settling for the lower ground to the east. The flood swept Orleans entirely away. Marysville thrived and later changed its name to Corvallis.

At Salem the Willamette River poured through the business district, carrying away many wooden buildings. The *Oregon Statesman* wrote that the flood was "not Noah's," but "the next deepest one to that." When the floodwaters receded, the river settled into a different bed. Instead of flowing between Browns Island and Minto Island, the current detoured west, merging the two islands and annexing them to the Salem shore. Today, Minto-Brown Island Park has become Salem's backyard wilderness, prized by joggers and birdwatchers.

Ten miles north of Salem the river changed course again. Methodist missionaries had built a log cabin settlement on the riverbank there in 1834, but had abandoned the outpost in favor of higher ground at Salem in 1840, a move hinting at divine foresight. The 1861 flood swept away the old log buildings and left the site stranded on a slough that became known as Mission Lake. Across the river at the thriving mill town of Wheatland, the current swept away the lower half of the city, including a grain warehouse with 7000 bushels of wheat. Wheatland never recovered. Today all that remains are a few farmhouses and a road sign near the Wheatland ferry landing.

Downstream another 15 miles, the 1861 flood wiped out the historic city of Champoeg, where Oregon's government began. The seemingly gentle stretch of Willamette River at Champoeg curves along the northern edge of the Willamette Valley's prairies. American fur trappers from Astoria liked the spot so much that they set up a trading post nearby from 1811 to 1813. French-Canadian trappers from the Hudson's Bay Company fort in Vancouver began retiring here in 1826 to try their hand at farming. Wheat grew as if by magic. It looked so easy that American mountain men started settling here too. By 1836, the farmers were producing a thousand bushels of wheat a year. In 1837 the crop increased to a staggering

The 1852 Newell House was the only home in Champoeg to survive the 1861 flood. It is now open as a museum from 1pm to 5pm on weekends from March through October.

5000 bushels. The Hudson's Bay Company built a warehouse and store at Champoeg in 1841 to handle the trade.

Oregon was held jointly by Britain and the United States at the time, but it seemed to the Americans that the Hudson's Bay Company was calling the shots.

American settlers called for a showdown at Champoeg in 1843 to determine whether Oregon should form an American-style government. Only white males were allowed to vote, and the Oregon Country was so sparsely populated that the gathering was small. After a line had been drawn in the sand and the men took up sides, the vote stood deadlocked, fifty to fifty. Then two French-Canadians joined the Americans. With that decision, Oregon took an irreversible step toward rule by the United States.

By 1860 Champoeg had blossomed into a steamboat port with 200 buildings, including a hotel, a Masonic hall, two blacksmith shops, an Episcopal church, and several saloons.

Then came the flood of December 1861. The river filled Champoeg's streets with seven feet of water. No one died, mainly due to the quick work of four young men in rowboats. But log cabins and frame houses simply floated away. When the waters retreated, only one home remained — the 1852 Robert Newell house, on high ground south of town.

Two saloons had also survived. The once-proud Hudson's Bay Company warehouse drifted 150 feet downstream before it ran aground, askew and derelict. All that remained of the town's church was a bell that turned up later in the mud of Champoeg Creek. The rest of the townsite was as barren as a sand beach.

Some of the buildings from Champoeg and other riverside towns floated downriver toward Oregon City. You might think the drop at Willamette Falls would churn such structures to kindling, but the flood had smoothed the falls into a roaring brown rapids. Below the falls the river stood a staggering 48 feet above flood stage. Oregon City's mills and breakwaters vanished.

In Portland, a crowd gathered along the waterfront to marvel as houses, docks, bridges, and barns floated past. The pilot house of a riverboat steered by, somehow separated from its boat. One man rowed out to catch a scow loaded with apples, but his rope broke and the scow sailed on. Then a stack of oat sheaves floated by with a rooster on top. The rooster strutted about, pecking oats as calmly as if he were back home in his barnyard. A daring boy in a small boat rescued the rooster and sold him as a novelty for a quick five-dollar profit.

Meanwhile, the water kept rising in Portland. One family stayed in their riverfront house until they were trapped. By the time a man in a

A year after the Flood of 1861, Champoeg farmer Donald Manson built this barn on high ground. A visitor center for the Champoeg State Heritage Center now stands nearby.

The flood of 1890 hit Salem particularly hard. Water extended almost to the old Marion County Courthouse (at left) and the First Methodist Church (behind the power pole).

rowboat heard their cries for help, a hole had to be cut in their roof to rescue them.

After the 1861 flood, canny businessmen on Portland's waterfront began building their wharves with two stories. The lower level served in summer and fall when the river was low. The upper deck, about eight feet higher, came in handy during floods. As Portlanders soon learned, the city is just close enough to the Columbia River that it can expect two flood crests a year, one from each river. Floods on the Willamette are a result of western Oregon's winter rainstorms, and generally hit from December to February. The Columbia River's floods, on the other hand, are triggered by spring snowmelt in the Rocky Mountains. When that high water arrives in May and June, it can back up the Willamette River as far as Oregon City.

Floods of the Late 1800s

The flood of 1876 came down the Columbia River in June, filling Portland streets for three weeks. Because the sidewalks and many of the streets themselves were made of wood, citizens quickly weighted the planks with bricks, millstones, chains, nail kegs, and scrap iron to keep them from floating away. Store merchants moved their wares to second stories. The prestigious Clarendon Hotel, conveniently located on the waterfront at First and Flanders Streets, hired workmen to build a false floor throughout the lobby so guests wouldn't wet their feet. A few days later, the workmen had to raise the floor.

The flood of 1880 was another June freshet from the Columbia. It crested a trifle higher than the 1876 flood, measuring 27.4 feet in Portland. With five feet of water in the Clarendon Hotel, guests had to check in by boat.

In 1890 a snowy January turned into a warm, rainy February, launching a major flood down the Willamette River. In Eugene the water crested at 36 feet, dunking that city's downtown for the first time since 1861. Because the rainstorm moved north with the flood, the crest was particularly high in Salem. In that city the young Oswald West, a future governor, watched in astonishment as debris backed up behind the area's only Willamette River bridge and carried it away.

Portland's first bridge across the Willamette had been built on Morrison Street by a private company in 1887, just three years prior to the flood. The bridge's toll of five cents was considered so high that most people still preferred the Stark Street ferry. Portlanders watched as the 1890 flood backed logs, houses, barns, and other flotsam against the relatively flimsy bridge. When the Powers furniture factory floated downstream and smashed into the other debris, onlookers thought sure the bridge wouldn't hold. It did, but it remained so shaky that the city bought it and replaced it with the current structure 14 years later.

The flood of 1894, a Columbia River event, covered Portland more deeply than any flood in history. Water rose to 33 feet—almost six feet higher than the 1880 flood—and filled the streets for the first two weeks of June. Because the water had backed up from the Columbia, however, there was so little current that many Portlanders larked about the flooded streets in pleasure boats, dubbing the event a "Carnival of Waters."

Temporary plank walkways were erected five or ten feet above the streets. Because there were no handrails, incautious or inebriated pedestrians often fell in. Up to 1500 boats plied the streets. Chinese locals staged a gala boat race from the Skidmore Fountain up Second Avenue to Stark and back on First. Winning time for the eight-block course was five minutes flat, a record that is likely to stand for some time.

At night, the city's newly installed electric lamps lit the temporary

A view of the 1890 flood in Salem shows the unfinished Capitol, at left, without its dome.

Salem had only one bridge across the Willamette River before the 1890 flood.

Venice. The fire department installed a steam-powered pump on a barge and towed it around the city, putting out fires in the upper stories of flooded buildings.

Business boomed at lumber yards, selling planks for boats and walkways. One carpentry firm turned out forty crude boats a day. The waters extended up Burnside almost to Ninth Avenue, just shy of what is now Powell's Books. At every edge of the urban sea, men with boats called out to passersby, offering their services for a dollar an hour, exclaiming that their craft was superior to others because of its dry floor, carpeted seat,

Salem's bridge after the 1890 flood. Oswald West, who served as Oregon's governor from 1911 to 1915, wrote on this photograph, "I saw this bridge carried away by the flood."

colorful bunting, or flag.

East Portland was all but cut off, with the Albina and Stark Street ferries unable to run. The Steel Bridge raised its center span for safekeeping. The Morrison Bridge would have been passable for vehicles, but its approach ramps were underwater. Elevated walkways permitted only pedestrians to cross. The city's many electric streetcars stopped when water poured into the power station. A few horse-drawn cars were still running, "but in the main the citizens are gaining health and saving nickels by walking," the *Sunday Oregonian* reported.

The world's longest bar did not shut down altogether for the flood. To be sure, the winding 684-foot counter in August Erickson's record-breaking tavern on Burnside between Second and Third Avenues was underwater. But Erickson simply moored a houseboat in the middle of Burnside Street and shifted operations there. A barber set up shop on a

Scenes from the 1894 flood in Portland. Upper left: Front and Ash Streets. Upper right: Third and Oak Streets. Lower left: Front and Morrison Streets. Lower right: Cable car.

The flood of 1894 inundated 150 blocks of downtown Portland.

barge nearby.

Portland's sometimes festive atmosphere was not shared in towns along the Columbia River itself. At The Dalles the river rose 53 feet, flooding all of downtown. Below Portland the Columbia surged 20 miles wide, entirely covering Sauvie Island. The current swept away salmon canneries, fish wheels, houses, and railroad trestles.

The five devastating floods between 1861 and 1894 taught people in western Oregon hard lessons about avoiding disaster. Floods had become part of Willamette Valley life. Riverside towns like Champoeg, Wheatland, and Orleans were abandoned. Others, like Independence, were replatted on higher ground. Everyone remembered the high water marks before building bridges, barns, or businesses. Oregonians had learned to stand back from the brink and to respect the power of rivers.

Then a surprising thing happened. For almost fifty years, western Oregon had no major floods. Gradually, people began to forget the lessons they had learned.

Dams and the Flood of 1943

Throughout the early 1900s people seemed more alarmed by the deadly flash floods in eastern Oregon than by flood problems in the western half of the state. After Portland's dunking in 1894, neither the Willamette nor the Columbia caused much trouble for decades.

When trouble came, the rivers weren't entirely to blame. During the Depression of the 1930s, thousands of unemployed workers had fled the cities. Families were desperate for cheap housing, ideally on cheap land where they could grow their own food. More and more homes sprang up in the paths of old, half-forgotten river floods. Cut-rate housing developments crept across the flats north of Portland. Similar sprawl speckled the Keizer bottom land north of Salem and the River Road flood plain north of Eugene.

Meanwhile the federal government launched massive projects throughout the country to build dams, control floods, generate power, and put the unemployed back to work. The Flood Control Act of 1936 authorized $300 million in federal funds to address the problem. In 1937 President Roosevelt dedicated Bonneville Dam on the Columbia River. World War II slowed the dam-building effort in Oregon, but two modest earth-and-gravel-filled dams were completed in 1942. The Fern Ridge

The 1943 Flood (in gray) spread across the flood plain where the Willamette and McKenzie Rivers join. Between 1943 and 2006, Eugene's city limits expanded into the flood zone.

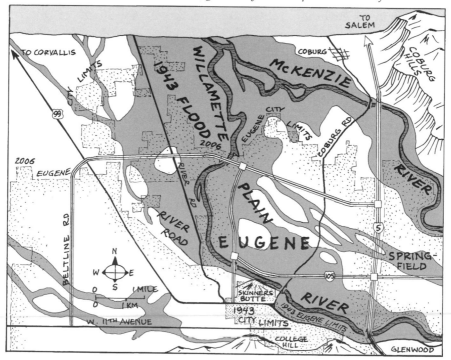

Dam backed up a reservoir on the Long Tom River a dozen miles west of Eugene. The Cottage Grove Dam impounded the Coast Fork of the Willamette River.

In December of 1942 it rained and rained in western Oregon. The dam engineers, not used to Willamette Valley floods, filled the reservoirs too early, making the Fern Ridge Dam useless when the flood's crest hit. The Cottage Grove Dam lowered the floodwaters only six inches in Eugene. By New Years Day of 1943, hundreds of homes in the new Glenwood and River Road districts near Eugene stood in four feet of water.

Marvin Smith was driving along a wet highway near Albany with his wife and five-month-old son when the current swept their car into the ditch. Behind them was Clinton Franklin, a military police sergeant from the nearby Camp Adair base. The sergeant leapt out, swam to the sunken car, and pulled Marvin out by his hair.

The Willamette River at Independence in the flood of 1943.

After trying in vain to save Marvin's wife and son, the sergeant swam with Marvin to a tree. The two men clung to the branches for half an hour until a local farmer rescued them in a boat.

In Salem, the flood floated the Mellow Moon, a dance hall and roller skating rink at the eastern foot of the city's new Willamette River bridge. For years the conservative administrators of Salem's Methodist-run Willamette University had condemned the dance hall as a disreputable venue that lured their students astray. When the river rose, the Mellow Moon's wooden floors rose too. The entire structure floated downstream, lodged against the bridge's piers, and began backing up debris.

Alarmed that Salem might lose its only Willamette River bridge, as had happened in 1890, Oregon Governor Charles A. Sprague ordered the state highway department to dynamite the Mellow Moon. Workers were setting the charges when the building disintegrated, sweeping away Archie Cook and Michael Maurer.

Salem's bridge closed while crews searched in vain for the missing men. Meanwhile, a thousand soldiers from Camp Adair who had been in Salem for New Year's celebrations now found themselves AWOL, cut off from their base. Some of the servicemen helped search for the lost workers. After two days, the Southern Pacific Railroad provided a special train to take the soldiers back across an intact railroad bridge to their camp.

In Oregon City and Portland, crowds watched as thousands of logs from sawmills tumbled down the river, tearing away houseboats and docks. Water was deep enough in Portland's Old Town that one quick-thinking angler managed to catch a 15-pound steelhead *inside* Union Station.

The total toll from the 1943 flood was ten dead and $6 million in damage. Although the flood's depth ranked it as a mere "twenty-year" event, far lower than Willamette River floods in 1861 or 1890, it had caused more damage than any flood in Oregon history.

And what lesson was learned? Rather than suggest the need to curb development in flood plains, people demanded more dams. As soon as World War II ended, the U.S. Army Corps of Engineers set to work on a plan to deal with western Oregon's floods. In 1948 they announced an ambitious project to dam nearly all of the Willamette River's tributaries. Twelve new concrete dams, all of them larger than the first two, would back up reservoirs into the McKenzie, Santiam, and Clackamas canyons.

The age of disastrous floods would be over! Instead a modern age would begin of carefully regulated river flows, cheap electricity, and plentiful hatchery fish.

The Vanport Flood

One sign of trouble for the modern age of dikes and dams came when the flood of 1948 washed away the entire city of Vanport, Oregon.

Why had Vanport been built in a flood plain? Part of the cause of the eventual disaster was racism.

Racism?

No one called it that in 1941, when ship-building magnate Henry Kaiser asked the city of Portland to house 24,000 out-of-state workers. Kaiser needed laborers to build Liberty Ships at the Portland docks for the war effort. The new residents would mostly be black families from the East Coast. Unaccustomed to black neighbors, Portlanders squirmed.

Oregon's Constitution had banned Negroes from the state until 1926. Many cities still had "sundown laws" that forbade blacks from remaining overnight. Oregon was one of the few states that still had not ratified the 15th amendment to the U.S. Constitution giving blacks the right to vote. In 1940, only 0.6 percent of Portland's population was black.

Portland welcomed the 150,000 shipyard jobs that Kaiser promised. But the city made little effort to provide housing for Kaiser's out-of-state workers.

Built in World War II as a government housing project, Vanport was surrounded by flood plain dikes. By 1943 the city was Oregon's second largest, with a population of 42,000.

Kaiser rolled his eyes at Portland's response. He asked the federal government to acquire flood plain land outside Portland's city limits. Then he built his own city — Vanport.

Named for Vancouver and Portland, Vanport was the largest government housing project in the nation. Clusters of two-story apartment buildings, arranged with military precision, spread across a square mile of bottom land between the Columbia River and Columbia Slough. The keystone-shaped city covered what is today the West Delta Park golf course and the Portland International Raceway, immediately west of Interstate 5.

Well-built 33-foot-tall dikes surrounded Vanport on three sides. The fourth side, downriver to the west, was sealed off by a long railroad embankment, which seemed to be the broadest and tallest dike of all.

By 1943 Vanport had become the state's second largest city, with 42,000 residents. The city boasted five nurseries, five schools, a theater, a library, a hospital, a police and fire station, a post office, two recreation centers, a college, and two shopping centers — all of it laid out with the efficiency of an Army camp.

The dike that breached to flood Vanport on May 30, 1948 was actually just a railroad embankment, filled with dirt instead of rock.

Throughout the war, Henry Kaiser's 150,000 local employees worked around the clock in three shifts, building two ships a week. The Allies desperately needed freighters to carry food and munitions from the United States across the Atlantic to Britain and Russia. The goal of the Liberty Ship program was to turn out freighters faster than German U-boats could sink them. Of the 2,751 Liberty Ships produced, 322 came from the Portland shipyard just north of the St. Johns Bridge. Other Kaiser workers built escort ships in Vancouver and tanker ships at Swan Island. After each shift change, cars jammed the roads to Vanport.

The frantic pace of shipbuilding ended along with the war, but Vanport remained. Many of the out-of-state workers did not want to leave Oregon. They had developed a sense of community in Vanport. They were proud of their schools, their hospital, and their college. To be sure, the buildings themselves were poorly constructed, with cheap plywood paneling, pull-chain lights, and outdoor-style water faucets. But racial discrimination continued to make it hard for Vanport residents to find better housing in Portland itself. Three years after the war, 18,700 people lived in Vanport, and most of them were black.

Sunny weather in May of 1948 melted so much snow in the Rocky

Mountains that an ominous flood crest began moving down the Columbia toward Portland. As reports came in from Umatilla and The Dalles, officials predicted the crest might hit 30.5 feet in Portland on Tuesday, June 2, nearly as high as the record 33-foot flood of 1894. Crews piled sandbags along the city's new seawall, hoping to keep downtown Portland dry.

In Vanport, engineers checked the dikes on Saturday, May 29, and pronounced them sound. Mimeographed letters distributed to Vanport residents urged them not to panic or flee. Although the flood would be twelve feet higher than the city itself, the dikes were 30 inches taller than necessary to keep out the river. If water rose higher, sirens and sound trucks would spread the alarm for an orderly evacuation.

Nonetheless, nervous Vanport residents kept calling the town's switchboard operators to make sure. Until at least four o'clock on Sunday afternoon, the operators methodically repeated, "There is no immediate danger. Everyone will be notified in ample time."

Calvin Hulbert, a private flight instructor, happened to be flying over Vanport at 4:17 that Sunday afternoon. Below him, the city looked like a tidy Dutch polder surrounded by a muddy sea. The dikes really had been tall enough to hold back the flood.

But then Calvin noticed a tiny gap beneath the railroad tracks to the west. As it turned out, the railroad embankment had not originally been designed as a dike. Instead of rock, it had been built with fill dirt. Perhaps that had seemed sufficient because the railroad was on the downstream side of Vanport, away from the flood's current.

As Calvin watched in amazement, the fill dirt simply sagged beneath the rails and dissolved. Within seconds the gap grew from six feet to sixty, and then to six hundred!

A wave of water ten feet tall surged into the city from the west. Apartment buildings splintered, burst, or floated aside. Calvin saw people rush out to their porches. Moments later, the porches and people were swept away. An old man ran ahead of the wave, pulling two small children in a toy wagon. Then they, too, were gone.

Calvin circled back over the city, anguished. The people of Vanport didn't know what was coming. Even after sirens finally started wailing, most people were methodically carrying furniture and pets out to their cars. Calvin wanted to warn them somehow to drop everything and run for their lives! He circled again, frantically wiggling the tips of his wings. People looked up and waved.

At that point Calvin got sick to his stomach.

In Vanport itself, the initial wave looked like a breaker at the beach. After smashing aside several rows of houses, the wave spread, slowed, and flattened out. Within two hours, the entire city was under twelve feet of water.

Henry Doeneka shook his head at the honking cars crowding the street three abreast outside his Vanport apartment. The sirens hadn't worked at all in his part of town, so Henry just laughed at the dozens of panicky drivers. He even got out his camera and climbed up onto his porch roof to take a picture of them.

That's when Henry noticed what looked like fog, moving along the pavement behind the last cars. With a start, he realized it was actually water. A surge 18 inches deep was spreading through the street. It splashed against cars and buildings. Then it just kept coming, rising higher and higher. Henry suddenly realized that none of the cars was going to escape—including his own.

Henry jumped down from the porch roof and ran into his apartment,

Within two hours of the dike breach, Vanport had filled with twelve feet of water. Considering that residents had little warning and that every building was ruined, it's surprising that only 15 people died.

wondering frantically what he should try to save first. What was so valuable that it couldn't be replaced?

That's when Henry thought of the family upstairs. Nancy Cyrus had lost her husband in the war. She was raising three small children by herself.

For the next ten minutes Henry helped his neighbor carry all three of her children through the flooded streets to a road atop a dike. By then cars, logs, and debris were floating everywhere, and the water was chest deep.

But Henry waded back once more. This time he would save something of his own—the camera. If nothing else, Henry would have pictures.

When water burst into Norman and Marcelle Butcher's ground-floor apartment, the young couple grabbed their two children and ran to an empty apartment upstairs. Little Sally was only eleven months old. Michael was two—old enough to be almost as frightened as his parents.

A few minutes later the entire building lifted off its foundation and began slowly floating east, spinning with the current. Norman was hoping they would drift to the dike, where they could escape. But after 40 minutes the building started sinking. Water seeped up through the floorboards of the second story. Norman considered swimming to the dike to get help, but he didn't want to leave Marcelle and the kids. They opened the windows and sat together on the sill, calling for help. Despite the flood, some of the buildings they floated past were in flames. Electrical shorts had sparked fires on the upper story.

Then an eddy caught their building and spun it to one side, crashing into another apartment house. The jolt threw the entire family out into the muddy water. The children flew out of their parents' arms. Marcelle hit her head on a piece of wreckage and blacked out.

In that horrible moment, Norman had to make a terrifying decision. He could not save both his children and his wife. He had no time to think twice. He grabbed Marcelle.

Norman struggled to keep his wife's head above water. While he was swimming with her toward a raft of debris, however, he saw his two-year-old son slip under the floodwaters and disappear.

Norman and Marcelle were rescued an hour later by men poling a boat through the ruins. The bodies of their drowned children would not be found for five days.

Considering how little warning Vanport had, it's astonishing that only 15 people died. Every building in the city was a total loss.

Vanport was abandoned as a townsite after the flood, but the city left its mark on Oregon in other ways. Hundreds of Vanport refugees had found emergency shelter in Jefferson High School after a vice principal took the initiative to open the school's doors to them. That humanitarian gesture was never forgotten. The school became the heart of a thriving black community—at long last, a community that had found a welcome *inside* Portland's city limits. Later, city councilors renamed a street near the high school Martin Luther King Jr. Boulevard. Vanport Square, a tax-supported center developed by the son of a Vanport Flood refugee, with shops owned primarily by local businesspeople of color, opened on Martin Luther King Jr. Boulevard in 2008.

Vanport College also survived. Students and staff managed to rescue the school's records and equipment moments before floodwaters arrived. The unsinkable institution moved to Portland and became Portland State University, now the state's largest center of higher education.

The health care program developed by Henry Kaiser for Vanport residents survived as Kaiser Permanente, the state's largest hospital system.

Another long-term effect of the Vanport disaster was the acceleration of dam-building projects throughout the Northwest. Almost every year from 1949 to 1966, major new dams opened on Willamette tributaries. Meanwhile a string of even larger dams on the Columbia turned that once-wild river into a series of lakes.

The network of dams got its first real test in 1964.

The Christmas Week Flood of 1964

Chaos! Every major highway in Oregon was closed, cutting off entire cities from emergency supplies. Fifteen people were killed and more than 11,000 were homeless. Governor Mark Hatfield activated the Civil Defense emergency radio network for the first time in Oregon history to declare the entire state a disaster area.

The holiday season of 1964 had cooked up the perfect recipe for a giant winter flood—rain, ice, snow, and then lots more rain.

The storms began in late November, when rain saturated the soil. Then Arctic air moved south into Oregon on December 17, freezing the ground statewide. The next day a front from the tropics collided with the cold air, dumping snow on top of the ice. The Coast Range had a foot of snow, the Cascades had three feet, and even Portland got eight inches.

Then the temperature rose sharply on December 19. Warm, torrential rains melted the snow. The water couldn't soak into the frozen ground below, so everything came barreling down the rivers.

Half of the state's weather stations set all-time records that December.

Towns along the lower Rogue River staggered under 41 inches of rain that month, and Eugene had 21 inches. Even on the dry side of the Cascade Range, nearly nine inches of rain fell in the cities of Bend, The Dalles, and Lakeview. In just five days, some stations received two-thirds of their average *annual* rainfall.

Rivers jumped up, looking for their old flood plains. Soon hundreds of homes in recent subdivisions near Eugene, Salem, and Portland were under water. Thousands more were being evacuated. Federal dams had made low-lying land seem safe for development. Now television reporters were featuring the ominous memories, nightmares, and warnings of Vanport survivors.

Portland police awakened houseboat owners along the Willamette River at three o'clock in

Keizer in the 1964 flood.

the morning of December 23, demanding that they evacuate immediately. The residents were angry for a few minutes, until the flood actually began tearing docks loose. Soon 27 houseboats had floated into the night.

"We had two cats and two dogs in that house," Frank Grimble complained. His wife added, "It happened so fast I couldn't even save my animals. I don't know where my house is. I don't feel very good."

A powerboat from the Harbor Patrol spent the night watching for flotsam at the Ross Island Bridge. The crew snagged a section of dock that included the Willamette Sailing Club's clubhouse and managed to tie it to a ship at the Zeidel dock. Meanwhile, deserted houseboats wound up strung along the shore for miles.

The next morning, houseboater W.L. Washams was griping to reporters. His wife was sitting nearby, listening to the police radio for clues about their home. "Honey, guess what?" she interrupted him. "We moved to Swan Island."

The Clackamas River flooded as never before, jamming thousands of drift logs against power company dams. At its mouth the Clackamas

River backed the Willamette River into a lake that stretched all the way to Oregon City, flooding shopping centers and businesses.

Every helicopter and airplane in the state was pressed into service to rescue people and deliver emergency supplies. Coast Guard choppers plucked more than 60 refugees from farmhouse roofs in the Newberg area. Helicopters were the only way to reach Oakridge, Idanha, Rhododendron, and other Cascade Range communities cut off by the raging rivers.

Louise Moody owned a restaurant in Rhododendron, at the foot of Mt. Hood. She woke up at 5 am on December 22, planning to open her cafe. She discovered that the water supply was out, six inches of snow had fallen overnight, and the wind was blowing 60 miles an hour. Louise thought about this a minute and then went back to bed.

At ten o'clock the local postmaster called Louise to say the Highway 26 bridge was about to go out at Zigzag. Louise put on her ski clothes and walked down to see for herself.

The Zigzag River was booming along, constantly changing course as it explored the canyon floor, undermining banks on one side and then the other. Five houses had already fallen in. Trees 100 feet tall tumbled in every minute or two. Her neighbor's rental cabins were slowly pitching into the river, one at a time. The highway bridge was long gone.

By the time Louise got home the power and phones were out. She turned on the gas grill and hung blankets over the kitchen doorways to keep warm. Then she found three candles and lit one.

The next day, helicopters flew repeatedly through the canyon, ferrying emergency supplies and powerline repairmen. Without water or power, the only shop open in Rhododendron was the liquor store. Business was booming there.

By Christmas Eve, Louise was wondering out loud if there could be a nicer holiday present than a highway bridge. A little boy who was visiting scoffed, "We don't need a bridge very bad, because they can bring Santa Claus in one of the helicopters."

Up the Columbia River, Joe Dickson, a 60-year-old doctor from Montana, was driving the freeway east of The Dalles with his wife Norma and their 21-year-old son George. It was December 22, and they were heading home for Christmas. They had just passed a highlight of the trip—the half-finished, $511-million John Day Dam on the Columbia River. A spectacular new stretch of freeway along the future reservoir crossed a new quarter-mile bridge that spanned the side canyon of the John Day River.

The ride was even more scenic because the John Day River was growling beneath the bridge at flood stage.

Joe stopped the car for a better look. The bridge itself was a monumental, two-and-a-half-million-dollar work of art. Half a dozen 200-foot spans perched atop pillars 15 stories tall. Eventually the dam's reservoir would rise to within 40 feet of the roadway, covering most of the bridge's beauty. For now, the pillars soared up from dizzying depths.

When Joe, Norma, and George looked down into those depths they could feel the bridge railings vibrate. The normally shallow John Day River was caroming down the canyon 40 feet deep, tearing out giant chunks of the bank on either hand. The roiling water churned beneath them past the bridge pillars.

Suddenly a pillar shifted and a crack opened in the roadway.

"Get off the bridge!" Norma shouted. She grabbed her son's arm and pulled him back.

Joe took out his car keys and jumped across the crack. "I'll move the car!"

But the bridge moved first. Undercut by the flood, one of the pillars twisted to one side. As slowly as a drawbridge, the entire 200-foot span beneath him began tilting away. The car rolled toward the gap. Joe scrambled a moment on the inclining pavement. Then he and the car tumbled together into the swirling brown water, nearly 100 feet below.

"Dad!" George ran to the broken bridge's edge. He tore off his jacket.

"George, don't!" Norma cried.

But the young man had already jumped feet first over the brink.

Joseph Dickson was one of the first casualties of the flood. His son George was later pulled from the river and taken to the hospital in Goldendale, where he was treated for shock.

The 1964 flood destroyed 33 highway bridges, but it also washed out many railroad lines. More than 300 passengers in two trains spent Christmas Eve stranded by slides on the Washington side of the Columbia River. When railroad crews radioed for help, Santa Claus responded — in the form of the Air Reserve. The 939th troop carrier wing sent a C-119 Flying Boxcar to parachute emergency rations of bread, butter, butane, and Christmas treats to the marooned railway travelers. The only parachute that failed to deploy properly held the treats. Turkey, ham, mayonnaise, and milk plummeted into the rocks. In a Christmas miracle, all but the mayonnaise and milk survived the plunge.

On Portland's waterfront, drift logs broke loose the *River Queen,* a former San Francisco ferry that had been converted to an upscale restaurant. Tugboats caught the drifting eatery and moored it half a mile downstream on the far bank.

When floodwaters rose at The Oaks, a 1905 amusement park on the Sellwood shore, workers knew what to do. The flood of 1948 had already ruined the park's roller skating rink once. After that flood, park owners had replaced the expensive wood flooring with a new floor atop a layer of empty 55-gallon drums. Now workers simply cut the floor loose. It rode out the storm safely, floating inside the building.

At the height of Portland's flood, the crew of a Coast Guard cutter found a legless man rowing a small boat down the middle of the Willamette River past Swan Island. The man identified himself as Hall Templeton, a 53-year-old member of the Boise Cascade Corporation board of directors. And no, he didn't want to be rescued. Hall said he had lost his legs in an accident years ago and had taken up rowing as a way to keep fit.

"I row almost every other day for exercise," Hall explained. "I start feeling a little out of sorts if I don't exercise."

"In a flood?" the crew asked. Logs, trees, and buildings were churning past. "Where do you think you're going?"

"To Woodland, Washington, to visit a college friend."

The crew scratched their heads. Woodland was 34 miles downstream. The trip would require crossing the flooded Columbia. They told Hall this was not a good idea, especially for a double amputee in a small craft.

"Everyone needs a certain element of foolishness," Hall replied. He asked if he was violating any laws.

No, the crew admitted, not if he had a regulation life preserver on board.

Hall showed them his flotation vest and rowed on.

Thirty-four miles later, Hall's friend met him in Woodland with a pickup truck and trailer, and they drove safely home.

The 1964 flood damaged every county in Oregon. A foot of water poured through the streets of Condon, an eastern Oregon city that is not in a canyon and really shouldn't flood at all. The town of Mitchell, no stranger to flooding, was cut off from the world for days. Near Medford, half a dozen bridges washed out along the Rogue River. Along the upper Rogue a four-foot wall of mud poured through the resort community of Shady Cove. The mud left a mobile home in a mill pond, and shoved a beauty parlor and a Busy Beaver Motel cabin across Highway 62.

Throughout Oregon, 570 homes had been destroyed, and the storm season wasn't over. December's deadly recipe of rain-ice-snow-rain repeated itself three weeks later in January, 1965. This time eastern Oregon was hit hardest, with the Umatilla, Walla Walla, and Grande Ronde Rivers reporting record flows. In all, the series of storms tallied up 47 deaths and $400 million in damage in Oregon, northern California, southern Washington, and Idaho.

Planners considered the Christmas Week Flood a "100-year event" because it rivaled the flood of 1861 as the largest in Oregon's recorded history. One important difference between the two events was the network of dams that had been built on the Willamette and Columbia river systems in the intervening century. To be sure, many of the reservoirs filled early in the 1964 storm. When the flood crest hit at the Dorena Dam south of Eugene, for example, eight feet of water was already pouring over the top.

Still, the U.S. Army Corps of Engineers estimated that the dams lowered the 1964 floodcrest in Eugene by 14.8 feet, in Salem by 7.5 feet, and in Portland by 4.5 feet. The day the flood crested at 29.8 feet without spilling into Portland's downtown, the U.S. Army Corps of Engineers issued a statement that the "cost of the destruction to Portland alone would have more than paid for all of the Willamette flood control projects."

Or might there have been a less expensive way to cut Oregon's losses? After 1964, the possibility of alternative flood-control methods was not widely discussed for years. In the meantime the state would face more floods and yet more damage.

More High Water Marks

What does it mean if "100-year" floods start occurring every 30 years — and then every *ten* years? The floods of 1996 and 2007 affected slightly smaller areas than the flood of 1964, but in each case, some rivers flooded higher than ever. Damages also were high each time. Disturbingly, damage reports often came from the same properties as before.

The **flood of February 1996** is perhaps best remembered from frantic scenes in Portland, where hundreds of volunteers helped shore up downtown's harbor seawall. The 1996 flood killed seven people in Oregon, forced 22,000 to evacuate their homes, and left behind $400 million in damage. In hard-hit Tillamook, 1200 dairy cattle drowned. Two-thirds of the state was declared a disaster area.

The weather pattern leading up to the 1996 flood varied only slightly from the dangerous recipe of 1964. Heavy rains late in 1995 soaked the ground. Then a surprise December windstorm toppled trees. In January, cold storms dumped as much as two feet of snow a day in the mountains and foothills. A freeze in the final week of January dropped temperatures in the Willamette Valley into the teens, paralyzing Portland with ice and sealing the ground.

Then came the "Pineapple Express," a warm, wet front from the tropics. Temperatures shot up 40 degrees. In just four days (February 6-9), the storm dumped a record-breaking 27.88 inches of warm rain on Laurel Mountain in the Coast Range. Records were also topped in Astoria, Corvallis, Hillsboro, Portland, and Oregon City. In the Cascades, melting snow doubled the runoff. Streams went wild. The flow at Hood River, for example, swelled by a factor of 20 in just two days.

Dozens of expensive new riverbank homes toppled into the Sandy River east of Portland.

Harold Jank, a retired 70-year-old truck driver, lived with his wife Jacqueline in a one-story house wedged between the Sandy River and the East Historic Columbia River Highway. Harold had just come home from the hospital the previous day to recover from back surgery. He was watching television when a Troutdale police officer banged on the door. The officer urged them to evacuate. The river was rising, he said, and the mountain slope on the other side of the road looked unstable.

The 1996 flood reopened some of the Willamette Valley's flood plain channels.

Jacqueline wanted to leave, but Harold balked. He couldn't go anywhere without a walker. And what about his medicines? Jacqueline insisted they needed to move to a motel. She brought their car and left it running outside the front door. She got the walker and three pillows for Harold's back. She was just fetching his medicine when a rumble grew outside.

"Uh oh," Jacqueline said, opening the door. "Here it comes."

A second later a mudslide smashed into the front wall. The damaged house slid into the raging Sandy River.

Harold found himself adrift on a plaid sofa atop a section of floor. The ceiling was gone, and so was Jacqueline.

For nearly an hour, Harold yelled for help. Meanwhile his raft of

wreckage drifted beneath three bridges and sailed out onto the raging
Columbia River. The house tilted and the the sofa started sliding into the
flood. Harold managed to climb a wall to a fragment of roof, where he
clung to the remains of a chimney.

On the Columbia, tugboat deck hand Bryan Miles spotted a plaid sofa
amidst the usual storm flotsam of trees and stumps. Then he saw a tilted
rooftop with a white chimney and what looked like a person.

"There's someone on that house!" Bryan yelled to the tugboat's pilot.
The pilot turned the boat to chase the wreckage. When the tug pulled
alongside, Harold gasped, "My wife. My wife was here. There's her
boots."

One blue-and-white snow boot remained, floating with the other debris. But Jacqueline Jank was gone.

Later, after rescue crews had searched in vain by helicopter and boat,
Harold tearfully said, "If she'd have made two more steps she just might
have made it."

Charlie Harper had bought his dream house on the Sandy River near
the Stark Street bridge. Then he spent $250,000 landscaping the home's
two-and-a-half-acre riverfront yard. With five years of hard work, he replaced native willows with decorative shrubs. The river's old gravel bars
became manicured lawns. He turned a slough into a koi pond with an
artificial waterfall.

But the Sandy River had other ideas. In a few hours on February 7,
1996, the flood undid all of Charlie's work. The river not only restored its
original, back-to-nature landscaping motif, but it came six inches away
from removing Charlie's house as well.

Near the Willamette Valley town of Scio, eight-year-old Amber Bar-
greele drowned while walking to the corner mailbox. When searchers
later found her body in a culvert, the entire community mourned.

Rising water tested the new subdivisions that sprawled across low,
soggy, flood-plain land in Washington County's upscale "Silicon Forest."
With water lapping at her doorsill, Denise Wertzler of Cedar Hills yelled
"Slow down!" to people driving the flooded street. Each passing car sent
waves into her home.

In the South Emerald Loop development in Cornelius, 22 new
homeowners discovered that their builder had cut costs by connecting
stormwater drains to the sewer system. February's heavy rains backed

up the sewers, forcing raw sewage out of showers and toilets as if they were fountains.

Along the Molalla River, boats and logging machinery evacuated people from 115 homes that had been built in the river's flood plain. Roy Ferris, watching the muddy water pour past houses, mused aloud, "I wonder what we did to make Mother Nature so mad?"

In Portland, sandbagging crews and giant pumps were working around the clock to save the Oregon Museum of Science and Industry (OMSI). The museum had moved to a remodeled power plant beside the Willamette River just eight years earlier. Now water stood two feet deep in the museum's sub-basement. Ironically, the only exhibit that actually closed for the flood was the *USS Blueback*, the museum's submarine.

Volunteers helped sandbag downtown Portland's seawall in the 1996 flood.

In Tillamook the Wilson River crested 5.4 feet over flood stage—a foot higher than the previous record. Coast Guard rescue boats motoring through the city stalled unexpectedly. One boat hit its propeller on the roof of a sunken car. Another had its propeller snarl in a barbed wire fence. That boat's crew had been on their way to rescue a marooned farm family. Instead the crew wound up marooned too, forced to spend the night in the family's flooded home.

George and Dulcie Doyle of British Columbia had decided to tour scenic Highway 101 on their vacation through Oregon. What a rainy place! And why would a little town like Tillamook have a traffic jam on a Wednesday afternoon? As the couple waited impatiently, water suddenly filled the road. Moments later the flood was seeping in their car doors. Tires from a nearby tire store started floating past the windows.

Dulcie snatched up her backpack and crawled through the car's sunroof. George grabbed a blanket from the backseat and crawled up too. They sat there shivering on the roof, hoping that somene would come rescue them. When no one did, they waded up the road to a Laundromat.

While washing and drying their clothes, the Doyles got to talking with Jessie Embum, a Tillamook resident who was also doing her laundry. Jessie told them all the motels in town were full of either water or people, but she would be willing to share her own house. The Doyles accepted gratefully. That evening, finally warm and dry, Dulcie mused, "I wonder what our next vacation will be like?"

Along the Willamette River, the 1996 flood threatened the low land north of Salem yet again. Two things had changed since the 1964 disaster, however. Dikes had been built north of Salem in 1965, and the area had incorporated in 1982 as Keizer, Oregon's newest city. When the river rose in 1996, Keizer mayor Dennis Koho ordered half the new city's population to evacuate. Water lapped to the rim of the dike, but it held.

In Oregon City, the entire lower business district was under water, with more than 80 businesses damaged or destroyed. Boat owners offered tours of the submerged city for $5.

In Portland, the rising flood threatened to top downtown's harbor seawall. If water spilled into the streets, Old Town would quickly become a lake. Mayor Vera Katz ordered the railing atop the seawall barricaded for extra protection. Volunteers and city works sprang into action, placing 438 concrete highway dividers, 600 sheets of plywood, and 30,000 sand bags along a mile of railing between the Hawthorne and Steel Bridges. The flood finally crested at 28.6 feet, just inches below the impromptu barricade.

The flood of December 2-7, 2007 repeated the theme of the 1996 deluge, with variations. Once again, all roads were closed to Oregon's northern coast. The Coast Range town of Vernonia again was under water, worse than ever. Again, high water closed Interstate 5 near Chehalis. Many of the same businesses flooded in Tillamook. Floodwaters crested at record highs on the Nestucca, Wilson, Wallapa, and Chehalis Rivers.

The storms of 1996 and 2007 left people wondering if major floods are becoming more frequent in Oregon. If so, what do we need to learn to limit their damage?

Why All the Floods?

Western Oregon is a notoriously rainy place to live. Rivers here can be expected to flood periodically. And rainstorms are sufficiently random that it's not possible to draw solid conclusions from a few unusually flood-prone decades. But now that scientists agree our planet's atmosphere is warming, for a variety of reasons, one widely predicted effect is an increase in the severity of Oregon's winter rainstorms.

Here's the logic. Warmer air heats the oceans. That increased energy

The flood of 1890 near Salem.

generates more storms and more clouds, especially in the tropics where the water is already warm. Because warmer air is able to carry more moisture, the clouds are packed with rain. Normally this would be a problem only in the tropics, where hurricanes really may be more frequent, but the storms are now starting to spread farther north as well. Studies show that the tropical belt has widened alarmingly in the past quarter century as the energy in the storms has grown.

The result is that more and more wet winter storms are flung north as far as Oregon. The "Pineapple Express" that freights wet clouds our way is stoked and picking up steam. The December storm in 2007, for example, began as two tropical typhoons in the Pacific Ocean. Instead of dying out at the Tropic of Cancer, the storms picked up power from the warmer sea and walloped the West Coast with a wall of wet clouds 4000 miles long.

If our rivers really are getting wilder, what can we do?

Thinking Like a River

"It must be apparent that such a flood is likely to occur any winter; and hence the proper thing to do is prepare for it," *Oregonian* owner Harvey Scott editorialized after an 1881 flood in Portland. "As the scientists would put it, we must get into harmony with our environment."

That lesson from the 19th century became a casualty in the 20th century when military engineers assumed command of flood preparations. After World War II, the U.S. Army Corps of Engineers set to work combatting high water as if it were an enemy to conquer and control. For years, dams and dikes were the two primary weapons in the Corps' arsenal. The public urged the engineers on, demanding nothing short of victory.

After half a billion dollars of dam-building failed to prevent $157 million in damage from the 1964 flood, the engineers admitted, "We've known all the time we never had complete control of the river."

The Army backpedaled further after the flood of 1996. Major General Russell Fuhrman, commander of the Corps' Pacific division, pointed out that most dams are designed to generate power, and not to hold back

Do you have flood insurance?

Private homeowner insurance policies don't cover flood damage unless you pay for extra coverage—and then the premiums can be alarmingly high.

Theoretically, buildings in designated flood plains cannot be sold without flood insurance. Because of the cost, however, private buyers rarely demand the extra coverage, and even most mortgage companies look the other way. As a result, only about 20 percent of the buildings in Oregon's flood plains are properly insured.

Flood insurance is so expensive that 80 percent of buildings in flood plains lack it.

Ironically, floods are the most common kind of natural disaster, accounting for 90 percent of all disaster-related damage, according to the Federal Emergency Management Agency (FEMA).

How expensive is flood insurance? Even if you live in a low-risk area outside of a flood plain, and even if you don't have a basement, the extra coverage can double your annual insurance payment. If you wait until the rivers are rising, it will be too late to call your insurance agent, because policies have a 30-day waiting period. On top of all this, the policies generally don't cover personal possessions, so you'll end up paying for damaged clothes and furniture anyway.

Congress created the controversial National Flood Insurance Program 40 years ago to cover risky properties that private insurers wouldn't touch. Oregonians lucky enough to snag this coverage pay an average of $632 a year, but the program is subsidized so heavily by taxpayers that it's $17.5 billion in debt. Most of the money goes to rebuild the same flood-prone structures over and over.

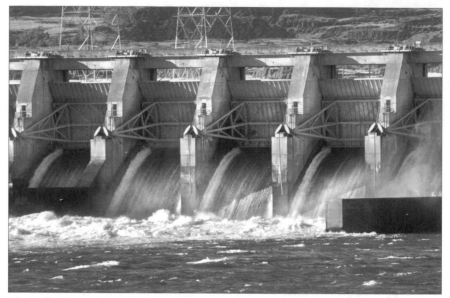

The Dalles Dam drowned Celilo Falls in 1957. Fifty years later, a memorial effort to briefly drain the reservoir ended when sonar revealed that the old falls lay under 30 feet of mud.

floods. Only 14 of the 40 dams on Willamette River tributaries can store floodwaters. Less than 30 percent of the watershed's runoff is regulated by dams. "The other 70 percent," the major general said, "is the act of God."

Control remains even more elusive on the Columbia River, where only two dams, the Grand Coulee and John Day Dams, have the capacity to store floodwaters.

Nor are we likely to gain full control of the rivers by building more big dams. It turns out that dams create enough problems of their own that momentum has grown to start *removing* certain dams, rather than to build more.

Salmon and other fish have been the most publicized collateral damage. Older dams without fish ladders have blocked salmon runs entirely from most of the Northwest's headwaters. Even dams designed to let adult fish swim upstream present enough of an obstacle that runs have shrunk. Fingerling fish trying to swim downstream are often chopped up by power turbines or poisoned by the nitrogen in spillway bubbles. Retrofitting dams to solve these problems has proven expensive and prone to failure.

Dams seem permanent, but they are not. River silt gradually settles in the still water behind dams. Within a few centuries, reservoirs become mudflats, useless for flood control or recreation. To commemorate the fiftieth anniversary of The Dalles Dam in 2007, Indian tribes and history buffs proposed draining its reservoir for a few days to briefly restore Celilo Falls, a spiritual site that once was the Northwest's greatest salmon fishery. The proposal died when sonar revealed that the drowned falls had already been buried by 30 feet of mud.

The dams themselves were mostly built before the Northwest's earthquake risks were understood in the 1980s. Massive quakes or volcanic mudflows could breach the dams, unleashing catastrophic floods. Even without a sudden disaster, dams develop weaknesses with age. Cracks form as the ground shifts or as the concrete degrades.

The aging Marmot Dam on the Little Sandy River east of Portland was removed in 2007. Removal of the Little Sandy Dam in 2008 is opening 100 miles of streams for salmon and steelhead habitat. The Savage Rapids Dam on the Rogue River and a series of dams on the Klamath River are likely to be next.

If dams aren't the answer, what about dikes? A seawall saved downtown Portland in 1964. Dikes saved Keizer in 1996. Rock embankments, known as *riprap*, have successfully protected riverfront homes along mountain rivers.

One of the difficulties with dikes is that they don't actually solve the problem — they just move

Great blue herons are among the many birds that need the wetlands of flood plains.

it someplace else. Diking a flood plain is like pushing on a waterbed. Building dikes in Keizer increases the risk of flood across the river in West Salem. Dikes along the Columbia River in North Portland raise floodwaters that threaten Vancouver. Riprap in front of a streamside mountain cabin increases the risk that neighboring cabins will be swept away.

Channeling rivers not only shifts problems, but it also creates new ones. The straighter a river runs, the faster its current flows. And faster currents cause more erosion.

Rivers like to meander for the same reason that downhill skiers like to make S-shaped turns — to slow down. Each curve eats up energy and speed. Slower is safer. Fast water picks up boulders, digs deeper, and

The Walla Walla River broke its channel dikes in the 1964 flood to restore its natural meander rhythm.

eventually slams into riverbanks, creating meanders whether people want them or not.

Recent research shows that the S-shaped bends of a river are part of the current's *wavelength*. Like a vibrating string or a beam of light, a river oscillates back and forth in its channel with a definable rhythm. The width and speed of the river's current determines how large the meanders will be. Straightening a river with dikes sets up a long-term battle with the river's urge to meander. Eventually, a big enough flood will come that the river will win the war.

For an example of this futile fight, look at the northeast Oregon city of Milton-Freewater, where the U.S. Army Corps of Engineers channelized the Walla Walla River into a straight and narrow path. In 1964 the flooding river broke its straightjacket of dikes every few hundred yards, reasserting its natural wavelength with spectacularly rhythmic precision. That same year the corps developed an insightful definition for the

A map of the Marys River near Corvallis shows how meanders migrated down its flood plain from 1956 to 1994. (Source: U.S. Forest Service)

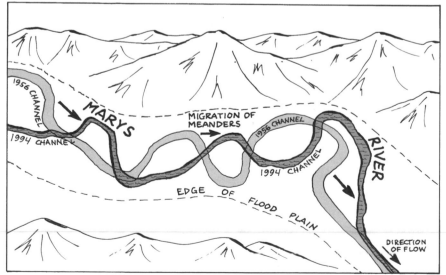

Minto-Brown Island Park has restored wetlands in the Willamette River flood plain near Salem while providing room for joggers, geese, and dog-walkers.

term *flood plain.* "It is actually a part of the river channel," the engineers recognized. All of the flat land bordering the river, within the margins of the meanders, is part of the flood plain, and all of it carries water in times of flood.

Even without major floods, riverbends gradually "migrate" downstream, as maps of historic river channels clearly show. The current cuts strongest on the downstream part of each meander. Meanwhile, sediment settles on the calmer, upstream edge. Eventually riverbends march downstream until they have covered every part of the flood plain. If there are structures in the flood plain, one day they will find themselves on the current's cutting edge.

Wetlands have only recently won recognition as a natural flood-control mechanism. These seasonally soggy lowlands were long derided as worthless. Especially in the Willamette Valley, mile after mile of wetlands were diked, ditched and drained for farms or commercial development.

Now it turns out that wetlands serve as natural reservoirs in times of flood. Just like the reservoirs behind dams, wetlands fill when the rivers rise. If the flood plain is allowed to pool up, it holds back water until the floodcrest passes. Building concrete dams certainly is one strategy to reduce flood damage. But restoring wetlands can do a lot of the same work with less expense, less maintenance, and less risk.

Does this mean we should reopen old sloughs full of weeds and bugs? Actually, it does. Wetlands turn out to be astonishingly important for wildlife. Most of the "weeds and bugs" in wetlands are native species that

The icon of Oregon's state flag, beavers have long known how to "think like a river" by encouraging the wetlands that hold back floodcrests.

evolved here ages ago. Without them as food, the populations of our fish, birds, and other wildlife will continue to decline. Beavers and salmon may survive only as icons for our flags and license plates. The western pond turtle, for example, lives to be a hundred years old, but has become as rare as the wetland habitat it needs. Ominously, the few turtles that remain seem all to be over 30 years of age. Unless we pay attention, a key part of Oregon's ecosystem is in danger of dying out.

Think like a river! Just as people need exercise, rivers need to flood. It's never healthy to lie in a bed too long. Every once in a while a river needs to get up, stretch its muscles, and shake its gravel bars around.

Most people get the idea—standing in the way of a river is asking for trouble. Why, then, are so many homes and businesses damaged by floods? And why do people keep building in harm's way?

The answer here is also painfully simple. People build on riverfront land because it's beautiful, convenient, and generally not prohibited. Private flood insurance may be expensive, but who needs it? If disaster strikes, the federal government will bail you out.

Each time the President declares an official disaster area, people can file claims for federal relief. Congress has created a National Flood Insurance Program for properties that are so prone to flooding that private insurers won't issue them policies. These programs cost taxpayers billions of dollars.

Unfortunately, most of the money has been spent to rebuild the same structures in flood plains over and over again. Proposed reforms would encourage repeat claimants to raise their buildings or move to higher ground, but those reforms stalled when Congressmen in flood-prone states complained that their constituents were victims.

Loten Hooley, owner of a Tillamook lumberyard that has received more than $1.5 million in federal relief, said he isn't about to move from his high-visibility location on Highway 101, even though it's suffered 20 floods in 40 years. After the flood of 2007 he told *Oregonian* reporter Brent Walth, "If they want to talk about buying me out or paying the full cost of moving me, then we'll talk."

Ken Kesey's fictional flood fighter, Hank Stamper, would have clapped him on the shoulder and said, "Never give a goddam inch."

Maybe we'll never all think like rivers.

CHAPTER VII

Wind and Weather

Weather throws a little of everything at us here in Oregon.

Almost every winter, ice storms turn Portland into a skating rink of frozen roadways for a day or two. The Columbia Gorge is a perfect crucible for stirring up ice storms known as *silver thaws*. When wet clouds from the Pacific meet icy winds from the Rockies, a fairyland of silver lace spins traffic, sags powerlines, and cracks trees.

Oregon's gigantic snowstorms have become legend. Crater Lake saw a cumulative total of 73 feet of snow fall in the winter of 1932-33, topping their average of 45 feet. A snowfall in 1884 entombed trains for weeks at Starvation Creek Falls, forcing Columbia Gorge travelers to dig their way out for food. In January 1950, a storm dumped 22 inches of snow on Portland. Three

Winter ice storms often shut down Portland's airport – as here in January 2004.

feet of snow buried Eugene in January 1969, closing the University of Oregon for the first time in history.

Other wild weather includes an Arctic blast that froze the eastern Oregon town of Seneca to 54 degrees below zero in 1933. And despite our rainy reputation, droughts in eastern Oregon have bankrupted farmers, drained reservoirs, and wiped dozens of towns off the map. Oregon's spectacular weather has left everyone with a favorite story. No book can cover them all, so let's focus on windstorms. Why windstorms?

Many of the most enduring memories date to 1962, when a surprise gale walloped western Oregon on Columbus Day, Friday, October 12.

The Columbus Day Storm

The weather report for October 12, 1962 suggested breezes and light clouds. The first sign of trouble came just after noon when a coastal power company manager at Crescent City tried to alert Portland officials to the scale of the approaching disaster. "Streets are blocked! Crews are unable to move!" And then telephone lines to the coast went dead.

The remnants of two typhoons, Emma and Freda, had crossed the Pacific Ocean in early October and joined forces off the northern California coast. The new storm made a sharp left turn and raced north along the coast, dropping air pressure so suddenly that barometers appeared to be malfunctioning. At Cape Blanco, Oregon's westernmost point, the weather station anemometer spun so fast it flew to pieces. By 1 pm the station's attendant estimated the wind speed at 170 miles per hour.

Flying tree limbs, signs, and roofing shingles killed several people in Eugene.

In Gold Beach, 400 children had just gone home from Riley Creek Elementary School when winds blasted the building apart, scattering pieces for a quarter mile. A six-by-six-inch beam from the school punctured a nearby home, missing a sleeping man by inches.

In Bandon the wind lifted an empty motel cabin and dropped it on an unoccupied trailer, destroying both. The lights went out at Coos Bay when the wind blew a 200-foot powerline tower into the bay, dropping a 115,000-volt line across the port's channel.

In Newport the wind measured 138 miles per hour before the storm destroyed the gauge. The second story of the city's Elks Lodge blew into the street, crushing two cars. Exposed in the roofless first floor were a bowling alley, restaurant, tavern, and barber shop.

At the Air Force radar station atop Mt. Hebo, south of Tillamook, the official wind gauge broke at 84 miles per hour, but winds probably blasted as high as 170. The gale ripped 200-pound tiles off the station roof and hurled them down the mountain, splintering trees.

Two dozen people were killed in the Willamette Valley, most of them crushed by falling trees. Some losses bordered on the bizarre.

Curtis Ray, 85, was already upset that he'd had to entrust his 84-year-old wife Martha to a nursing home. On the afternoon of the storm he stopped by the Sunset Home in south Eugene to visit. The wind outside the windows was so loud they could hardly talk, especially now that Curtis was a little hard of hearing. Suddenly there was a crash as the adjacent barn-sized brick chapel collapsed in the wind. Bricks began tumbling through the ceiling. One brick broke Martha's wrist. But the husband she had just been talking to was dead, entirely buried by debris.

The Columbus Day Storm damaged most barns in western Oregon. This grain storage building near Newberg collapsed.

Larry Johnson, 21, was expecting a baby with his wife. They felt lucky to find a place with cheap rent while Larry finished up his degree at the University of Oregon. Their apartment had been built as temporary housing in World War II, just like the apartments in Vanport. After the war the university had bought nearly a hundred of the old Army buildings, brought them to Eugene on railroad flatcars, and set them up on swampy land near Roosevelt Junior High School to house veterans under the G. I. Bill. By 1962 the rows of two-story apartment buildings had become Amazon Married Student Housing.

The Amazon buildings were so drafty that candles on the windowsills sometimes blew out even when the windows were closed. Now the wind outside was screaming. Tiles had begun to peel off the roof of the junior high school down the street, spinning fragments through the air.

Larry leaned out the window, trying to tape cardboard over the glass as protection. Suddenly one of the flying roof tiles sailed down out of the sky, angled through the open window, and sliced into Larry's chest like a circular saw.

His pregnant wife screamed. Blood was everywhere. She called an ambulance, and they rode together to the hospital.

Larry was dead. His wife was admitted for shock. The next day, Sacred Heart Hospital announced that her condition was "good."

Where were you in '62?

Those who lived in western Oregon in 1962 have vivid memories of the Big Blow on October 12. When the wind began on that Columbus Day I was walking home from the third grade at McKinley Elementary School in Salem. Wow! Each time I spread out my jacket and hopped, the wind carried me five feet down the sidewalk.

J. Wesley Sullivan was news editor of the Oregon Statesman *when the Columbus Day Storm hit in 1962.*

By the time I got home, all the kids on the block were outside, reveling in the wind. You could kick a football a full block. You could stand at a crazy angle and let the air hold you up. Leaves and branches were sailing by. Trees started falling. Wires tore loose and jerked about like snakes. It was great fun, and the roar was so loud you could hardly hear parents frantically shouting to "Get in off the street!"

When Mom dragged us in I watched out the window with my brothers and sister, snickering at the crazy neighbor who was trying to keep his walnut tree from falling by propping it up with a board. Then Dad came home from his job as news editor at the *Oregon Statesman*. He took a look around, got some boards, and propped up our two cherry trees.

Then the lights went out. Dad looked as serious as I'd ever seen him. "I've got to get back to the newspaper."

While Mom cooked us a candlelight dinner of hot dogs on a Coleman camp stove, Dad fought his way a mile back downtown. Trees had crushed cars and blocked streets. Signs flew past, slicing through the air. Shattered store windows covered downtown sidewalks with glass.

The newspaper office buzzed like a war command center. Radio and TV stations were off the air, so people would be relying on the paper for news. The managing editor found kerosene heaters to melt lead for the typesetting machine. Someone got a generator. Photographers rushed in with film to develop. Dad collected stories and wrote headlines. At 2 am the presses rolled, and Dad walked back home through the dark, ruined city.

In the morning, the people of Salem awoke to find the newspaper on their porches, as always. The news had gotten through. But what seemed to matter most were the personal memories of where you had been and what you had been doing during the Columbus Day Storm.

Although the October 12, 1962 windstorm cut power to Salem, the city's Oregon Statesman *managed to publish on time the next morning, with a cover shot that became an icon of the storm — a collapsing Monmouth college tower photographed by student Wes Luchau.*

Roy Johnson, 62, was walking down the street near the University of Oregon when the wind suddenly picked up a plywood ticket booth from the track at Hayward Field, sailed it through the sky, and landed it on top of him. Roy survived with a broken rib and a damaged kidney.

Sawmills in the 1960s still burned bark and wood scraps in giant wigwam-shaped incinerators. The wind flattened burners in Eugene and Junction City, scattering sparks. One blaze destroyed two blocks of downtown Junction City. Eugene firefighters battled 75 fires.

In Corvallis, Bud and Hazel Capen had been fixing up their suburban home for six years. When the wind tore off their roof, they cowered on the kitchen floor with their black cat Shmoo. Glass shards and tree branches blasted over their heads. Wall after wall crumpled. They crawled to the utility room. Incredibly, the telephone was still working. Bud called his mother and told her he didn't expect to survive. When the wind finally stopped, however, they were still alive. Their house, on the other hand, had become a field of wreckage.

Outside of Oregon City, Ed Gross had finished building a garage for six school buses one week before the storm. When the wind hit, the entire

five-ton garage flew into the air, sailed entirely over the top of Ed's house without damage—effortlessly clearing his television antenna—and then landed 300 feet downwind on his *neighbor's* house, smashing it to rubble. Meanwhile the only damage to the six school buses was a single missing rearview mirror.

In the Columbia Gorge, the Northwest power grid short-circuited when the Bonneville Power Administration's main transmission tower across the Columbia River collapsed at Bonneville Dam.

Most of the trees blew down at Salem's Capitol Mall. Willson Park, once a grove of giant firs, became a firewood lot.

In Portland, wind gusted to 116 miles per hour on the Morrison Bridge. Near the Ross Island Bridge, a 350-foot World War II landing craft broke loose from the Zidell scrap metal docks and crashed into the Hawthorne Bridge, destroying one of the lanes.

At the Totem Pole Marina beside the Columbia River's Interstate Bridge, the wind scattered 17 cabin cruisers that had been on display. One boat landed atop a parked car. The marina's store windows shattered. Struggling in the wreckage, manager John Lenz, age 50, died of a heart attack.

At the Portland International Airport, a new 300-foot-long hangar collapsed on the planes inside. Winds destroyed 175 airplanes at airports across the Northwest.

Hundreds of giant Douglas fir trees blew down at Council Crest, dramatically widening that popular viewpoint's panorama. Nearby, the wind mysteriously skipped the Washington Park zoo, merely blowing over a few garbage cans.

Windows blew out throughout downtown Portland, showering the streets with glass and debris. The Park Blocks resembled a half-finished logging operation. Signs flew down the streets, smashing cars. Shingles peeled from roofs like playing cards from a casino deck. Power blinked on and off as crews struggled to bring alternative generators online. Transmission towers crumpled, blacking out all five television stations.

Tornadoes in the Pacific Northwest?

We may not be in Kansas anymore, but Oz-like twisters really can tear through the Northwest. For some reason, Vancouver, Washington seems to tally more than its fair share.

One of the most devastating tornadoes in recent memory touched down on April 5, 1972 in Vancouver, ripping the roof off a Waremart market. The Peter S. Ogden Elementary School was destroyed, injuring 70 children. Damages topped $3 million.

Sixty tornadoes have struck Oregon in recorded history, including a Morrow County twister that killed six and wrecked 30 buildings in 1888. A tornado lifted a barn 300 feet in the air near Eugene's airport in 1951. A mysterious, unseen tornado in Wallowa County jackstrawed 3000 acres of timber in 1968. In 1993, people saw a funnel cloud that crossed Marion County near Salem, killing six cows and sucking water from the Willamette River.

Tornadoes are rare and small in Oregon. Here, a waterspout at Neskowin.

Tornado strength is measured by the Fujita scale from F0 (with winds up to 72 miles per hour) to F6 (with winds greater than 261 miles per hour).

An F1 tornado on Thursday, January 10, 2008 arced through Vancouver, Washington just a trifle north of the 1972 path. In just two miles the twister uprooted 200 trees, damaged a dozen homes, and snapped four power poles with 100-mile-per-hour winds.

Some of fiercest winds hit the Vancouver Lake Crew's docks, where more than 50 rowing shells, worth thousands of dollars each, lay smashed on the shore like so much straw. The rowing club's founder, Bill Kalenius, was a 55-year-old cancer survivor who had "dedicated his life to this," according to his wife Mary Kay. "It kept him afloat." Donations and volunteers have helped rebuild the club since the unlikely windstorm.

KGW-AM played spooky music, but when the staff realized theirs was the only station still on the air, they broadcast warnings to stay off the streets.

In Seattle, the 1962 World's Fair closed early for the day when wind set the Space Needle's airy tripod humming like a giant tuning fork.

In all, the Columbus Day Storm killed 38 people, left 150 homeless, knocked down eleven billion board feet of timber, and caused $250 million dollars of damage from northern California to British Columbia. The insurance industry reeled. Most homeowner policies *do* cover wind damage. Two hundred additional insurance adjusters flew to Oregon to help settle the claims.

Will the Winds Return?

Although Oregon's windstorms are less focused than the summer spiral hurricanes of the tropics, there are patterns. Our big gales come from the south. They hit in winter every few years. Usually we get old typhoons from the tropics that have wandered east across the Pacific, gathered strength, and barged ashore.

The 1962 Columbus Day Storm may have been rivaled by a ten-hour gale on January 9, 1880. That blast killed 30 and flattened forests. Four of the dead were children who were eating lunch when the wind felled a tree across their schoolhouse in Vancouver, Washington. Twenty-five others were sailors who drowned when Astoria's fishing fleet sank in the Columbia River's mouth.

Windstorms have raked the state in the winters of 1921, 1931, 1936, 1951, 1955, 1958, 1962, 1967, 1971, 1981, 1995, 2002, and 2007.

One of the storms with the most bluster hit on December 2, 2007, when gauges clocked 129-mile-per-hour winds at Bay City near Tillamook. Two of the government's three weather buoys off the Oregon Coast were torn loose. A third of a billion board feet of timber blew down, mostly in Clatsop County. Church steeples, warehouses, and roofs were lost from Tillamook to Astoria.

The 2007 gale also toppled one of Oregon's largest living things, the 206-foot-tall, 18-foot-diameter Klootchy spruce in a county park east of Seaside. It had shared the title of world's biggest Sitka spruce with a tree in Washington. Oregon's top contender, unless a windstorm one day fells it too, is now Big Spruce, a 193-foot-tall, 16-foot-diameter tree in Cape Meares State Park, ten miles west of Tillamook.

CHAPTER VIII

Landslides

After a mudslide tore through a home west of Roseburg in the rainy winter of 1996, killing four people, Oregon's governor called for a landslide action plan to warn people of risks. Legislators authorized nearly a quarter of a million dollars to map the state for landslide hazards.

The resulting map of high-risk areas was so alarming that officials decided not to publicize it. The map revealed that western Oregon is riddled with thousands of steep slopes where potential landslides lie waiting, aimed at downhill properties like loaded guns.

And what pulls the trigger? The more we learn about the causes behind Oregon's landslides, the more controversial the subject becomes.

Of Lakes, Rapids, and Beach Cliffs

Catastrophic landslides are not news to Oregon geologists. Slides created many of the lakes in the Cascade foothills, and nearly all of the lakes in the Coast Range. In 600 AD, for example, a gigantic jumble of sandstone boulders dammed Lake Creek in the Coast Range to create Loon Lake. East of Reedsport 20 miles, the two-mile-long lake now attracts crowds of campers, swimmers, and boaters each summer.

In about 1000 AD an even larger landslide created three lakes in what is now the Rogue-Umpqua Divide Wilderness, northwest of Crater Lake. Half of Grasshopper Mountain collapsed, launching a four-square-mile slide that dammed Fish Lake. Slumps atop the landslide debris later filled to form Buckeye and Cliff Lakes. Those pools beside the broken mountain's cliff are now popular day-hike destinations.

Many of our river rapids have been created by landslides too. A gigantic slide in the Columbia Gorge dammed the entire Columbia River for several months around 1460 AD. That event inspired the legend of

Stripes on a cliff face show where a landslide cut Grasshopper Mountain in half in about 1000 AD, creating Buckeye Lake.

the Bridge of the Gods, and may well have wiped out an Indian village. The entire south side of Table Mountain rumbled into the Columbia River across from the present-day city of Cascade Locks. The slide covered 14 square miles with debris and formed a natural dam 270 feet tall. The dam soon washed out to create the Cascades, a stretch of whitewater that terrified pioneer travelers. Although the rapids has since been drowned by Bonneville Dam, it left its name to an entire mountain chain, the Cascade Range.

Oregon geologists are particularly unsurprised by beachfront landslides. The Pacific Ocean is eating away our coastal cliffs at an average rate of about two feet a year. Soft sandstone bluffs, such as those at Newport, are retreating about ten times that fast. In 1942 a large slump at Newport's Nye Beach sent 15 homes sliding toward the sea.

In 1997 a similarly soft seacliff near Oceanside threatened to undermine 32 townhouses at a five-year-old development called The Capes. Owners of the upscale, gated subdivision asked permission to shore up the cliff by putting "riprap" boulders on the beach.

Both Tillamook County and the governor denied The Capes' request. Officials noted that the developers had been warned of the threat of erosion. According to geologists, rock barricades actually *increase* beach erosion. Although a property with riprap boulders may be briefly protected from the waves, neighboring properties will erode more quickly, in the same way that riverside dikes divert floodwaters to other exposed areas. If all the properties along a beach use boulders, the sand will simply wash away. Then the public will be left without any beach at all. This is why it's illegal to place riprap boulders on Oregon's publicly-owned beaches without a permit.

The Mountains Are Restless

Even when the Cascade snowpeaks aren't erupting, they can still cause trouble. If you stack volcanic rubble 10,000 feet high, add some glaciers, and then soak the whole pile with rain, landslides are inevitable.

On an unhappy Christmas Day in 1980, a man drove his truck up to Mt. Hood to be alone. Cold rain was drenching the woods. He pulled into the Pollalie Creek Campground along Highway 35, crawled into the back of his truck, and went to sleep.

Four miles up the mountain, a crack was opening in the ground at the head of Polallie Creek.

If you've hiked the trail to the Cooper Spur shelter, high on Mt. Hood's east shoulder, you're familiar with the area's stark alpine terrain of steep cinder fields. Over the centuries Pollalie Creek had cut a V-shaped notch into one side of this slope. Now, saturated by rain, the entire head of the canyon slumped downhill. Suddenly the gully turned into a vast, quarter-mile-wide bowl. As the landslide gained speed over the next four miles, it tore out the canyon slopes on either hand, growing larger as it went. By the time the avalanche of cinders, trees, and mud surged across the Pol-lalie Creek Campground, it was 60 feet deep. The roar probably awakened the man only seconds before he was swept to his death.

The landslide fanned out, plowed into the cliffs on the opposite side of Highway 35, and then stopped, damming the East Fork Hood River.

For the next twelve minutes the East Fork Hood River backed up behind the wall of debris, form-

Steep canyons and melting glaciers trigger landslides at Mt. Hood.

ing a muddy lake where the campground had been. Then the impromptu dam broke, sending an even larger torrent of mud and rock down toward the Hood River Valley. Five miles of the highway vanished. By the time the slide finally ground to a halt, it had left one man dead and $13 million in damage.

Mountain landslides are often triggered by melting glaciers. On the south side of Mt. Hood, the lower end of the White River Glacier periodically crumbles, launching a slurry of rocks and mud three miles down its canyon to close Highway 35. On the north side of the mountain, the Eliot Glacier's floods have closed the popular Timberline Trail around Mt. Hood twice in 15 years.

At Mt. Jefferson, backpackers marvel at the open wildflower fields of

Jefferson Park, a mile-square plain snugged against the mountain's cliffs. Glacial floods and landslides created this remarkably flat valley by fill-

ing it repeatedly with muddy debris. Jefferson Park's lack of large trees suggests that the most recent of these devastating slides hit as recently as the 1930s.

On the west side of Mt. Jefferson, the melting Milk Creek Glacier launched a landslide in 2006 that tore out the Pacific Crest Trail and spread four miles down a wooded valley. The flood buried the first mile of the popular Pamelia Lake Trail with four feet of mud. Most of the trees in the flood's path survived, but the trunks now emerge from a bed of mud and rocks instead of a carpet of green moss.

Glacial mudflows from Mt. Jefferson filled and leveled Jefferson Park.

Pamelia Lake itself was created a few centuries ago by similar land-slides from the melting Milk Creek Glacier. Pamelia Lake's rockslide dam is still so porous that the lake outlet is mostly subterranean, audible as an underground gurgling. Each summer the lake level drops ten feet, leaving a broad grassy beach.

These mountain landslides raise the question of why the glaciers are melting. Let's discuss that in a later chapter.

Rainstorms, Roads, and Clearcuts

After a 1975 rainstorm, hundreds of landslides roared down the steep Coast Range canyons of the Mapleton Ranger District west of Eugene. No people died and no houses were destroyed, but the slides created an en-vironmental disaster. Muddy debris scoured out streambeds, killing fish and ruining spawning beds. Entire hillsides were stripped of soil, leaving scablands that might not be able to grow trees for centuries.

Was the rainstorm really the cause of the disaster? The Forest Service conducted a study to find out. Researchers examined 70 percent of the Mapleton Ranger District and found 245 landslides. Of these, only nine percent were "natural" events, caused by the rain alone. Fourteen percent of the slides had clearly been triggered by roadcuts, primarily from logging roads carved into steep hillsides. But an astonishing 77 percent of the slides had originated in recent clearcuts. In a clearcut logging area, all of the trees are harvested. Then other plants are poisoned or removed by hand in an attempt to help new tree seedlings get started.

Despite the 1975 study, Forest Service officials had a hard time believing that clearcut logging could have been a factor in more than three-quarters of the storm damage. The Forest Service ordered another survey in 1978. That study investigated 99 landslides and found that 77 of them were related to clearcuts, confirming the earlier results almost precisely.

P.B. Wickham, the Forest Service ranger in charge of the Mapleton District, sent an internal memo to his boss, suggesting that their long-term practice of clearcut logging might be having a catastrophic impact on Oregon's Coast Range.

Wickham's superiors in the Forest Service were outraged. They responded by demoting him to a less important post far away.

Wickham's replacement at the Mapleton Ranger District kept up the pace of intensive logging, but with a few adjustments. New logging roads would be built by hauling dirt away from roadcuts, rather than merely dumping it down the slope. Trees in steep clearcuts would be lifted out by helicopters or aerial cableways, rather than by dragging the logs uphill through the dirt. And small patches of forest would be left at the steepest parts of canyon headwalls, where it's hard to log anyway.

To see if the modified clearcutting strategy was working, the Forest Service ordered an aerial photo survey of the Mapleton Ranger District in 1982. The photos revealed 50 new slides caused by roads and 79 more slides in clearcuts. Torrents of debris had scoured an additional 14 miles of streambeds.

The Forest Service decided more time was needed for study. Meanwhile, the Mapleton Ranger District announced a Seven-Year Plan that would continue clearcutting 100 million board feet of timber per year.

At this point, local environmental groups decided time was running out for the Coast Range forests. The homespun Siuslaw Task Force and the Oregon Wildlife Federation appealed to the National Wildlife Federation for help. Together they filed suit against the U.S. Forest Service in 1984, arguing that the government was violating its own environmental laws.

The U.S. District Court agreed. In a decision that shook the forestry business, Senior District Judge Solomon shut down *all* timber sales on the entire 200,000-acre Mapleton Ranger District.

Logging operations on Forest Service land came to a halt. In the years

After heavy rains in 1996, Andy Stahl of Forest Service Employees for Environmental Ethics counted 180 landslides in clearcuts. Forest Service studies show that more than three quarters of slides are related to clearcut logging, and many begin at logging roadcuts.

that followed, the Forest Service developed much stricter guidelines to limit the threat of landslides. The new rules banned clearcuts altogether on steep slopes. But state and private forests adopted weaker restrictions. And some of the most dangerous areas had already been logged.

Potential landslides had been strewn throughout the hills like time bombs. One of the most devastating slides would wait until 1996.

Western Oregon had already been walloped by one deluge in 1996 — a February storm that flooded Tillamook and nearly topped Portland's seawall. So the state was weary when another monster rainstorm hit just nine months later. Four inches of rain drenched Corvallis and Eugene on November 18, breaking records. Rivers from the Siletz to the Umpqua rose higher than they had for years.

It was a Monday evening, and Susan Moon was glad to have made it home to her husband Rick and their two teenagers, Rachael and Justin. Susan had to commute 27 miles from her nursing job at Roseburg's Mercy Medical Center, but she loved their woodsy home on Hubbard Creek Road, beside a little brook in the Coast Range.

Susan had become a nurse because she cared about people. That evening, for example, she had invited Ann Maxwell, a lonely Roseburg friend, home for dinner. Ann had just lost her husband after a four-year struggle with Lou Gehrig's disease. Susan thought an evening out would do Ann good. To make sure Ann felt comfortable, Susan also invited Sharon Marvin, a neighbor who had just turned 40, the same as Ann.

While Susan waited for Ann to arrive, she and Sharon set the table. What a lovely dinner party it would be! The lights flickered, so Rick got out candles, and that was even better. Their 13 year old, Justin, was out side watching the rainstorm with the neighbor boy, Todd. Perhaps Rachael felt a little left out, but then that was part of being 16.

By six o'clock Rick was complaining that the evening newspaper hadn't yet arrived. Must be the weather, he thought. Susan began worrying that Ann might have lost her way in the storm.

And then the strangest booming noise rattled the windows.

"Get out of the house!" Rick shouted.

Susan and Sharon looked puzzled. Rachael, however, bolted for the door.

A second later the back wall of the house caved in and the lights went out. A mass of mud and trees smashed the windows and churned across the room. The debris buried Rick, Susan, and Sharon before pushing out the front wall and moving on.

Rachael screamed to her brother Justin. They grabbed the neighbor boy, Todd, and scrambled up a wooded hillside away from the mud.

Ann Maxwell was still searching for the Moons' house, worried about showing up late for dinner. Hubbard Creek Road had been a mess of tree branches and puddles. Finally she parked her car, walked up a likely driveway, and stopped short.

A wall of landslide debris was roaring out of darkness. Ann tried to run, but the mud caught her first.

The newspaper delivery man had been struggling with Hubbard Creek Road too. Arnold Ryder was 70, but after retiring from his job as a baker he had been just bored enough that he agreed to take on a rural route for the Roseburg *News-Review*. He was already two hours late with his newspaper deliveries when a fallen tree blocked the road altogether.

Arnold thought for a minute. He would have to call the county road department to clear the road. He needed a phone. After sitting in his car awhile, he finally got out into the rain and started walking toward a house.

Suddenly a mudslide churned across the road. Arnold managed to grab a tree. Then the debris knocked him loose, swept him down the hillside, and left him pinned under a log.

Two hours later rescue crews arrived on Hubbard Creek Road. They found three frightened teenagers, shivering in wet clothes. They found the remains of the Moons' house, now a debris field strewn with scraps of vinyl siding. A purple vinyl raincoat and a credit card lay in the mud.

A few minutes later the searchers found Arnold Ryder. They cut him loose from his tree. Arnold had fractured his knee and broken a rib. He couldn't talk and he was coming down with pneumonia, but in time he would recover.

The search crews also found the bodies of Susan Moon, her husband Rick, her neighbor Sharon, and her friend Ann.

The landslides that night in 1996 claimed one more victim. Delsa Hammer, 48, was driving back from Roseburg to her home in Coos Bay when mudslides blocked Highway 38 near Scottsburg. Delsa waited in a string of 30 cars and trucks for the road to reopen. Hours passed and people grew anxious, but what could they do?

As people sat in the string of vehicles, rocks kept sliding down the hillside, hammering the cars like bowling pins. Still, it seemed safer to stay inside than to go out in the storm.

About 9 pm, truck driver Jack Gillen heard a crack like a rifle shot.

A wall of debris crashed onto the highway. The slide swept away his truck and several of the cars. Everything tumbled down into a riverside pasture. Jack found himself upside down, wedged against the controls in his truck's cab. He hung there for more than two hours, hoping help would come. Finally, some people from the cars on the highway managed to free him by using a hacksaw to cut off the truck's steering wheel and gearshift.

By then everyone agreed they couldn't expect outside help. The 50 people stranded in the cars and trucks were cut off from the world. The crowd broke into a nearby house, carried Jack inside, built a fire, and settled in for the night.

The next morning a Coast Guard boat sailed up the Umpqua River from Reedsport, looking for survivors. The boat took Jack back for medical attention in Reedsport. Later a road crew managed to plow through the slides on the highway and free the other travelers. When the floodwaters lowered, however, they also found one car that had been swept into the Umpqua River. Delsa Hammer was still in her car.

A map of landslides in 1996-1997 shows that western Oregon is particularly at risk. (Source: Atlas of Oregon)

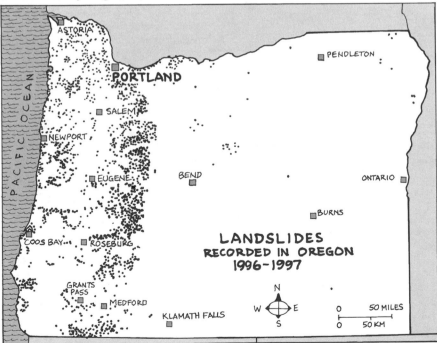

Which Ground is Most Likely to Slide?

Rain increases the risk of landslides, and western Oregon seems to have more than its share. But certain areas have slippery soils that make them particularly treacherous.

The Portland Hills have frustrated developers for years, shrugging off roads and buildings. The problem is a ten-foot layer of slick soil that dates to the Ice Age. Glaciers in Canada kept sending floods down to the Portland area. The floods left a vast outwash plain covered with fine silt. Winds blew that powdery silt onto the hills. Rain turns this layer into a goopy mess with a consistency halfway between potter's clay and quicksand.

The 30-mile Wildwood Trail traverses Portland's Forest Park on unstable soils held in place by the forest itslf.

In 1915 developers built an 11-mile access road, Leif Erikson Drive, across the face of the Portland Hills, hoping to subdivide the slope into view lots. Landslides bedeviled the project so badly that the area was finally dedicated as a wilderness park in 1948.

Trees seem to anchor the Portland Hills' silt pretty well. Forest is what keeps Forest Park from sliding downtown.

Oregon's Coast Range has a similarly slippery story. Almost the entire range is made of seafloor mud and sand that doesn't belong above water at all.

About 20 million years ago, as the North American continent was jerking its way west across the Pacific, the contact zone got so badly stuck that the continent ripped loose a 60-mile-wide chunk of seafloor. This slab of ocean bottom has been shoved ahead by the continental plate ever since, like debris caught on a bulldozer blade.

The mudstone of the Coast Range hardly qualifies as rock. You can break it with your bare hands. Dry a piece in the sun and it crumbles. No wonder the steep canyons of the Coast Range are so prone to landslides!

Want to see if your home is threatened? The state's landslide hazard maps are available online at *www.coastalatlas.net/learn/topics/hazards/landslides*. The maps are astonishingly detailed, but the site isn't particularly user friendly, so it may take awhile to find out if the ground beneath your feet is likely to slide.

Four days after the 1996 landslide tragedies, state forestry officials revealed that the deadliest slide had begun in a ten-year-old clearcut on steep terrain.

"At this time I'm not thinking anything happened due to logging or road building," Douglas District forester Steve Truesdell said. He felt that the slides were caused only by the heavy rainfall.

But an aerial survey by Andy Stahl, director of Forest Service Employees for Environmental Ethics, found that at least 180 slides had started in clearcuts during the storm. The Hubbard Creek slide had begun in a ten-year-old clearcut on a 168-acre parcel owned by a private timber company.

"The state Forest Practices Act allows harvest to occur on steep unstable soils," Francis Eatherington of the environmental group Umpqua Watersheds told a reporter. "We're going to have to change this and start taking into account not only people's watersheds, clean drinking water and fisheries, but we also have to take into account people's lives."

The clearcut above the Moons' home was so steep that the state Department of Forestry had recommended logging with aerial cables to minimize erosion. The state had also suggested removing logging debris from draws to reduce the risk of slides. The private timber company had followed all those suggestions, and had replanted the area as required by law.

But the clearcut had still launched a devastating slide ten years later. Why?

The answer came partly from research at Mt. St. Helens. The volcanic blast of 1980 had flattened mile after mile of forest. In effect, the volcano had created one of the largest clearcuts in history. Since then, scientists have been studying the blast zone intensively to monitor its recovery. They were surprised that the barren area seemed virtually immune to landslides for the first 15 years. The soil was stable until about 1996. Then trails and roads suddenly started disappearing as the ground slid loose. Maintenance crews could hardly keep up with the damage.

Researchers realized that the roots of the killed trees had been holding the soil. After 15 years the old roots were so rotten that they no longer stopped landslides. To be sure, new trees had grown as tall as 20 feet by then, but the new roots were still too small and shallow to have much effect. Until the new trees grew larger, they were merely adding weight to the slopes.

In the high, cold country of the Cascades, the most dangerous period for landslides seems to be ten to 25 years after a clearcut. In the lower, warmer woods of the Coast Range, where wood rots faster and new trees grow quicker, the landslide hazard peaks earlier—about four to 15 years after a clearcut.

Roads can trigger landslides, especially in clearcuts that are 4-25 years old, sending mud and debris into streams.

The winter of 2007-2008 brought more rains and more landslides, renewing the controversy over clearcut logging on steep slopes. The most publicized slide started on property that had been clearcut near Woodson, 70 miles northwest of Portland.

Woodson isn't so much a town as a wide spot in Highway 30 between Clatskanie and Astoria. Logging goes way back in this neck of the woods. Even before logging trucks or railroads, timbermen hauled logs down the hillside to Woodson, dumped them into Westport Slough, bundled them into rafts, and floated them to sawmills along the Columbia River.

Only a few people lived at Woodson by 2007. High water from the Columbia River had flooded Jeff Peterson's home in 1996, so he had built a new house on higher ground. Seventeen-year-old Ian Robinson and his roommate Don Crom lived in a trailer nearby. And then there were Mike and Misty Roubal. A garden of berry bushes and fruit trees surrounded the house they had bought only a year and a half earlier. Their eight-year-old son Lukas was out of school for a few days, recovering from oral surgery.

A week had passed since big rainstorms and floods had made headlines. It was Tuesday morning, December 11, and Miisty was away at work. Mike was thinking he would spend the day replacing the damp insulation underneath their house.

Suddenly a state official pounded on the Roubals' door. "Open up! Evacuate immediately! Flood danger!"

"What flood?" Mike wondered. The floods were supposed to be over, and his house was on high ground anyway. It wasn't even raining.

But the official was adamant, so Mike got Lukas in the car and drove away.

Minutes later a wall of mud and debris came crashing down the hillside canyon behind their home. When the torrent hit Woodson, a lake of mud spread out five feet deep, filling the Roubals' home and burying Highway 30. Ian Robinson's trailer floated to one side and smashed open. Half a dozen empty cars, including Mike Roubal's classic 1955 Chevrolet, swirled around in the mud like potatoes in a stew. Two boats drifted up out of the backyard were they had been stored. The Roubals' garden of berry bushes and fruit trees became a mud flat.

Everyone had been evacuated in time. But how had officials known the mudflow was about to hit?

As it turned out, the mudflow had actually begun eight days earlier, at the height of the rainstorms. In the hills two miles behind Woodson, rain had triggered two landslides on logging areas that had been clearcut in 1992 and 2004. The slides had blocked a culvert in an abandoned railroad berm, allowing water to back up 40 feet deep. When officials feared the berm was about to break, they ordered the evacuation of the community below. The warning had come just in time.

The day after the Woodson disaster, crews were still working to open Highway 30. Ian Robinson was allowed to search his ruined trailer briefly for valuables, but he couldn't find his prized Tae Kwan Do medals in the wreckage. Misty Roubal cried, mourning the loss of her house and garden.

Jeff Peterson bitterly told an *Oregonian* reporter, "They keep logging in these steep canyons, and the big money goes to the timber companies. They don't give a damn about us."

In this case, however, the money had not gone to a timber company. It had gone to the Oregon State University College of Forestry. The 2440-acre forest property above Woodson had been donated to OSU in 1929 for research into reforestation. Instead the school had repeatedly clearcut the property to raise funds. The two landslides began on slopes that were steep enough to raise concern, but not quite steep enough to be off-limits to clearcut logging under the Oregon Department of Forestry's landslide restrictions.

The landslides left people wondering why the state hadn't done more to cut risks and give people warning. Then *Oregonian* reporter Michael Milstein discovered that the state *had* made detailed maps of landslide zones, but the maps were so alarming that they had been withdrawn.

Jon Hoffmeister had spent almost three years developing new land-slide hazard maps of 19 western Oregon counties for the state Department of Geology and Mineral Industries. He had linked up the department's computers on weekends to get enough computing power to combine data about soil types and terrain. He had checked his work with field trips. He had even made a trip to Woodson, where he knew a landslide had killed four people in 1933.

When Jon's department released the maps in 2002, some city and county officials complained that the maps designated too much land as hazardous. The Legislature had passed a law limiting development in official landslide hazard zones, and now it seemed that hazardous zones were everywhere. How were cities going to grow? What right did the state have to restrict development on private land without compensation? And how could anyone trust maps that had been generated mostly by computers?

Reeling from this pressure, the state geology department withdrew the maps. The next year the Legislature removed the limits on construction in landslide zones designated on official maps.

Since then, geologists have praised Oregon's landslide hazard maps as among the best of their kind in the world. The maps have accurately predicted more than 90 percent of the areas covered by landslide debris.

Not all warnings are welcome.

CHAPTER IX

Forest Fires

Just a few years ago, forest fires were considered horrific disasters, to be extinguished at all costs. Now they are recognized as a natural and essential part of Oregon's forest ecology. What has changed? Aren't forest fires still a threat to our homes, wildlife, and timber?

A Brief History of Fire

Oregon Indians and pioneers alike set fires on purpose to manage the land. For the native tribes, fires in the Willamette Valley improved deer hunting, promoted willow shoots that could be used for basketry, and renewed fields of edible camas bulbs. In the hills, fire improved hunting, renewed beargrass sprouts for basket weaving, and expanded huckleberry fields.

Pioneer farmers praised the Willamette Valley prairies as an Eden, but that grassland existed only because fires every few years had killed the encroaching fir trees. Similarly, Central Oregon's park-like groves of ponderosa pine

The Biscuit Fire of 2002 ignited a debate about the role of fire, the concept of healthy forests, and restoration efforts.

were so inviting because fires had burned along the forest floor every five to 25 years, tidying things up. Eastern Oregon's grasslands, which fed a boom in cattle and sheep in the early 1900s, existed only because wildfires killed the junipers and knocked back the sagebrush every few years.

When the Forest Service took over the newly created National Forests in 1905, fire management was the hottest issue of the day. One faction of foresters argued that small, low-level fires improved soil fertility and prevented catastrophic fire. Another group felt that all fires were destructive and dangerous.

The anti-fire faction emerged victorious after the Great Fire of 1910. That year a record-setting blaze in Idaho and Montana torched three million acres and killed 86 people. In the backlash that followed, more than 8000 fire lookouts were built to watch for smoke, including 849 lookouts in Oregon. By 1935 the Forest Service adopted a "10 am policy" to put out all fires by mid-morning on the day after they start. Roads and airplanes became part of the battle plan.

The Charlton Lake fire of 1985 near Willamette Pass. The Forest Service now relies primarily on airplanes to monitor fires.

Meanwhile the Forest Service launched a campaign to reeducate the public about fire. A psychologist hired by the Forest Service in 1939 analyzed the traditional use of low-level fire and announced that it represented the "defensive beliefs of a disadvantaged cultural group." A Forest Service movie, *Trees of Righteousness,* warned in Biblical terms of "demon fire." By World War II the anti-fire slogans had shifted to patriotic themes, such as "Careless Matches Aid the Axis."

By far the most successful Forest Service anti-fire campaign began with the creation of Smokey the Bear in 1944. The advertising mascot, later identified with a fire-scarred cub at the National Zoo in 1950, was so widely loved that his popularity rating eventually exceeded that of the President. Coordinated with "Keep Green" campaigns in individual states, Smokey targeted children with great effect. Human-caused fires dropped 50 percent between 1950 and 1980.

But other voices were questioning the anti-fire strategy. Harold Weaver, for one, warned in 1943 that fire suppression was changing Central Oregon's ponderosa pine forests in dangerous ways. A government forester, Harold had graduated from what is now Oregon State University. He noticed that dry branches and brush were piling up on the forest floor throughout Central Oregon. Thickets of young trees were also choking the understory. If a fire did start, he predicted it could flame up from the new tinder on the ground, explode through the new thickets of small trees, and torch the crowns of the old ponderosa pines, killing everything.

Ponderosas are normally wizards at surviving fire. The outer layer of their thick bark is able to flake off during a blaze, shedding heat. Older ponderosas rise limbless for 30 or 50 feet to keep their needles safely above the reach of ground fires. By eliminating small fires, Harold reasoned, the Forest Service was stocking the woods with fuel for later, catastrophic burns.

A National Park Service report on Yellowstone in 1963 found many of the same problems Harold had noticed in Central Oregon. In 1969 the National Park Service began letting some natural wildfires burn. The new policy recognized fire as a natural part of forest health, reducing fuel supplies and making way for new growth.

The public was a little suspicious when the National Park Service introduced "prescribed burns," where rangers actually *set* fires. A ranger explained at a biological sciences convention in Oregon that the goal of the National Park Service had "progressed from a protection of natural objects to a protection of natural processes."

By 1971 the Forest Service had begun changing its attitude toward fire too. They edged Smokey the Bear toward retirement by introducing a new mascot, Woodsy Owl. But Smokey's ringing challenge, "Only YOU can prevent forest fires!" was not easily displaced by Woodsy's slogan, "Give

A prescribed fire, intentionally set to reduce fuel on the forest floor, burns in Central Oregon without hurting the larger trees. Historically, low-level ground fires burn in the area every five to 25 years. The construction of homes in the woods has created conflicts.

a hoot, don't pollute."

Biologist Richard Vogl echoed the public's mood in a 1973 article for the *Saturday Review*:

> "Who could believe, as we sat securely in mother's lap and lis-tened to the story of Bambi, that we were being pumped with a great deal of nonsense? Who could mistrust the honest-looking, clean-cut man wearing a green uniform and badge who visited our fifth grade and told about Smokey the Bear and the destruction wrought by forest fires?"

In Oregon, the reluctance to embrace wildfire went deeper than memo-ries of Smokey the Bear and "Keep Oregon Green" posters. Oregonians had learned to fear fire because of the recurring nightmare that had been the Tillamook Burn.

The Tillamook Burn

Half a dozen forest fires in Oregon's history have burned more terri-tory than the Tillamook Burn of 1933, but none has seared public opinion so violently.

The Tillamook Burn was a holocaust on Portland's doorstep, a disaster that darkened skies across the most populated area of the state. An entire generation of Portlanders grew up horrified by the endless miles of black snags that lined highways to the beach.

In the summer of 1933, however, Portlanders had a lot of other things on their minds. Oregon was in the depth of the Depression. When the Til-lamook Burn began on August 14, the whole issue of forest fire seemed so unimportant that Portland newspapers didn't mention the blaze for a week.

At the time, almost all the forest in Oregon's northern Coast Range was privately owned, primarily by a half dozen large timber companies. Logging railroads snaked up into the hills on precarious-looking trestles to logging camps of plank buildings. Men with crosscut saws and axes felled giant trees twelve feet in diameter and 250 feet tall. Steam-powered "donkey" engines winched the enormous logs to the tracks. Work in the woods was dangerous and the pay was low. Many woodsmen died or were injured in accidents, but during the Depression it was just as danger-ous to join a union and complain.

Clearcuts stretched for miles behind the crews. Branches and smaller trees were left on the ground as slash—debris that dried out in the sum-mer sun, raising the risk of fire. Lightning is rare in the Coast Range, so natural fires are uncommon. But the logging operations themselves created sparks from locomotives, donkey engines, and camp stoves. Aware of the danger, timber companies hired their own lookouts and fire crews. The federal government had thousands of additional firefighters on hand — the Civilian Conservation Corps (CCC), unemployed young men hired to work in the forest to reduce the welfare rolls.

August of 1933 opened dry and hot, with 90-degree temperatures. Oregon Governor Julius Meier closed state forests to logging. The ban had little effect because the state did not own much forestland. On private land, the governor's edict was merely advisory.

Just after lunch on August 14, word of the recommended shutdown reached the Gales Creek Logging Company, a small private outfit working the woods 15 miles northwest of Forest Grove. Bill Lyda, the owner's son, had been back at the job only fifteen minutes after his lunch break. He decided to let the donkey engine pull out one last log before calling it quits.

The engine whistle tooted and the cable tautened. A big Douglas fir

---

Oregon's Largest Forest Fires

The memorable Tillamook Burn and the 2002 Biscuit Fire certainly aren't the largest blazes Oregon has seen. The rainy forestlands west of the Cascade summit often don't burn for centuries, but when they do, the fires can be huge. Here are the largest since official record-keeping began.

1848 – Nestucca Fire, **295,000** acres southeast of Tillamook.
1849 – Siletz Fire, **800,000** acres northeast of Newport.
1853 – Yaquina Fire, **484,000** acres southeast of Newport.
1865 – Silverton Fire, **988,000** acres in the Cascades, reducing the future Silver Falls State Park to slopes of snags.
1868 – Coos Bay Fire, **295,000** acres east of Coos Bay.
1902 – Yacolt Burn, **1,000,000** acres in the Cascades, mostly on the Washington side of the Columbia River. Lives lost: 38.
1933 – Tillamook Burn, **240,000** acres northeast of Tillamook.
1936 – Bandon Fire, **145,000** acres, including the city of Bandon; 11 dead.
1939 – Second Tillamook Burn, **190,000** acres.
1945 – Third Tillamook Burn, **180,000** acres.
1987 – Silver Fire, **96,000** acres west of Grants Pass.
1996 – Simnasho Fire, **109,000** acres on the Warm Springs Reservation, including eleven homes.
2002 – Biscuit Fire, **499,000** acres west of Grants Pass.
2003 – B&B Fire, **91,000** acres at Santiam Pass northwest of Bend.

*In 1940, seven years after the first Tillamook Burn swept through the area, a bus on High-
way 20 crosses the Quartz Creek Bridge, five miles east of Elsie.*

log began plowing up through the slash toward the landing. Then the log
bumped into an old, fallen cedar. The engine growled and the cable sang
tight. When the log finally budged, a tiny flame puffed up.

At a later inquest into the origin of that fateful spark, experts testified
that it most likely was caused by the friction of wood against wood, or
perhaps by the rubbing of the steel cable. The Gales Creek Logging Company tried to downplay their responsibility. They claimed that suspicious
flashlight lenses had been found at the site, suggesting arson by a rival
logging company. Some witnesses claimed other fires might have started
in different canyons earlier that day. In the end, the exact cause didn't
matter.

As soon as Bill Lyda saw the smoke, he raised the alarm—"Fire!" His
logging crew ran to get their fire tools. By the time they returned, however, the fire had already climbed an ancient snag, turning it into a torch
that strewed flaming debris across Gales Creek's canyon. A lookout on a
nearby peak telephoned for backup. Soon, wind-borne sparks had ignited
spot fires miles away.

The next day the weather was even drier, with temperatures soaring to 104 degrees. A crew of 450 firefighters managed to control the fire at Gales Creek, but sparks had lit a blaze on the Wilson River that was running wild. By August 18, three days later, 1000 men were fighting a fire that covered 16,000 acres.

By August 21 the heat of the fire could be felt in Forest Grove. Women and children stamped out flaming debris that fell in the town's streets.

By August 23 the fire had spread to 40,000 acres, but a patch of misty rain brought hope. Two thousand men were fighting a fire line 15 miles long. Maybe now they would be able to hold the line.

Then the wind changed direction, and the damp ocean breeze gave way to a hot, dry gale from the east.

On the morning of August 24, the humidity plummeted.

The fire took a deep breath and roared.

Fire bosses frantically ordered their crews out of the woods. Behind them the forest exploded. Gray, mushroom-shaped thunderheads blasted 40,000 feet into the air. The firestorm created its own hurricane-force winds, sucking air toward its center. Winds ripped whole trees out of the ground and hurled them across canyons. Phone lines snapped, cutting communication to fire crews. Logging trains raced the flames over burning trestles toward Tillamook.

Frank Palmer was among the young CCC men still attempting to fight the fire. When Frank had signed up for President Roosevelt's "Forest Army" back in Illinois, he had imagined building trails and campgrounds in a forest paradise. Instead he had found hell on earth—flames in the darkness, sweat-drenching heat, howling winds, and chaos. As he rested from his work on the fire line, sparks whipped through the air. His hat flew off. Someone shouted. Frank looked up—and saw too late the giant tree trunk tilting toward him.

On that "Black Thursday" the sky grew so dark by noon that streetlights turned on in downtown Tillamook. Hot fir needles pattered on roofs like hail. Ash fell two feet deep from Wheeler to Tillamook. People shoveled their sidewalks. Cows stood bewildered in the fields, unable to find grass. Ships 500 miles at sea were showered with ashes. That evening, sunsets turned blood-red as far away as Montana.

In just 20 hours the Tillamook Burn had exploded from 40,000 acres to 240,000. The holocaust had swallowed barns, farmhouses, trestles, logging camps, and virtually every living thing for more than 300 square miles. Incredibly, Frank Palmer was the only person who died.

The scale of devastation on that one day, August 24, 1933, would not be matched in the Northwest until Mt. St. Helens blew up in 1980.

On the morning of August 25, 1933, the fire was still burning on the doorsteps of McMinnville, Forest Grove, Vernonia, and Tillamook, but the firestorm had spent its fury. A hard rain on September 5 allowed the weary firefighters to go home. Hollow snags would still be found smoldering a year later.

Timbermen tallied the fire's toll in terms of lost production. The killed trees contained twelve billion board feet of lumber, enough to build a million homes.

By June of 1934 salvage crews had started to reclaim the lost timber. They took only prime logs at least two feet in diameter, cut into 80-foot lengths. They left dead limbs and smaller trees behind as slash. Later crews sometimes salvage-logged the same area two or even three times, taking progressively smaller trunks and leaving more slash.

Meanwhile timber companies refused to pay property taxes on the burned land, forcing counties to foreclose. This allowed the companies to avoid the task of replanting, yet keep the timber rights to salvageable snags. Donkey engines, steam locomotives, and small unregulated logging crews continued with the salvage effort even on the hottest, driest days of summer.

The second Tillamook Burn began on August 1, 1939, almost exactly six years after the first. Once again the fire started in Gales Creek's canyon. Once again the blaze was sparked by a logging crew. This time the fire burned 190,000 acres, including 140,000 that had burned in 1933.

Salvage loggers stepped up their efforts during World War II to keep pace with wartime demand for lumber. By 1945, a total of four billion board feet of logs had been hauled out of the Tillamook Burn, removing about a third of the timber volume of the fire-killed trees.

The third Tillamook Burn began on July 10, 1945, almost exactly six years after the second fire. Again the cause was not natural, but was traced to sparks from summertime logging. This time the fire burned 180,000 acres, including 115,000 that had burned in either 1933 or 1939.

At the height of the third Tillamook Burn the United States detonated an atomic bomb over the Japanese city of Hiroshima. The world's attention turned to a mushroom cloud in Japan. Newspapers in Oregon, however, dedicated just as much space to the black mushroom cloud on Portland's horizon.

Even before rains put out the third Tillamook fire in September 1945, loggers began talking about a "six-year jinx" that might keep sparking fires in the area forever. A Forest Service report in October 1945 suggested that the most cost effective solution to the Tillamook Burn problem would be to build a "super-fireline" around the perimeter and let nature take its course, even if it took 100 to 300 years for the forest to regrow.

Many Oregonians demanded immediate action to restore the forest. A governor-appointed committee recommended a massive reforestation project. The Legislature drafted a Consitutional amendment to raise up to $750,000 in state taxes a year for the task. The ballot measure passed in 1948, winning approval from voters in all parts of the state.

Armed with approval for the largest state restoration project in history, Oregon took control of 255,000 acres of foreclosed land from the counties, creating what would become the Tillamook State Forest. By 1949 crews were hard at work surveying, replanting by hand, reseeding by helicopter, building roads, and felling snags for fire breaks. Busloads of school-children helped plant seedlings amid the ashes.

Everyone watched to see if the six-year jinx would strike again in 1951.

A smaller, fourth Tillamook Burn did occur in 1951. The fire was started by a snag-removal crew in a fire break. The fire began when workers dynamited a treetop to create a spar pole for hauling out the salvaged snags. The fire burned 33,000 acres, none of it in green timber.

In the years that followed, Oregon taxpayers funded the cutting of 1.5 million snags for fire breaks, the construction of 164 miles of fire roads, the planting of 72 million Douglas fir seedlings, and the aerial seeding of 116,000 acres with 72,000 pounds of Douglas fir seeds. The tax bonds authorized in 1948 were retired 25 years later in 1973. The first replanted trees to be sold for profit were cut in 1983.

Many lessons about fires and reforestation had been learned from the harrowing experience of the Tillamook Burn. Disturbingly, nearly all of those lessons would later be called into question—especially in the aftermath of Oregon's next great burn, the Biscuit Fire of 2002.

The Biscuit Fire

More than half a century after the Tillamook Burn, an even larger blaze in southwest Oregon would stir old nightmares. But the 499,000-acre Biscuit Fire of 2002 burned in a very different kind of forest, and the role of fire was starting to be viewed very differently. As it turned out, the real firestorm was a controversy over fire management and salvage logging, and it would begin only after the smoke of the Biscuit Fire had cleared.

Mike Webley was one of 7000 people called to the front lines of Oregon's Biscuit Fire, the nation's largest wildfire in the summer of 2002. Mike had a home, a pregnant fiancee, a business, and a city council seat in Waitsburg, Washington. He left it all behind to fight fire.

The previous summer Mike had battled the Thirty Mile Fire in Washington, where four fighters died. After that he had tattoed his chest with a skull and crossbones.

"It made me want to do this even more," Mike told reporter Andy Dworkin of *The Oregonian*. "Even if I save an outhouse, it makes me happy."

Fred Houston, a ranger from Utah on his 30th fire season mused that people "get hooked on fire. You either like it or you hate it. If you hate it, you quit the first day."

Pat Velasco, a veteran of 42 years of firefighting, did not come to the Biscuit Fire because of the thrill. For him, it was a chance to use a rare skill. "I just had a knack for fire behavior and capitalized on it." By outguessing the flames, Pat figured he could save lives.

The Biscuit Fire began with a thunderstorm July 12-15 that lit up the mountains of the Siskiyou National Forest between Grants Pass and Brookings with 12,000 lightning strikes. The lightning sparked 375 small fires. Nearly all of the blazes were in remote, roadless areas where

The Illinois River Trail, near one of the starting points of the 2002 Biscuit Fire, overlooks a typical mix of old, live trees and burned underbrush in the Kalmiopsis Wilderness.

firefighting was not a high prior-
ity for the Forest Service. Officials
monitored the fires and mostly let
them burn.

After a few days the fires co-
alesced into two larger conflagra-
tions, the Florence Fire on Florence Creek of the Illinois River in
the Kalmiopsis Wilderness, and
the Sour Biscuit Fire near the California border. The Forest Service
began calling in fire crews and
mapping containment lines.

August brought dry weather
that caused the two fires to grow
alarmingly. In just six hot days,
the fires burned two-thirds of the
area they would eventually cover.
Suddenly officials worried that
fire might spread east into the rural community of Selma. It might
also threaten lodges on the Rogue

*Vulcan Lake, on the western edge of the
Kalmiopsis Wilderness, was overswept by
the 2002 fire but most large trees survived.*

River or cabins on the Chetco River near Brookings.

On August 11 the fire's name changed. The city of Florence, on the
central Oregon Coast 150 miles north of the actual fire, had lodged a com-
plaint. News reports of the "Florence Fire" were causing tourists to cancel
seashore reservations. Forest Service officials decided to merge the two
blazes and rename it the Biscuit Fire.

The consequences of that decision were not merely semantic. Fire
crews were withdrawn from the five-mile-wide strip between the two
fires, where escape might have been difficult if things got hot. The withdrawn crews lit new fires to encourage the two blazes to burn together.
This made the perimeter easier to defend but torched thousands of additional acres.

For the next month the fire slowly expanded toward the perimeter lines
that fire crews were building. Television crews interviewed homeowners
in Cave Junction and Galice who waited nervously, unsure whether they
would be ordered to evacuate. Reporters in fire camps featured "hot shot"
firefighters who had come to Oregon from New Zealand, Alaska, and
Arizona.

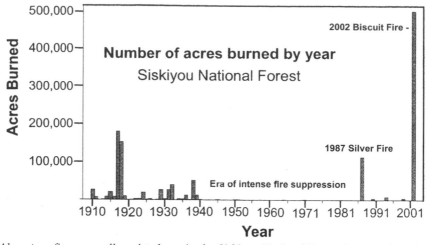

Almost no fires were allowed to burn in the Siskiyou National Forest for more than four decades from 1940 to 1986. The 2002 Biscuit Fire reset the area's historic fire cycle.

By September the perimeter fireline was complete. Cool, damp weather made it easier to mop up blazes. Newscasts began airing shots of homemade "Thank You Firefighters" signs in Brookings and Selma. Local business owners marveled at the millions of dollars fire crews had spent on food and supplies.

On November 8, the last smokes of the Biscuit Fire were extinguished. It had been the largest Oregon wildfire in a century. It had also been the most expensive in history, running up a tab of more than $154 million. In all, four rural homes had been destroyed, along with nine outbuildings, one lookout, and some picnic tables. Nearly three quarters of the burned area had been in officially designated roadless areas, including virtually all of the Kalmiopsis Wilderness. Only seven percent of the area had been designated for timber production.

How much forest had the Biscuit Fire actually destroyed? How much of the burned timber should be salvaged? And what was the best way to restore the forest?

The smoke had hardly cleared before these questions started provoking controversial and sometimes contradictory answers. Dan Donato, a 29-year-old graduate student at the OSU College of Forestry, came up with one of the most explosive answers of all.

A Firestorm of Controversy

Dan Donato didn't think of himself as a troublemaker. A native

Oregonian, he had grown up in the shadow of Mt. Hood. He liked to study hard and play hard. His garage was full of boats—sea kayaks, rafts, and canoes. After finishing his undergraduate degrees in oceanography and forest ecology, Dan took off for five years. He lived out of his car, working whatever seasonal biology jobs he could find. He surveyed populations of lynx in Montana and tortoises in the desert. He worked as a fire ecologist and botanist for the National Park Service. And so when Dan went back to OSU for his doctorate in 2003, it seemed natural that he would study the Biscuit Fire.

To understand the emotional reactions that Dan's study provoked, it helps to consider how different the Biscuit Fire was from the Tillamook Burn.

The region within the Biscuit Fire's final perimeter totaled 499,965 acres, 40 percent more area than was covered by the Tillamook Burn. Although the Biscuit Fire was larger, it killed far fewer trees. Especially the largest trees seemed to survive. Only about half of the forest canopy burned, and even this was a mosaic of green and black—a spotty pattern that skipped entire valleys.

What had burned most thoroughly was underbrush. Mile after mile of manzanita and poison oak had been reduced to ashes. The fire had also cleaned up the dead wood that had been accumulating on the forest floor. Flames had trimmed the lower branches of large trees.

The Illinois River flows through the heart of the Biscuit Fire area.

For much of the burned area, the Biscuit Fire had simply cleared out the forest's understory. Environmental groups and many scientists argued that the fire had performed many of the same maintenance tasks that the Forest Service had been paying crews to do elsewhere.

On the other hand, the Biscuit Fire really had killed hundreds of thousands of trees. The standing snags contained a billion board feet of merchantable timber. Many people felt the burned trees should be salvaged before they rotted. The salvage operation would create needed jobs. Some of the profits could be used to pay for replanting, fire break construction, and reseeding—the same kind of restoration projects that had been used after the Tillamook Burn.

President George W. Bush proposed a Healthy Forest Initiative, a plan to encourage salvage logging and to clean up woody debris in the forests to reduce the risk of future catastrophic fire. After visiting the Biscuit Fire site in the fall of 2002 he told a crowd in Medford, "We need to make our forests healthy by using some common sense. We need to — "

Applause and cheers interrupted the President. When he was able to continue he said, "We need to understand if you let kindling build up and there's a lightning strike, you're gonna get yourself a big fire. That's what we've got to understand."

Douglas County commissioners hired John Sessions and four other professors at OSU's College of Forestry to analyze the benefits of a speedy salvage operation. The university released the Sessions Report in July 2003, along with a press release titled "THE CLOCK IS TICKING ON BISCUIT FIRE RESTORATION." The Sessions Report said that prompt salvage logging could raise $100 million to pay for tree planting, brush removal, and other forest restoration work. "Delays in decisionmaking and implementation," the report warned, "will likely destine much of the most intensely burned area to cycles of shrubs, hardwoods, and recurring fires for many decades."

The Forest Service agreed, recommending 19,000 acres for salvage logging and restoration. None of the logging would be in designated wilderness. Salvage in roadless areas would be by helicopter.

Timber companies looked at the proposed salvage sales — mostly small burned trees in remote canyons — and asked if they could also cut some large, green trees to help pay expenses.

Environmental groups cried foul, insisting that the forest did not need restoration at all. Protesters chained themselves to logging road gates and tied themselves to treetops.

The Forest Service closed salvage areas to the public, and officials removed the protesters. The first truckloads of salvaged logs rolled out of the Biscuit area in 2004.

That same summer Dan Donato and Joe Fontaine, two young OSU graduate students, together with four established research biologists, were allowed into the salvage zone to conduct a scientific study with grant money from the Bureau of Land Management.

"We were interested in data that tested the commonly held assumptions about forest regeneration after large wildfires," Dan recalls. "We were measuring everything after the burn — the residual biomass, shrubs, mosses, seedlings — everything. We noticed a lot of seedlings and thought, wow! This seems really important. Maybe we ought to publish it." Dan's advisor, OSU professor Beverly Law, encouraged the graduate students in their work.

Dan and his team platted out squares in different types of burned forest and took measurements. Then they measured a few unburned areas as a control. The next summer the graduate students came back and compared the salvaged areas with the unsalvaged sites.

What Dan found went against everything he had been told. The burned areas had resprouted with an average of 300 conifer seedlings per acre—more than enough to restock the forest naturally. Rather than help with reforestation, salvage logging had made conditions *worse*. Heavy equipment had compacted the dirt, killing more than two-thirds of the volunteer seedlings.

Dan was also surprised to discover that the salvaged areas seemed *more* likely to burn again. The loggers had removed the least burnable part of the forest, the blackened trunks. Instead they had left piles of combustible branches on the ground. Unsalvaged areas had four times less of this flammable debris.

Dan's group returned to the College of Forestry, wrote up their findings in a paper, and succeeded in getting it accepted by the prestigious journal *Science*. The journal sent the one-page article to be checked by scientists at other universities. They found no flaws. The journal announced it would be published in January 2006 under the title, "Post-Wildfire Logging Hinders Regeneration and Increases Fire Risk."

When OSU professor John Sessions heard the news, he was furious. He tried to get *Science* to delay and alter the publication. The editors refused, noting that the article had been properly peer-reviewed by qualified scientists.

A one-page scholarly article in the January, 2006 issue of Science *magazine shook assumptions about salvage logging, divided Oregon State University's College of Forestry, undermined Presidential policy, and launched a Congressional hearing.*

352   20 JANUARY 2006   VOL 311   **SCIENCE**   www.sciencemag.org

BREVIA

Post-Wildfire Logging Hinders Regeneration and Increases Fire Risk

D. C. Donato,[1]* J. B. Fontaine,[2] J. L. Campbell,[1] W. D. Robinson,[2] J. B. Kauffman,[3] B. E. Law[1]

Recent increases in wildfire activity in the United States have intensified controversies surrounding the management of public forests after large fires essary. Postfire logging subsequently reduced regeneration by 71% to 224 seedlings per hectare (Fig. 1A) due to soil disturbance and physical burial by woody material during log-

after postfire logging, including in the Biscuit plan, but resources to complete them are often limited (7). Our study underscores that, after logging, the mitigation of short-term fire risk is not possible without subsequent fuel reduction treatments. However, implementing these treatments is also problematic. Mechanical removal is generally precluded by its expense, leaving prescribed burning as the most feasible method. This will result in additional seedling mortality and potentially severe soil impacts caused by long-duration combustion of logging-generated fuel loads. Therefore, the lowest fire risk strategy may be to leave dead trees standing as long as pos-

As soon as the article appeared, College of Forestry dean Hal Salwasser met with a timber industry group to brainstorm ways of discrediting his graduate student. Unless something was done, the study's implications might derail federal legislation that was going to put salvage logging on a fast track.

Salvage logging operations after the Biscuit Fire did not speed forest recovery.

The Bureau of Land Management announced it was canceling its funding for Donato's grant.

Congressman Greg Walden of Oregon called Donato to appear at a public hearing in Medford. Walden and others blasted the graduate student's ethics, science, and reputation, accusing him of making up data.

Dan stood firm. He pointed out that he had conducted his study with scientific rigor using widely accepted methods. He had gone to salvage logging sites and analyzed what he found. His study was repeatable. His article had been properly reviewed. It had been published in a journal so esteemed that it rarely published work by graduate students. If the professors and politicians standing up to denounce him wanted to be believed, they should study a salvage logging operation for themselves. Then they could write their own scientific articles.

Dan was so upset that he couldn't sleep for days. Normally a shy person, he was so barraged by requests for media interviews that he had trouble keeping up with his college classes.

Meanwhile, John Sessions and his colleagues at the College of Forestry wrote a scientific article attempting to discredit Donato, but they didn't have on-the-ground data. After peer review, their article was reduced to merely suggesting that Donato's findings might not be applicable to other types of forests.

Senator Ron Wyden of Oregon stepped in to defend the beleaguered graduate student, saying that government should never reject scientific findings for political reasons. Under pressure, the Bureau of Land Management reinstated Donato's grant.

Newspaper headlines and editorials began accusing College of Forestry leaders of unprofessional behavior and industry bias. OSU's faculty senate denounced John Sessions' attempt to stop the *Science* article. A crowd of more than a hundred packed a hall at OSU demanding reform and academic freedom. Faced with the possibility of a vote of no confidence, dean Salwasser apologized for "getting too involved in the debate." He appointed an independent panel to investigate College of Forestry practices and suggest improvements.

A few months after the *Science* article appeared, a Congressional report revealed that salvage logging in the Biscuit Fire area had cost taxpayers $1.9 million more than the timber was worth. Editorials across the nation denounced the salvage effort. The Hartford, Connecticut *Courant* wrote, "The Biscuit Fire has given proof that salvage logging is not only bad for the environment, but bad economics as well."

Since then, a series of scientific studies has confirmed Dan Donato's findings and added new evidence that forests are healthier when allowed to regenerate naturally after a fire. One survey found that brush actually *helps* conifer seedlings get established, providing shade when the trees are small and fragile. According to the study, tree seedlings keep sprouting as much as 19 years after a fire, even when seed sources were far away.

"These places have been burning for centuries, and they've been regrowing for centuries," researcher Jeff Shatford told *Register-Guard* reporter Greg Bolt.

Another study confirmed that subsequent fires are worse in manually restored areas, and not just because of the woody debris left on the ground by salvage logging. Flames flash through the even-aged stands of young Douglas firs planted by restoration crews. Natural regeneration provides a mix of ages and tree types that slows fire.

Like many pines, knobcone pines are adapted to fire. This cone is glued closed by pitch that melts during a fire, releasing seeds.

"It was the conventional wisdom that salvage logging and planting could reduce the risk of high-severity fires," researcher Jonathan Thompson told Associated Press reporter Jeff Barnard. "Our data suggest otherwise."

Dan Donato and his team had inspired others to challenge the conventional wisdom about fire recovery. Their work had not only survived scientific scrutiny, but it had also broadened public awareness of the role of fire in forests.

Dan himself learned that it is important to believe what you discover, and not just what you are told. He told reporter Erin Halcomb, "Ask important questions regardless of outside controversy. Do solid work. Stick to your guns."

The Many Roles of Fire

President George W. Bush returned to Oregon in August 2003, again promoting his Healthy Forests Initiative. This time his helicopter flew over two fires burning in the Mt. Jefferson Wilderness. The blazes would soon merge to become the 91,000-acre B&B Fire, but already a scene of desolation stretched below. Mile upon mile of smoking, black snags lined the crest of the Cascades north of Santiam Pass. Unlike the previous year's Biscuit Fire, nothing appeared to have survived.

"The worst thing that can happen to old stands of timber is these fires," the President told a crowd of 600 invited supporters at a county fairgrounds in Redmond. "They destroy the big trees. They're so explosive in nature that hardly any tree can survive. The problem has existed for years. Let's be the ones who start solving it."

The B&B Fire of 2003 killed entire stands of mountain hemlock near Santiam Pass, but billions of replacement seedlings sprouted.

The issue of fire has proven to be more complex than it once seemed. The plants of the High Cascades forest that burned in the 2003 B&B Fire, for example, have adapted to a very different pattern of fire than plants in the dry Siskiyou forest of the 2002 Biscuit burn. How different are Oregon's forests?

Imagine you are packing clothes for spring vacation. If you're going to the ponderosa pine woods of Central Oregon you might pack shorts and sunglasses. If you're going to the rainforest of the Oregon Coast you had better take an umbrella and a windbreaker. For the alpine forests of the High Cascades you'll want snowshoes and a down parka.

Just as vacationers adapt their wardrobes for the state's different climate zones, forests have had to adapt by using fire in different ways.

Perhaps the biggest difference is the *historic fire interval*—the average number of years between fires. Before intensive fire suppression efforts began in the early 1900s, every Oregon forest burned periodically. The intervals between individual wildfires varied a lot, but on average the forests in the drier parts of the state burned every few decades, while forests in rainy or snowy areas burned only every few centuries.

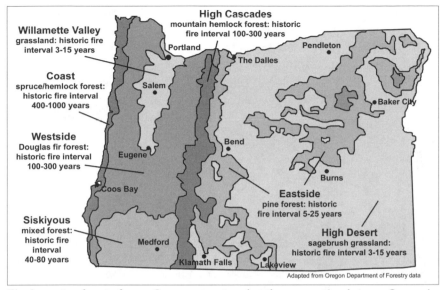

Fire is a natural part of every Oregon ecosystem, but the average time between fires varies greatly. Historically, low level fires sweep through the dry forests of southern and eastern Oregon every few decades, leaving most large trees intact. Rainforests in western Oregon don't burn for centuries, but then large blazes tend to replace entire stands.

These fire cycles have been going on for thousands of years, so forests learned to deal with it long ago. Trees came up with many different strategies to survive. In essence, some packed umbrellas, some packed snowshoes, and some packed sunglasses.

Let's take a closer look at the trees of the Biscuit Fire. The historic interval between fires in this area is fairly short—just 40 to 80 years. The older trees here have already lived through many fires. The big Jeffrey pines, for example, suck up ground moisture so other trees cannot grow nearby. This natural spacing makes it harder for brush fires to "crown out" and burn the forest canopy. Like ponderosa pines, their limbs are high and their bark is thick. Both Jeffrey pines and ponderosa pines spread their seeds by air into burned areas after a fire, but several other local pines use a different fire strategy. The cones of knobcone and lodgepole pines are sealed shut with pitch. The pitch slowly melts in the heat of a fire, releasing seeds after the blaze to start a new pine forest.

The hardwood trees of the Biscuit Fire area, including canyon live oak, chinquapin, and madrone, have adapted to the frequent fires by learning to sprout back from the roots. Three months after the 2002 fire, green leaves had already formed wreaths around the bases of trunks, even in scorched areas that fire crews had thought were completely dead.

In the High Cascades, trees have a very different strategy for dealing with fire. Forest fires sweep through these snowy mountains far less often than in the Siskiyous, and the resulting fires appear more destructive.

President Bush saw a sea of blackened snags when he flew over the B&B Fire in 2003. The view was alarming, but in fact was typical of the

fires that burn these high-elevation forests. Surprisingly, it's exactly the plan mountain hemlock trees have developed to remain the dominant species here.

If you've been on a day hike along the Pacific Crest Trail in Oregon you've probably seen a mountain hemlock forest. The hemlocks are so dense that there aren't many other kinds of trees. All the trunks are about the same

Beargrass resprouts quickly after fire.

size. That's because the trees are all the same age. Fires in the Cascades occur on average every 200 years. Typically, a fire will burn almost every tree in the area. Mountain hemlocks love this regimen because they're masters at reseeding.

Billions of mountain hemlock seedlings sprouted naturally after the B&B Fire. Already the new trees are on their way toward creating another even-aged forest. Fire is the mountain hemlocks' tried-and-true tactic for knocking out competing tree species.

Cascade fires also turn out to be essential to many species of mountain wildflowers. Beargrass, for example, bloomed more profusely

Beargrass bloomed profusely the second year after the B&B Fire. Wildflowers and huckleberries rely on fire in the High Cascades.

in the Santiam Pass area after the B&B Fire than it had in ages. Likewise, fires give huckleberry plants the light they need to thrive. Without fire to open up the forest canopy, the huckleberry bushes of the High Cascades would hardly have berries at all.

Fire may work fine for the Cascade forest ecosystem, but it has a public relations problem. The mountain forests live on a 200-year cycle. People

The Rising Cost of Fighting Fire

Fighting the Biscuit Fire cost $154 million, a record in Oregon's history. Nationwide, the cost of fighting wildfire has soared from an annual average of $1.1 billion to $2.9 billion between 1997 and 2007.

Why has firefighting become so expensive?

First, there really are more fires. Decades of fire suppression have allowed flammable debris to build up. Many forests and grasslands are overdue for a burn. In addition, summers have become hotter and drier in the United States—a climate change that is predicted to increase.

Another reason firefighting has become expensive is that so many people have built homes in harm's way. Planners call this danger zone the "wildland urban interface," where developments sprawl into grasslands or forests that are likely to burn. In Southern California, seven people died and 2000 homes burned when brushfires swept through rural areas in October 2007. In Central Oregon, residents of Black Butte Ranch have to evacuate their forestland homes every few summers because of fires.

The amount spent by the Forest Service to put out fires has skyrocketed to more than 40 percent of the agency's entire budget. As a result, funds have had to be cut for recreation and wildlife projects. Could money be saved by letting more fires in remote areas burn?

The 2002 Biscuit Fire is a case in point. Much of the area's remote, roadless forest emerged from the fire healthier than before. Most of the severely scorched areas burned during a few days of extremely hot weather when firefighting efforts were ineffective. The fire burned out largely on its own when damp weather arrived in the fall. And yet $154 million was spent.

What about saving buildings from fire? The Biscuit Fire's final damage tally included four houses, nine sheds, one lookout, and some picnic tables. These structures might have been preserved by wrapping them in advance with fire-resistant Kevlar paper or installing temporary sprinkler systems—relatively inexpensive techniques that have since saved buildings at Santiam Pass, in Hells Canyon, and elsewhere.

Defending vacation and retirement homes in the forest has become the single largest reason that fires are fought. As firefighting budgets tighten and the natural role of fire grows in importance, new strategies may be needed to keep people safe.

Increasingly, homeowners in rural areas are having to take fire precautions on their own. Tips include removing landscaping and trees near the house, storing firewood at a distance, and replacing wood shakes with less flammable roofing.

do not. Fire zones can look shocking for years. When fires burn at popular recreation destinations like Olallie Lake, Marion Lake, and Waldo Lake, it's hard not to mourn.

It's harder still to grasp the enormity of the historic fire interval in the Coast Range forests, the region where the Tillamook Burn occurred. The damp rainforests near Tillamook typically see fire only once every 400 to 1000 years!

The 2003 B&B Fire opened up views, especially for skiers on the Pacific Crest Trail.

When Oregon's coastal forests do finally burn, the plants *expect* the fire to be catastrophic. After a millenium without fire, the forest needs fertilizer. Alder and Douglas fir often grow back first. The roots of red alder host a special fungus that fixes nitrogen in the soil as a natural fertilizer. Two centuries may pass before shade-loving red cedar and western hemlock emerge above the alder and Douglas fir to form a new forest crown. Still more centuries may be required before the upper branches are big enough to provide habitat for tree voles, flying squirrels, murrelets, and other strange denizens of the coast's ancient rainforest.

Compared to the life cycle of such forests, a human lifespan is but a moment.

The Tillamook Burn, the disaster that horrified a generation of Oregonians, was sparked by humans. But eventually a giant fire would have burned in that area on its own. And just like the other giant fires that have burned in the Coast Range over the past millenia, it would have recovered on its own.

"Fire is not an event," forestry ecologist Tom Atzet told an audience at the OSU College of Forestry after the Biscuit Fire. "It is a process."

Sometimes it can be difficult to accept that process. It helps to take a long-range view.

CHAPTER X

Beyond the Cycles

Every natural disaster in this book began as a surprise—the flash floods, the wildfires, the sudden earthquakes. And yet on a larger scale there is also an underlying predictability to these events.

The natural phenomena we view as disasters are actually part of larger, ongoing processes. Floods, fires, and even earthquakes occur in cycles. To be sure, the rhythms of our planet can be wildly irregular. It is quite possible to have two "100-year" floods in consecutive years, for example. A fault zone that usually ruptures every 300 years might not cause an earthquake for 1000. But if we step back far enough, patterns do emerge.

Therein lies a secret that might help us sidestep future disasters. If we can understand the natural cycles, we can start to make predictions of what might happen next. And once we can predict, we can prepare.

Understanding Cycles

If Earth's cycles were simple to understand, avoiding natural disasters would be as easy as skipping rope. You would just watch for patterns and learn when to jump.

Unfortunately, some of the cycles are so large and so erratic that we still get tripped up. Let's look at the cycles behind Oregon's natural disasters and see what, if anything, we can do to get ready.

Ice Age flooding: every 10,000-50,000 years. When people settled in Oregon 13,000 years ago, the first Ice Age flood they experienced must have come as a real surprise. Can we imagine a modern catastrophe on such a scale?

If a similar flood were to roar down the Columbia River today, two-thirds of Oregon's population would be killed or displaced. Every city, dam, and tree within miles of the Columbia River would be swept away. When the water finally drained from Portland, nothing would remain but a vast gravel plain. The Willamette Valley would be a single sheet of mud.

But Ice Age floods happen only during ice ages. That's a cycle with an interval of some 30,000 years. Before another such flood could threaten Oregon, enough snow would have to fall in Canada to cover that country with a mile of ice.

We don't completely understand what triggers the cycle of ice ages. Natural variations in the Earth's orbit play a major role, bringing the planet closer or farther away from the Sun. But asteroid impacts, volcanoes, and sunspot cycles may also be influential. Some scientists believe global warming could set off a chain of events that could lead to another ice age.

In the meantime, we need not abandon Portland immediately because of the threat of ice age flooding. These colossal floods will certainly return. But we will have plenty of warning.

Subduction earthquakes and tsunamis: every 300-600 years. What makes the subduction earthquake cycle so frightening is that we *won't* have any warning when the next "Big One" strikes. Tension builds slowly for centuries along the great Cascadia fault zone, 60 miles off Oregon's coast. When the pressure suddenly releases, buildings and bridges will collapse throughout western Oregon and Washington. A few minutes later, ocean waves will surge through coastal cities.

Thousands of people must have died when the Cascadia fault zone last slipped on January 26, 1700. More than 300 years have now elapsed, so another giant earthquake and tsunami could hit at any time. Despite earthquake building codes for new buildings, despite sirens in coastal cities, and despite tsunami warning signs, we are not prepared. How can we keep thousands of people from dying?

When you read this sentence, stop to ask yourself what you would do if a magnitude 9.0 earthquake struck at this moment. Are you in a building with unreinforced brick walls or chimneys? What loose objects could fall on you from shelves or walls? If you are near the beach, could you get to high ground within 15 minutes without using your car? Do you know where your loved ones are?

The next subduction earthquake will trigger the most serious natural disaster in Oregon history. Ninety-nine percent of the people in Oregon are likely to survive the coming disaster with little more damage than broken dishware and a power outage—if they are prepared. The coming earthquake and tsunami will capture the attention of the entire world. They need to capture our attention *now*.

Volcanic eruptions: every 100-2000 years. Volcanoes can

erupt in cycles, but the patterns are so irregular that it's difficult to convince people to make preparations. In general, Mt. St. Helens erupts every century and Mt. Hood erupts about every two centuries.

The state's most recent lava flows oozed out of Newberry Crater and South Sister about 1200 years ago. These two volcanic hotspots tend to be active every millenium or two. A slight bulging of the ground suggests they may come due within the next century. None of Oregon's other volcanoes appears likely to erupt any time soon.

The biggest danger in an eruption is posed by glowing avalanches and mudflows. The problem is often compounded by quickly melting snow or crumbling glaciers. In the past, volcanic floods from Mt. Hood have scoured the Hood River, White River, Zigzag River, and Sandy River. Houses should not be built near these streams.

A sand moraine dams Carver Lake, high on South Sister. If an eruption broke the dam, the flood would inundate Sisters.

Near South Sister, Whychus Creek and the McKenzie River are high-risk areas where riverbank homes are also a bad idea. The city of Sisters and the community of McKenzie Bridge need to pay particular attention to the threat of volcanic floods.

All of Central Oregon might reasonably expect six inches to a foot of volcanic ash during an eruption. Roofs that have survived the region's winter snows probably will be able to handle the ash load. The biggest health hazard is likely to be respiratory disease, particularly for people with a history of asthma or lung ailments.

Unlike volcanoes in Italy and Indonesia, Oregon's fire mountains are not surrounded by intensive agriculture or urban development. Wilderness areas and national forests protect us from our volcanoes' eruptive cycles. This is a safety buffer we should preserve.

River floods: every 20-100 years. Historically, Oregon rivers experience major floods every 20 to 100 years. We have attempted to change this cycle in the past century by building flood-control dams. The dams have provided inexpensive power, irrigation water, and boating recreation in addition to lower floodcrests. Meanwhile, we are also learning that floods play a useful role in the ecology of the river environment.

Just like people, rivers need exercise. Rivers need to get up and shift their gravel bars around, put a little fresh silt on the fields, wash out old log jams, and make some new ones. Wetlands that flood every once in a while are not worthless — by allowing runoff to spread out they lower floodcrests almost as effectively as dams. Wetlands also provide important habitat for ducks, frogs, endangered pond turtles, and other species. Salmon rely on floods to stir up gravel for spawning beds, wash smolts downstream, and enable adult fish to clear the rocks on their way back upstream.

No major dams have been built in Oregon for two decades, partly because of the growing public awareness of river ecosystems. For the same reason, some old dams are being removed.

Dams remain an important flood-control tool, but they are not the only tool. Dams are also not a permanent solution. Reservoirs eventually fill with silt, reducing their storage capacity. Dams weaken with age and can fail in massive earthquakes. Climate change appears to be increasing the size and frequency of floods. All of these factors have encouraged renewed interest in the rivers' natural flood control system — wetlands.

In human terms, floods become disasters only when people get in their way. Since the flood of 1861, Oregonians have been told that the simplest way to lessen the risk of flood damage is to avoid building in the flood plain. The economic pressure to defy this logic is intense. Riverfront land is often extremely valuable to developers and very attractive to home-builders. In few other cases do private property rights conflict so violently with public need. Government policy can add to the confusion, restricting flood plain development while simultaneously providing disaster relief funds to rebuild in flood plains.

Unfortunately, avoiding flood damage in Oregon is not merely a matter of understanding the rivers' natural cycles. The issue is a thicket of conflicting interests that promises more disasters and more damage.

Forest fires: every 5-1000 years.

Like river floods, forest fires are part of a natural cycle that we have tried to stop — only to learn that the cycle was important after all.

A forest needs periodic fire in the same way that people need sleep. At times sleep can seem frightening — dark and full of nightmares. Sleep can even mimic death. But after a good night's sleep you wake up in the morning strengthened and refreshed. Similarly, fires can seem frightening but they actually renew forests. Fire clears out brush and dead wood, making room for vigorous young trees. Just as it is unhealthy to go without sleep for too long, a forest that's overdue for a fire can become dangerously unstable, loaded with unburnt fuel that can make the next fire even bigger.

All Oregon forests have natural fire cycles. There is no simple formula to predict these cycles because the historic interval between fires varies so much. In general, dry regions prefer frequent fires that creep along the ground every few years. These low-level fires leave most large trees intact. In wet regions, however, plants have adapted to giant, infrequent fires that wipe out entire stands of trees every few centuries.

Both kinds of fire cycles can have a disastrous impact on people. Today, the biggest danger is posed by vacation homes and retirement cabins in the woods. Now that scientists are revealing the importance of natural fire, the Forest Service and other agencies have adopted "let it burn" policies. This works fine in remote forestland, but becomes controversial when people live in the line of fire.

Fires that appear devastating can be part of the natural renewal process for Oregon forests.

Up to 80 percent of firefighting budgets are now spent defending rural homes, and costs continue to climb. Part of the problem is that zealous firefighters have put out so many blazes in the past. As a result, many forests are full of fuel, overdue for their natural burn cycle. Another problem is that summer weather really does seem to be getting hotter and drier, encouraging wildfires.

Trouble lies ahead. More and more people are building homes on forestland, particularly in the dry woods of central and southern Oregon. These are precisely the areas where frequent fires are important to forest health.

Will government tighten restrictions on development in forests? Will private homeowners be required to take responsibility for their own fire defense? All of the options seem to lead to conflict.

The Impact of Climate Change

The greatest natural disaster facing Oregon is a subject too large for this book to explore in detail. Our climate is changing.

The 2007 Nobel Peace Prize was shared by former Vice President Al Gore and the U.N. Intergovernmental Panel on Climate Change. The United Nations panel won the award for its scientific work, collecting proof that global warming is real and that it is primarily caused by humans. Al Gore won the award for publicizing the problem and suggesting solutions. His slide show about global warming, "An Inconvenient Truth," has been marketed around the world as a book and a movie.

Global warming is a complicated issue, but the core problem is that the level of carbon dioxide in the Earth's atmosphere is 40 percent higher today than it has ever been in the past 650,000 years. This sudden increase

has occurred largely within the past century. Scientists now agree that people are responsible for the sudden change. In general, the causes are industrialization and rapid human population growth. Specifically, the two main causes are the burning of fossil fuels (which release carbon dioxide into the atmosphere) and the destruction of forests (which absorb carbon dioxide).

Burning fossil fuels and cutting forests have increased the levels of carbon dioxide in the atmosphere, trapping heat from the sun.

Because carbon dioxide acts as a "greenhouse gas," trapping the sun's energy within the atmosphere, it has made the entire planet's surface an average of one degree hotter, in Celsius, over the past 40 years.

Global warming has already increased the number of storms over the oceans and led to record summer heat waves over the land. If carbon dioxide emissions continue to increase at the present rate, much of the Earth's polar ice will melt, raising sea levels by 20 feet or more.

In Oregon, summers are predicted to become hotter and drier, increasing fires and droughts. Winters will become wetter and warmer, reducing snowpacks while increasing floods.

We have already been able to observe some changes during our lifetimes. When I was a child, I re-

The warming effect of "greenhouse gases" like carbon dioxide has melted polar ice packs and glaciers, raising sea levels.

member the Collier Glacier was a river of ice, extending more than a mile between North and Middle Sister almost to a viewpoint on the trail. Now that glacier is barely half a mile long, and the trail overlooks a gravel field.

Other Oregon glaciers have retreated dramatically as well. The change has been tracked by the Mazamas, the state's largest outdoor recreation

In 1901, Mt. Hood's Coe Glacier covered most of the mountain's north face.

By 2005 the Coe Glacier had retreated far above Elk Cove.

Oregon's largest glacier in 1910 was the Collier Glacier at the Three Sisters.

By 1990 the Collier Glacier had shrunk to a patch of ice on the side of Middle Sister.

group. The Mazamas were founded in 1894 when 155 men and 38 women convened in inclement weather on the summit of Mt. Hood. To this day, climbing a glaciated peak is a requirement of club membership. Photo surveys sponsored by the Mazamas in the early 1900s and in 2007 reveal that the state's glaciers lost about half of their volume during those years. The dwindling ice supply has cut summer streamflows, hurting farmers and fish. Most of the summer irrigation water for Hood River Valley's fruit orchards, for example, comes from glaciers.

Oregon's warming climate is changing the types of plants that can grow here. Recent maps prepared for gardeners by universities reflect this new situation, shifting climate zones north across the continent. Some plants are able to move their range. Other species cannot move, and become extinct. In general, the rapid climate shift seems to favor non-native species that are accidentally introduced as weeds. About a quarter of all species on Earth will become extinct if temperatures continue to rise in the next few decades, as the U.N. climate change panel predicts.

As Oregon's forestland becomes hotter and drier, Douglas fir may give way to pine. Areas that are now pine forest may have no forest at all. Oregon's woods will look more like those in California, and California could resemble Baja California, where forest is rare.

Agriculture is at risk. Oregon has more ghost towns than any other state in the Union. Many of these abandoned villages date to the home-steading era of the early 1900s, when drought devastated farmers, espe-

The ghost town of Blitzen, near southeast Oregon's Steens Mountain, serves as a reminder and warning of climate change.

cially in eastern Oregon. As the climate continues to warm, farming in Oregon could become an increasingly precarious occupation.

Oregon's seacoast is also at risk. The U.N. panel on climate change anticipates sea levels will rise at least a foot by 2100, but the rise could be as much as 25 feet if the ice caps on Greenland and Antarctica continue to melt rapidly. At the same time, warmer oceans are creating more powerful storms with larger waves. The average height of waves off the Oregon Coast has been growing by more than a foot a decade. Together, the two trends spell trouble. Low areas will be permanently inundated. Giant storm waves will crumble beach cliffs and wash into coastal communities.

A strange "dead zone" off the Oregon Coast in recent summers appears also to be a result of the changing climate. Oxygen-poor water from the deep ocean wells up off shore, suffocating fish, crabs, starfish, and other marine wildlife. Fishermen say they have heard of fish-free zones for years, but scientists say the problem seems new.

Average temperatures in the Northwest are rising 50 percent faster than in the rest of the world, a panel of eleven independent scientists reported to the Northwest Power Planning Council. Oregon's climate has warmed nearly two degrees Fahrenheit in the past century, and is expected to gain another degree every decade. By the year 2090 almost half of Oregon's rivers will be too hot for salmon to survive.

Computer models suggest the melting of the Arctic ice pack will change currents in the Pacific, directing wet winter storms at Oregon.

A Greek Lesson: The Forests of Crete

What changes will global warming bring to Oregon's forests? For perspective, it might help to consider the Greek island of Crete, where the Minoan civilization thrived 4000 years ago. The Minoans repeatedly clearcut the

island's forests to build ships and palaces. But each time the forest was cut, some of the topsoil washed away. As the climate gradually warmed, it became harder for the trees regrow. Today Crete has no forests. Most of the island is barren and rocky, vegetated only by spiny shrubs.

Our history in Oregon is so brief that it is easy to imagine the forests will regrow forever. In fact, some steep areas might survive only a few bouts of clearcutting before the soil is so thin and the

A model of the Minoan palace at Knossus, Crete shows the use of wooden beams.

ground is so dry that trees will not grow. Already it is getting harder to replant forests in dry areas of southern and eastern Oregon.

Once a forested island, Crete was logged to build ships and palaces. Soil eroded from clearcuts. When the climate warmed, the forests did not grow back.

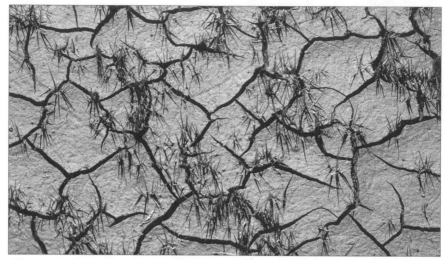

Climate change is predicted to bring Oregon wetter winters that increase the risk of floods, and drier summers that increase the risk of drought.

Skiing will dwindle and floods will increase. Summers, however, will be drier than ever. The annual acreage burned by Oregon forest fires is expected to double by 2040, compared to 20th century levels.

Earth's climate does change naturally in cycles. Our planet has seen other periods of warming. But the rise in greenhouse gases we have created is so far beyond anything in the geologic record that we are in danger of breaking the cycle.

What can we do? Should we switch our cars to alternative fuels such as ethanol or hydrogen? Actually, although these alternatives might reduce our dependence on foreign oil, studies show they don't really help with the overall emission of greenhouse gases. Smaller, lighter, more efficient vehicles are far more important. Bicycles are beautiful. Walking is wonderful.

Another surprise: Our single most damaging habit may be air travel. Jet engines pump out as much carbon dioxide per person per mile as cars—and they pump it directly into the upper atmosphere. Travel by train, ship, or bus is far less damaging.

We in Oregon have a special responsibility because our state is so heavily forested. Forests are the lungs of the planet. Each tree breathes in carbon dioxide, locks up carbon, and pumps out oxygen.

Beverly Law, a professor of global forest science at Oregon State University, set up instruments in a variety of Oregon forests to measure that exchange of carbon with precision. She found that clearcuts are like diseased

Comet and Asteroid Impacts

Fireballs from space may have killed the dinosaurs and caused several other ancient mass extinctions, but has an asteroid ever directly affected people in Oregon?

The answer may be yes, according to University of Oregon archeologists Douglas Kennett and Jon Erlandson. They are part of a team of researchers proposing that a comet or asteroid slammed into the Canadian ice shield 12,900 years ago, killing many of the people and animals in North America. The resulting forest fires, floods, and climate change could have helped wipe out mammoths, sloths, mastodons, camels, horses, and saber-toothed tigers–Ice Age fauna that became extinct at about the same time.

Critics of the theory say the animals were killed by human hunters. The first people in North America had arrived a few hundred years earlier from Asia. Critics also wonder why such a large impact from space didn't appear to leave a crater.

Kennett and Erlandson counter that comets are made of ice. If a comet landed on the Canadian continental glacier during the Ice

If a comet hit the Canadian ice shield 12,900 years ago, the impact of ice on ice might not have left a permanent crater.

Age, the impact of ice on ice might not have left a permanent crater. Blocks of ice hurled by the impact might have created the Carolina Bays, thousands of elliptical depressions between New Jersey and Florida. These lakes and bays are aligned in a northwest-southeast direction that points toward Canada. Excavations in the Carolina Bays have turned up iridium-rich magnetic grains that suggest an extraterrestrial source. A carbon-rich layer points to massive fires from the same era, perhaps sparked by heat from the impact.

The carbon layer is missing in Oregon. Excavations near Mill Creek in Woodburn's Legion Park show that Ice Age mammals survived in Oregon hundreds of years after the theoretical impact date. Kennett and Erlandson say the western U.S. may have been a refuge from the impact storm, but that hungry hunters eventually wiped out the megafauna anyway.

Fireballs from space probably have been the most violent of Oregon's natural disasters. Much mystery remains about exactly when extraterrestrial objects have hit Earth–and when they might strike again.

lungs. Rather than absorb carbon dioxide, clearcuts release it for 20 years, largely because logging debris emits gas as it rots. Forests do not become efficient engines for absorbing carbon until they are 50 to 90 years old.

"If I had the power to change things," Law told reporter Sharon Levy for an *OnEarth* article in 2008, "I would increase the length of forest harvest rotations so that more carbon is stored on the ground for longer periods."

Soil erosion may be the most insidious threat to Oregon's forests. Historically, large forests grew in Greece, the Alps, and the Himalaya foothills where trees no longer survive. Each time these steep areas were cleared, rains washed away a little more of the soil. Loggers didn't realize it at the time, but they were in effect mining the topsoil. Because the forest had been keeping the land cooler and damper, cutting the trees also sped climate change. Rivers dried up in summer. Forested hills became rocky badlands.

In areas where soils are thin, even two or three cycles of clearcutting can make reforestation difficult. Oregon's history is so brief that most forests here have not been cut more than two or three times. How often can Oregon's steep mountain slopes be logged bare before the soil is gone? Adding to the problem, roads and clearcuts trigger landslides that cause sudden, catastophic soil loss. In short, Oregon's forests are not necessarily a renewable resource.

If we are to slow global warming, the effort must be global. China, for example, now puts more carbon dioxide into the atmosphere than the United States. But Americans still have a much greater impact per person. Although we cannot change the world by ourselves, we have an obligation to do our part by preserving our forests and reducing our use of fossil fuels.

Our planet is alive, which of course is a good thing, but it can also be a little frightening. Sometimes we act as though the planet were entirely under our control. Natural disasters are proof that there are forces we cannot master. The risk of earthquakes and volcanic eruptions, for example, is simply the price we pay for setting up shop on a living planet.

The art of living with natural disasters lies in understanding the cycles of the Earth's forces. We still have much to learn.

CHAPTER XI

A Fictional Epilogue

Up to this point, this book has been a work of nonfiction. We have learned from the geologic record that devastating subduction earthquakes and tsunamis sweep the Oregon Coast every few hundred years. Another of these major plate-shifting events is inevitable. Legends of the Northwest's native tribes help give a picture of the damage and suffering caused by the last subduction earthquake and tsunami in 1700. How well will our modern civilization stand up when the next tsunami arrives?

Denial still runs high. Home prices remain high in designated tsunami zones. Voters complain about land use restrictions. Legislators balk at the cost of earthquake retrofits. Many people feel that building regulations are already too strict. Perhaps it's time to be slapped awake.

To be sure, we can only guess when the next subduction earthquake will strike. We don't know how large the accompanying tsunami will be, or what damage will be done. The foldout at the front of this book gives a glimpse of one such guess, with fictional news articles set in the year 2020.

Now we are about to launch into the human stories behind the headlines. Before you a fictional door is opening onto an imaginary future.

Welcome to the summer afternoon of Oregon's greatest natural disaster.

A Week of the Future

LINCOLN BEACH, 3:54 pm Tuesday, July 12, 2020.

Rod Barker had just decided it was time to put down his murder mystery and get a ginger ale when the floor of the beach cottage jumped up and did a sliding dance step to the left. Joan was already shouting at him from the bathroom, as if this was all his fault. Three rows of books cascaded into the room from the shelves, along with a basketball-sized Japanese glass float that exploded like a bomb on the hardwood floor. An unearthly groan rumbled from below.

When the house jerked again, Rod found himself bumped out of his chair. A fishbowl of agates collected by the grandkids narrowly missed his head, landing with a crash on the brick hearth of the woodstove.

"Rod!" Joan cried. The spray from the showerhead was wobbling at her as if from a loose fire hose. "Rod?" She had always been afraid of being caught unprepared—even as a teenager she'd had nightmares of showing up at junior high school in a slip—and now here she was fifty years later in the shower.

"There's an earthquake!" Rod called back. Hats and umbrellas tipped out from a closet as he staggered down the hall toward the bathroom. At first the doorknob seemed jammed, but then the wooden frame of the house flexed and the door flew open, venting a cloud of steam. Joan was wrapping herself in a towel. The floor rocked like a skateboard on a staircase.

Rod held out his hand. Joan hurried with him out through the house. Along the way she managed to grab a coat from a peg by the front door. Finally they were outside on the lawn. The ground yanked their feet sideways again, staggering them to their knees.

For minute the ground continued to ripple. Joan felt a little queasy. Shore pines in the vacant lot next door waved like giant blades of grass. The brick chimney of the empty house down the block crumbled in a cloud of dust. The old cabinetmaker across the street came out of his garage shop, holding his hand to his bald head.

Then at last the earth stood still.

The Barkers cowered on the ground. Was it really over?

Joan stood up and buttoned her coat. Rod peered past a salal hedge toward the little patch of beach he could see down the street. They had never had a very good ocean view. With prices the way they were on the Oregon Coast, they had only been able to afford a cottage a block up from the beach when they retired. More expensive vacation homes, most of them empty on weekdays, blocked much of their view.

As far as Rod could tell, everything looked the same down at the beach. Waves still curled in streaks of white foam. "I guess that was the Big One they'd warned us about," Rod said.

"Do you think there'll be a tsunami?" Joan asked.

Rod looked out to sea again. The swells were no higher or lower than usual, all the way to the horizon. A seagull flew past, seemingly unconcerned. "I don't know. I'm glad we didn't buy a place right on the beach, though."

"You tried to."

"I did not!"

Joan shivered in her coat. "Maybe we should move to higher ground."

"This is the highest ground for miles. Sixty feet above sea level. Remember? That's what I told that fast-talking real estate guy — what's his name, McCullough. I put my watch right here on the porch railing." Rod set his hand on the rail and pressed the global positioning system button of his wristwatch. He studied the GPS numbers and frowned. "That's funny."

"Funny?"

Rod tapped the device on his wrist and read the numbers again. "Yeah. This thing says we're only fifty feet above sea level now. And thirty feet farther west."

"Thirty feet west?" Joan asked, raising her eyebrows. "How can that be?"

Rod shrugged. "I don't know. My damned watch must be broken."

"Get the phone," Joan said. "Now I'm worried about the kids in Portland."

PORTLAND, 3:54 pm Tuesday, July 12, 2020.

Seth O'Neil liked to bicycle home along the river from Portland State. After struggling for five hours in a crowded Japanese immersion class each Tuesday, the last thing he wanted was to swelter in a crowded streetcar. He looked forward to the quiet of his apartment. He had spent most of June knocking out a wall for a balcony to let some air into the big, converted warehouse off MacAdam Avenue.

Two things always amazed Seth about the new condos he passed beyond RiverPlace. First, that people would spend two million dollars to live near the roar of the Marquam Bridge. And second, that they never came out to look at the river itself. A solitary duck waddled out of Seth's way as he rounded the empty Starbucks patio. Thunder rolled in the distance—strange for a sunny day.

Seth wasn't riding much faster than usual, but suddenly the pavement wobbled and his tires lost their grip. With a cry of alarm, he found himself flying down a grassy bank. His bike stopped short at a guardrail but he kept going. He landed painfully in a patch of replanted willow brush, practically in the water.

The fall had ripped bloody scratches through his skin-tight shirt. He unbuckled his helmet and groaned. Why the hell had he slipped? Why couldn't he stop shaking? And what was that weird sound, if not thunder?

Somewhere above him, an ominous shadow was moving.

When Seth looked up, he saw the two-story center span of the Interstate 5 freeway bridge slowly tilting off its pillars. As gracefully as a spaceship undocking, the monumental steel rectangle twisted half a turn and descended toward the river before him. With a colossal roar, twin arcs of water rose in slow motion above the rooftops of OMSI.

The whole scene was so astonishing and so strangely beautiful that Seth did not come to his senses until he realized that the broken toys skidding down the half-sunken freeway section were in fact tractor-trailer trucks. Those vehicles had real, live people inside. The traffic din overhead had changed to squealing tires and honking horns.

To Seth's horror, two cars suddenly flew off the far side of the freeway's stump. They sailed a hundred yards and splashed into the river near the distant shore. Then a van jolted into the sky directly overhead, tumbled end over end, and landed tail-first with a big splash, hardly thirty feet away. It had almost hit him!

The van bobbed up with a vacant white gaze in its one big eye. By the time it bobbed up a second time, however, the white behind the windshield had shriveled. Of course—the airbags were deflating.

By the third bob the van was drifting downriver and sinking lower. Then Seth saw something that made his heart stand still. A small white hand was reaching up from the darkness inside.

Instantly Seth was scrambling to help. He yanked off his shoes, grabbed a fist-sized rock from the bank, and dived into the river. The cold water stung his scratches. With the rock in his left hand, he could only manage a slow, awkward side stroke. It seemed like hours, but less than two minutes passed before he reached the van and crawled up onto the windshield.

Inside was a little girl, no bigger than his seven-year-old sister, struggling in vain with the passenger door handle. Next to her a woman in the driver's seat sagged from a seatbelt strap, her eyes closed. Water had risen to her chest.

The girl looked at Seth and screamed.

"I'm here to help!" Seth shouted. "Cover your face with your hands!"

"What?"

"Just cover your face!" Seth lifted his rock and smashed the windshield. The glass crumbled into what looked like little ice cubes. Water poured across the dashboard. He reached in and pulled the girl out onto the chrome grille. "Are you all right?"

She gasped a moment. "Mama! Get Mama out!"

The woman's face was almost underwater. Seth held his breath, stuck his head into the water, and probed around beside her until he found the seatbelt release button. Then he braced his knee against the steering wheel, put his hands under her armpits, and pulled. At first the unconscious woman seemed to be stuck in the bucket seat, but finally he managed to drag her up halfway onto the dashboard. He couldn't tell if she was breathing. At least there didn't seem to be any blood.

"We're sinking!" the girl cried.

The van was indeed tilting back, nearly full of water. They might have only a few seconds before the whole thing went under. Seth looked at the shore, now perhaps fifty feet away. Then he eyed the little girl. "Can you swim?"

She nodded fearfully.

"Good. Take off your shoes so you'll be lighter. Head toward that grassy spot, OK?"

The girl nodded again and began taking off her shoes. But she didn't actually leave the sinking van until Seth had dragged her mother all the way out of the broken windshield, gripped the unconscious woman across the chest with his arm, and set out first.

Never had Seth swum so hard, fighting to keep the woman's head above the waves. The weight of their wet clothing turned every stroke into a struggle.

He reached the shore exhausted, but still somehow managed to drag the woman up onto the grass. He cleared her mouth and breathed life back into her until her eyelids fluttered.

When the little girl waded ashore and crawled up to hug her mother, Seth was finally able to catch his own breath for a while. He staggered up the grassy bank, his torn clothes dripping. He headed for the Starbucks patio, foggily thinking that he would ask a barista to call 9-1-1.

But when he actually reached the gate of the patio, people were frantically running about, crying and shouting. Seth realized that thousands of people must have seen the bridge collapse. Hundreds would already be jamming the phone lines to call 9-1-1.

"Don't stand there blocking the gate!" A big man in a business suit shoved him aside. "If you can't help, at least get out of the way."

Seth had never felt so tired. He looked back to the riverbank lawn. A crowd had already gathered around the woman he had pulled from the river. The little girl was helping her mother sit up. A man was saying, "Take it easy, you're going to be all right," Another voice shouted, "Get back, everybody! Give us some room here! Move back!"

Seth hated crowds. The woman and her daughter didn't need him anymore. He was just in the way. Suddenly all he wanted was to go home, take a shower, collapse in his bed, and rest.

Seth slogged down through the willow brush to get his shoes. Then he put on his helmet, lifted his bike back up from the guardrail, and slowly rode home.

SEASIDE, 3:54 pm Tuesday, July 12, 2020.

At first Lynne Engalls thought the dancing sand must be part of some goofy carnival ride that Seaside merchants had installed beneath the beach to amuse tourists—sort of like the wave pool or the bumper cars they had seen yesterday among the saltwater taffy stands on Broadway. The Engalls had driven all the way from Baker City, and this was their first vacation in Seaside, so Lynne really wasn't sure what all to expect.

The bouncing sand spurted up a couple of inches, with tiny ripples that smoothed away the footprints and left her a little giddy. Her husband Dave looked worried but Makenzie and Sam, the five-year-old twins, were just giggling. Makenzie's new solar radio was playing *Rock Me Baby All Night Long*.

Then the ground beneath them suddenly dropped six feet, as if the entire beach were a trampoline that some giant had jumped on. When the sand sprang back it came up at an angle, sprawling Lynne sideways in a cloud of grit.

"What the hell?" Dave sputtered.

"Earthquake!" A voice near the water shouted.

Lynne grabbed up the twins, catching Makenzie by the wrist and Sam by the shoulder strap of his overalls. They were both howling, with sand in their hair and eyes. The carnival ride wasn't over yet. Three-foot-tall hummocks of sand pulsed up and down on the volleyball courts, sometimes spouting geysers of sand where they met. Lynne suddenly sank to her calves in loose sand. Then just as suddenly the sand hardened and jerked to one side, throwing her off balance.

"Run!" voices cried from the water's edge. "The tsunami's coming!"

Lynne and Dave exchanged a frightened glance. He lifted Sam to his shoulder. "Let's get the kids to the car."

"No!" Sam wailed. "Not without my telescope!"

"Dad!" Makenzie added. "You can't leave my radio!"

Dave muttered an obscenity that Lynne had never heard him use before. Driftwood sticks, shells, and suntan lotion bottles were surfacing and disappearing in the boiling sandstorm about their feet. Dave grabbed something shiny. "Here's the telescope. I hear the radio over there."

Lynne fished it out of the sand. "Let's go!"

Running was impossible in the rolling, jerking quagmire of sand. Everywhere people were falling as they struggled up the beach. The concrete stairs to the Turnaround were even worse. A crowd of more than a hundred beachgoers jammed the narrow steps, shoving to escape. The roar of water behind them made everyone frantic. A boy in a blue swimsuit fell and covered his head, but was trampled by sandy feet. The shouts from the beach were turning into screams.

Lynne didn't dare look back until all four of them had made it safely to the sidewalk. She clutched Dave and the twins. Down on the beach, one wave had already covered the volleyball courts. Now another, larger wave was cresting over the spot where they had just picnicked. Dozens of people, still struggling in the sand, vanished in the surf. The wave petered out at the edge of the steps and slapped against the concrete wall of the Promenade with a small splash.

"My God!" Lynne breathed. "We barely made it! All those other people — "

Dave pulled her back from the edge. "Let's get to the car."

Up on the Turnaround the earthquake was jolting the ground even more violently. The Lewis and Clark statue wobbled, jerking Meriwether's outstretched bronze arm as if he were no longer certain which way pointed west.

One look at Broadway was enough to convince Lynne that they couldn't drive out of town. An entire storefront had tipped into the street, smashing cars and blocking everything. Loose powerlines jerked and crackled. Dozens of cars honked, but weren't moving anywhere. The side streets didn't look any better. Every few hundred feet the pavement had buckled. If she remembered right, the only way out of town was on a narrow bridge anyway, and it was perhaps a mile away, across a city in chaos. They were trapped.

Suddenly sirens started to wail from the rooftops. A man gave a bitter laugh. "*Now* they turn on the sirens! The earthquake's over and the tsunami's gone."

Lynne stopped, uncertain. The ground really wasn't shaking anymore. It was also true that the ocean had retreated somewhat, leaving a bare stretch of wet sand where the picnickers and volleyball players had been. Lynne didn't want to think about what had become of all those people. She had to concentrate on what her own family should do.

Makenzie's radio squawked as if to offer an answer. It stopped playing music, emitted three grating buzzes, and then said, "This is an announcement of the emergency broadcast system. This is not a test."

People gathered around. Makenzie turned up the volume proudly. The droning radio voice continued, "An earthquake has struck the coast of Oregon and Washington. Earthquakes can generate dangerous ocean waves. If you are in a low-lying area near the ocean, move away from the beach to high ground or to a tall, solidly built concrete or steel building. Do not return to low-lying areas until you are told it is safe to do so. Tsunamis may consist of multiple waves over a period of many hours. Listen to this station for more information. This has been an announcement of the emergency broadcast system." After three more raucous beeps, the music returned.

Lynne made a decision. "Let's go up to our room. It's on the third floor. That's the highest ground we've got. We can't drive out of town until they fix the streets."

"But if there's a bigger wave, we might lose the car," Dave objected.

"If there's a bigger wave," Lynne said, "I sure as hell don't want to be in the car."

NEWPORT, 3:54 pm Tuesday, July 12, 2020.

The VanderStraats were just about ready to return to their car when the earthquake hit.

Frank and Irma had spent all day at the Oregon Coast Aquarium, trying to get full value out of their $20 admission fees. They had been through the exhibits twice, Irma had read every informative plaque, and Frank was looking tired—the way he did more often now, Irma thought. Years ago she had been one his students at the pedagogical institute in Amsterdam. She had worshiped the ground he walked on. She had been in heaven when he retired and they could finally be married. But now that they were actually on their dream vacation, driving around North America for six months in a Volkswagen camping van, she had started to notice little things. Frank would forget the names of her children. He suffered strange bouts of fearfulness. Lately he had started imagining that thieves were following them, intent on stealing their van. Was it ordinary aging, or something else? When they got back to Holland she would insist he saw a doctor.

"Look at the sea otter, Frank!" she said, trying to perk him up. "It's swimming on its back."

"I want to check on the Volkswagen," Frank replied. "We've seen all this before."

But then something happened they had not seen before. The ground jumped sideways, staggering the crowd to its knees. The otter's pond sloshed up from its tank, drenching a family beside them. People screamed. Rock crunched. Water roared.

Irma helped Frank struggle to his feet, but another jolt of the ground sent them sprawling toward a bench. Water surged down a nearby walkway, sweeping away a garbage can. When the surge subsided, a sea lion lay flopping in the gravel courtyard outside the gift shop.

The VanderStraats clung together on the bench while the ground rolled. The otter tank sloshed like an ocean liner's swimming pool in stormy seas. Frank was tense with fear, jerking his head to watch the chaos to either side. Irma had never been so scared.

By the time the earth finally stopped shaking a siren was blaring. A surprisingly calm man walked up to them, wearing the blue vest and blue baseball cap of the Oregon Coast Aquarium volunteers. He shouted above the siren, "We've had an earthquake! Stay calm! We need to evacuate everyone to high ground in case there's a tsunami!"

"A what?" Frank asked.

"*Een zeefloed,* " Irma translated. She had read all about tsunamis on the informational plaques. "It comes sometimes after an earthquake."

"Oh, I see."

The volunteer pointed toward the lobby. "Meet out front! We'll all walk together to the bridge! Don't go to your car!"

But when they actually got to the aquarium entrance, Irma couldn't stop Frank. The plaza was crowded with frightened tourists, and he absolutely insisted on checking the van. He told Irma, "If there comes a *zeefloed*, we will get away faster in the Volkswagen."

"Frank! They don't want people causing a traffic jam."

"With everyone else here, we won't have a traffic jam." He stumped off toward the parking lot, and she followed.

The van's engine started just fine, as usual, and although the asphalt was broken occasionally by cracks, it was nothing a careful driver couldn't manage. Traffic wasn't even that bad—except for a few crazies who honked, squealed their tires, or drove through stop signs. The first real trouble appeared when they passed the Rogue Ale brewery. Ahead of them the beautiful green steel curve of the Yaquina Bay Bridge still arched above the river, but there was nothing on either side of it. The graceful concrete arches that connected the steel span to the shore were simply gone. When Frank drove closer, Irma could see that the bridge's concrete segments had fallen like gigantic dominoes onto the docks and parking lots below. The bridge was unusable. No one was going to drive north into Newport on Highway 101.

"Well," Frank said. "I guess we drive south instead."

But fallen concrete blocked the route to the southbound highway on-ramp, and the line of honking cars behind them made it impossible to turn around. Everyone was driving up the Highway 101 off-ramp instead, past the "WRONG WAY" sign.

Frank frowned. Tight-lipped, he followed the others past the sign. He got about a hundred feet before traffic stopped altogether. People honked, some got out of their cars and yelled, a few tried to drive off across the grass, but no one was getting onto Highway 101.

For several tense minutes Frank and Irma said nothing. Then a crowd of perhaps a hundred pedestrians walked by the stranded cars, led by the blue-vested volunteers from the aquarium.

Frank scowled silently as they passed.

"Maybe we should go with them," Irma suggested.

Angrily Frank yanked on the emergency brake. "All right, we'll walk, if that's what you want!" He turned off the engine, locked the anti-theft bar across the steering wheel, and got out.

As they walked up past a "Leaving Tsunami Hazard Zone" sign, Irma saw with alarm that the area of high ground before them wasn't very high, and it certainly wasn't very large. A noisy crowd packed the two-lane highway on the bridge abutment, where the white stripes vanished into thin air. The ground was hardly fifty feet above sea level, but with the bridge out, this was obviously the highest place for what looked like miles. Below them on the flats along the bay Irma could see the brewery's big metal building, a couple of motels, a vast marina of pleasure boats, the roofs of the aquarium buildings, and an RV park speckled with what looked like little white boxes. She had thought about staying at that RV park tonight, but it was pretty expensive, and although it had lots of sites the best ones were probably full. To the south, the flats along the highway were cluttered with antique shops, fudge stands, crab markets, and used car lots. Other than the collapsed concrete of the bridge, she didn't see much earthquake damage.

"Our passports!" Frank said suddenly. "They're still in the lockbox under the seat."

"That's all right," Irma said. "We'll get them later, after it's safe."

Just then someone shouted, "Look!" and everyone turned toward the ocean.

At first Irma didn't see anything unusual. Certainly there was no giant wave. The two jetties of boulders stretched half a mile out to sea on either side of the river entrance, just as before. Or wait — when she looked more closely she realized that the jetties were shorter. The far ends were submerged! And the jetties were getting shorter all the time. Waves were beginning to crest in the river mouth — not the single, gigantic wave she had expected, but rather a series of smaller waves at the front of a long surge. It looked as if the tide had decided to come in all at once. Only when the swell passed the footings of the bridge twenty feet deep did she realize how large it was. The water effortlessly lifted away the public fishing dock and rammed the brewery building across a parking lot half full of cars. Then the surge began sweeping through the marina, clearing away boats as if they were pool toys. The RV park lay just ahead.

Hundreds, perhaps thousands of people were drowning! Horrified, Irma clutched for Frank's arm.

A stranger shook her hand loose.

Where was Frank? Panicked, Irma looked for him in the crowd. "Frank?"

She fought her way to the concrete stairs at the edge of the bridge abutment, suddenly struck with foreboding. On the highway ramp below, the door of the Volkswagen van was standing open.

"Frank!" she cried.

ASTORIA, 4;10 pm Tuesday, July 12, 2020.

Andy Proudfoot certainly had not felt an earthquake while working on the *Tyee Chinook*. He had been pulling crab pots all afternoon with his dad and his cousin Jimmy off Long Beach. All he had noticed was a patch of choppy water. Whitecaps without any wind.

They had pulled in the last pot — empty, of course. It was bad enough that the treaty salmon had died out, and now he could hardly break even with these low-life scavengers, the Dungeness crabs. Raccoons of the Sea, his dad called them. He was just sailing past the North Head lighthouse, heading home for the jetty mouth and Astoria, when the nagging memory of those strange whitecaps made him decide to flip on the radio.

Chatter everywhere! Andy quickly ran through the radio channels, picking up emergency broadcasts, Coast Guard alerts, and shouting boat captains.

"Holy shit," Andy muttered.

His dad poked his head into the cabin. "What's up?"

"I guess there's been an earthquake. Everyone's worried there might be a tsunami."

"A tidal wave? They say those waves aren't much at sea. But they get big close to shore."

"Land to port!" Jimmy called out from the deck. "You asleep in there?"

Andy looked up from the radio and gaped. "What the hell?" Surf was breaking on a strange cliff, hardly 400 yards to the left. He'd been sailing half a mile from shore! He spun the wheel hard and gunned the motor, turning the *Tyee Chinook* back toward open water. But it didn't seem to have much effect. Where on earth had the cliff come from, and why didn't he recognize it?

"It's McKenzie Head," his father said slowly. "Turn the boat."

"McKenzie Head?" Andy stared at the old man as if he were insane. "But that's a mile inland!"

His father let out a long breath. "Look at your GPS. You can't fight this one, Andy. We're already on top of the campground at Baker Beach."

"That's impossible!"

"Turn the boat around, Andy. Aim to the left of Cape Disappointment."

"To the *left*? Are you crazy? The goddam river is to the *right* of Cape D!"

"Maybe it used to be. A river has its own ideas."

Just then they sailed backwards past what looked like a piling. But it wasn't a piling. It was the top of a power pole. With a streetlight.

Andy gasped. "It really is the campground!"

For a moment he just stared at the churning, sandy water of the flood. He had camped here with his daughters just last year. Hundreds of people must have been swept away by the tsunami. A chill crept down his back. Hundreds? If the Cape Disappointment Campground was under ten feet of water, then the entire Long Beach peninsula would be too. Twenty miles of sand, roads, and beach cottages! Six cities and 8,000 people! All of it washed into Willapa Bay by the same impossible current that was dragging the *Chinook Tyee* backwards past the impossible north side of Cape Disappointment.

"Turn the boat, Andy," his father said.

Numbly, Andy turned the wheel.

SEASIDE, 4:12 pm Tuesday, July 12, 2020.

Dave and Lynne Engalls stopped briefly at their Ford to get a few last things from the car. Then they hurried up the stairs of the Sea Queen Resort to their third-floor room, tugging the twins along.

The suite was large, very nice, and so new you could smell fresh carpet. Sam and Makenzie ran to the television in their room while Lynne hung up their beach towels. Here in the hotel it almost seemed as if nothing unusual had happened. Had they really escaped an earthquake? Had they really watched waves sweep away dozens of people on the beach? The hotel's concrete walls muted even the sirens outside.

Dave opened the sliding glass door and looked out across the balcony to the smooth, empty beach. The sand actually looked tidier than it had yesterday, when it was pockmarked by crowds. The thought made him flush with a mixture of fear and guilt.

Guilt was what had brought him to the Oregon Coast in the first place. Dave had been embarrassed that their five-year-old twins had grown up in Oregon without ever seeing the ocean. They lived in Baker City, eight hours from the beach. He never seemed to get enough time off to make the trip worthwhile. So he had talked Lynne into it. Of course they'd had to wait until Dave had helped with the Fourth of July fireworks at the county fairgrounds, as usual. But then he had paid a neighbor boy to come feed the calves and move irrigation pipe until the 18th. Lynne had found a middle school teacher to fill in for her at the bookstore where she worked.

It was Lynne who had rented the suite online, in a brand-new resort with a spa in the bath, and a balcony overlooking the Turnaround right in the middle of Seaside's beachfront. "If we're doing the Coast, let's do it right," she had said. "We might as well be front and center." And so they were.

"Daddy?" A small voice cut above the mumble of the television in the next room.

Dave looked at Lynne. Together they went into the kids' room. Surprisingly, the twins weren't watching the cartoon shows that had kept them up so late last night. Instead the TV was tuned to a CNN announcer reporting from the Middle East. Makenzie was dialing through channels of music, Spanish, and static on her solar radio. Sam was out on the balcony, focusing his telescope on the horizon.

"Daddy?" Sam said. "What does a tsunami look like?"

"I don't really know," Dave admitted. "I've always imagined it would be a huge wall of water."

"I don't see anything like that," Sam said. "There's a fishing boat, though."

"Maybe the tsunami's already come and gone," Lynne suggested. "Maybe it's over."

Sam looked through his telescope. "Hey, bigger waves are coming now."

A moment later a wave smacked the wall of the Promenade, sending up a long line of foamy spray. Instead of receding back down the beach, however, the water stayed high. The next wave crested over the Promenade railing and washed up onto the parking lot. Again, before the water had time to retreat, another wave hit. This one rolled knee-deep past the Lewis and Clark statue and surged onward down Broadway.

People screamed. A man was yelling in a downstairs room. On Makenzie's radio an excited announcer at KYTE-FM urged everyone to stay calm. Dave clutched Lynne and Sam by the shoulders.

The next wave was perhaps only eight feet tall. The swell wouldn't have been particularly unusual if it had been down on the beach where it belonged. But now, on top of the rising surge from the first waves, the eight-footer plowed into Seaside like a Panzer division of battle tanks.

Parked cars at the Turnaround jumped up sideways and rolled before the breaking crest. Wooden buildings skidded backwards or crumpled to sticks. The wave crashed into the concrete wall of the Sea Queen with a roar, smashing the first-floor windows and splashing foam past the balcony where the Engalls huddled.

The man downstairs continued to scream for a moment, and then stopped. The bedroom light blinked out. The CNN reporter fell silent. The voice of Makenzie's radio announcer turned into a soft buzz. Even the sirens went dead.

"Oh. My. God." Lynne breathed the words quietly.

Before them stretched the ocean.

Where the beach and the Promenade had once been, there was now nothing at all but open sea. Even the sounds of chaos had stilled to a slosh. The view from their balcony would hardly have been different if they had been on a cruise ship in the middle of the Pacific.

"So that's a tsunami?" Sam asked.

Dave nodded, unable to speak. Their hotel was still standing. The flood had swept through the first floor and moved on. The people in the lower rooms must have drowned, but the Engalls were still alive.

Makenzie came up behind them. "Can we go look out the front door too?"

Lynne herded her family in off the balcony, closed the glass door, and latched it — although she knew the lock was now meaningless.

Dave walked to the front door. Despite himself, he couldn't help thinking about his Ford, new just six months ago. He had bought it with a trade-in and a full $10,000 down.

The twins peered from behind his legs as Dave cautiously turned the front door handle. He opened the door just a crack, as if today were some horrible Halloween and monsters really might be lurking outside.

The ocean looked quite different out the front door. The concrete stairs from the hotel's breezeway descended into a swirling, muddy maelstrom. Toward town the flood was studded with the upper stories of buildings. Dozens of Seaside's hotels, businesses, and homes were still standing, surrounded by water. If people were alive out there in the vast muddy chaos, Dave couldn't see them. In fact, he couldn't see the end of the water. The tsunami was still surging inland. The concrete Sea Queen had held out like a bunker, an island in the current of a great, backwards river.

"I can't believe it," Lynne said behind him. "I guess we're the lucky ones."

Dave nodded. "But now what do we do?"

LINCOLN BEACH, 4:17 pm Tuesday, July 12, 2020.

The Barkers tried three times, but couldn't get through to their daughter Susan in Portland. Finally Joan went into the house to get some clothes. Rod set up lawn chairs on the grass so they could watch for a possible tsunami.

Joan came out a few minutes later, shaking her head. "The house is a wreck!"

"I didn't see much structural damage."

"Rod! It looks like the grandkids threw a rock party in there or --"

"Shh!" Rod held up his hand.

"Don't you shush me!"

He pointed to the little patch of beach visible between houses. "The waves are coming up higher. See?"

Joan sat down beside him and squinted. "That's not very high. Waves came up farther last winter."

"They did not."

"They did so. Remember that storm?" Joan humphed and settled in to watch.

But the waves really were getting higher. Each one seemed to build on the last. Finally a good-sized breaker actually hit the lowest cottage by beach path. They heard the crash of breaking glass.

"See?" Rod said. "That's the Weidlers' place."

"Those people never come here anyway. They're from L.A. or somewhere."

Across the street the bald cabinetmaker had wandered back out of his garage. Rod waved to him. "Hey, Ernst! Come on over and watch the tsunami!"

Ernst crossed the street, frowning. Rod set up an extra folding chair on the lawn for him.

"Boy, that earthquake sure made a mess in my shop," the cabinet-maker said, sitting down. "Knocked a can of paint on my head. Are you two OK?"

"Yeah, we're fine." Rod said, watching the beach. "Hey, look at that one!"

A wave broke against the first row of beach cottages with a thunder-ous crash. The Weidler cabin jerked back, collapsed to half its height, and drifted out with the receding foam.

"Boy!" The old cabinetmaker gawked. "Are we safe up here?"

"Safe as anywhere, I guess," Rod replied.

Ernst was still staring at the hole where the house had been. "Wow. That place cost a million dollars. I was so mad when those California law-yers built it right in front of us."

They watched the waves in silence for a moment.

"Kind of opens up the view, doesn't it?" Joan said. Without the Wei-dler house, they could see the surf quite a bit better.

"I wonder if that other house down there will hold up?" Rod mused. "You know, the big empty one McCullough keeps trying to sell?"

Ernst shook his head. "I dunno."

"We always wanted a better view," Joan said, "But I sure didn't want it this way."

They sat watching for a long time.

SEASIDE, 4:20 pm Tuesday, July 12, 2020.

The Engalls stood on the third-floor breezeway watching the tsunami surge through Seaside. Soon other people began venturing out to join them. An elderly couple came out of Room 306. A group of four businessmen emerged from a room near the end. A couple in their twenties waded up the stairs from the second floor, their clothes drenched. No one talked much. They looked down at the sandy water boiling through the submerged first floor, where no one could have survived. They looked out at the growing gulf that separated them from the distant, forested hills of the Pacific's new shore. Sam steadied his telescope on the railing. The young wife from the second floor closed her eyes and quietly chanted an obscenity, over and over, until her husband put his dripping arm around her shoulder.

Finally the current slowed. The water level dropped a few feet, exposing empty windows on the gutted first floor. And then the tsunami turned around.

Now the current began flowing toward the sea, faster and faster, as if it were determined to suck Seaside into the depths. Several buildings that had withstood the inward rush of water now crumbled. A vast lake of wreckage floated toward the Sea Queen Resort, the last obstacle before open water.

The flood bulged before the hotel as if at the prow of a giant barge. Telephone poles, trees, smashed cars, and debris crashed into the second story before slipping to one side or the other. A log smashed the stairway, buckling the metal rail at a crazy angle. The hotel shuddered.

The old man from Room 306 ordered, "Get inside, everybody!"

"No, wait!" Lynne objected.

Everyone looked at Lynne. She had borrowed Sam's telescope. Now she put it down and said, "I can see people out there, floating this way on the wreckage. If we get ropes or poles, maybe we can rescue some of them."

Dave and the four businessmen fetched curtains and heavy curtain rods from the rooms. They knotted sheets into ropes. Soon the men were standing at each end of the breezeway, holding out the rods like fishing poles in a raging stream. A rooftop sailed past with a dozen shouting people, just out of reach. Several lifeless bodies floated past in the wreckage. But then a woman on a picnic table managed to grab Dave's pole and climb to safety. A maple tree with half a dozen people eddied against the breezeway long enough for all of them to scramble ashore.

When the current finally slowed, 23 wet and weary survivors had gathered on the breezeway of the Sea Queen. Hardly two dozen, Dave thought, exhausted. Out of how many thousands in Seaside?

Makenzie looked over the railing. "Daddy? Why isn't the rest of the water going away?"

Dave leaned over and looked. "I don't know, honey." If the tsunami was really over, why was water still standing in the streets two feet deep?

"The man on the radio said there might be another wave." Makenzie held her little radio in the sunshine and began slowly turning the dial, trying to find anything but static.

Then the walls began to shake. One of the new arrivals screamed.

Dave closed his eyes. "Dear God. Not another earthquake."

PORTLAND, 6 pm Tuesday, July 12, 2020.

The *ON AIR* light for the six o'clock news had just flashed at Angela Flint and Marcus Hampton when the whole studio bobbled. The tech guy struggled to keep his wheeled camera focused on the anchor, but Angela's head rolled around the screen like a marble.

"I'm Angela Flint with the News at Six," Angela said, trying to look earnestly into the wobbling lens.

"And I'm Marcus Hampton. Looks like we're having a little aftershock here from this afternoon's big earthquake. It's been that kind of day, hasn't it, Angela?"

"It certainly has, Marcus." Angela was still looking earnest. She gripped the table to hold steady. "This afternoon a powerful earthquake measuring nine on the Richter scale struck the Pacific Northwest just before four o'clock, triggering tsunamis on the Coast and destruction throughout western Oregon and Washington. We have Chris Payette live on the scene in Portland's Old Town, where rescuers are pulling victims from the rubble of more than thirty brick buildings that collapsed onto streets and a MAX train. Chris?"

The *ON AIR* light went dark.

"Yow!" Angela scowled, holding her head.

"Take it easy, Angie," Marcus cautioned. "We've still got a Webcast and a national feed."

"A *little* aftershock? I felt like some kind of televised ping pong ball."

A voice in their earphones said, "Marcus in five. Three, two."

"Thank you, Chris," Marcus said, lowering his eyebrows seriously at the camera. "We'll want to follow up on your story of the MAX driver. A true hero. Elsewhere in Portland, the Marquam Bridge collapsed into the Willamette River during the earthquake today, killing dozens and closing Interstate 5 indefinitely. But at least one family escaped without serious injury, thanks to the intervention of what the mother claims was an angel. Paul Koutsopolous has the story."

As soon as the *ON AIR* light darkened, Marcus clapped his hand over his earphone. "Bogus! This is so bogus! Here we've got people dying and you give us some wacko story about a woman rescued from a sinking van by an angel? Where do you get this stuff?"

The voice in the earphone said, "No one knows how the woman and her daughter survived. We're looking hard for upbeat news here. Angela in five. Three, two."

"That's amazing, Paul," Angela said, smiling again. "I think we all could use a guardian angel, especially on a day like this when so many have lost so much. That's particularly true on the Oregon Coast, where the surge from a tsunami has devastated low-lying areas. The big wave hit ten to twenty minutes after the earthquake. At a federal emergency headquarters at the Portland airport, spokesperson Robert Wonne now estimates that as many as four hundred people may be missing. Hardest struck are the communities of Seaside, Pacific City, Lincoln City, and Newport. With us by satellite telephone is Charles Krafeld, a volunteer with the Oregon Coast Aquarium in Newport. Charles, are you there?"

A shaky voice came through the static, "Yeah, I'm here."

Angela asked, "Can you tell us what the tsunami was like there in Newport?"

The *ON AIR* light blinked off, but everyone in the studio was quiet, listening to Mr. Krafeld. There weren't any pictures of him. The monitor was showing footage of beach debris taken from a helicopter.

"We'd practiced for tsunamis, so we knew what to do, but—"

"But what, Charles? Are the animals all right?"

"Animals?" Mr. Krafeld sounded puzzled.

Angela smiled, rolling her hands in the air as if this might help her explain something that seemed so obvious. "You're a volunteer at the aquarium. How are the animals?"

"Hell, lady, I guess seals are used to saltwater. The real tragedy out here is about people! We tried to evacuate the museum and get everyone up here to the bridge ramp where it's high."

Angela felt herself flush. The station would pay for letting "hell" slip into a live broadcast, and she would probably get the blame. She asked, "Which bridge did you say you're on, Charles?"

"We're on the ramp of the collapsed Yaquina Bay Bridge. It's the only high ground in South Beach. But some tourists wouldn't go, and then there were the people at the brewery and the marina and the RV park and the shops and the state park. We even had one guy who was safe until he ran back to his car at the last minute --"

The satellite telephone voice broke off. For a moment the entire studio was silent.

"And then what happened, Charles?" Angela asked.

"And then the water came up the bay, and they all just—they all just—"

"How many people are we talking about here, Charles?" Angela asked.

"I don't know. Hundreds? Maybe a thousand? They're just—just gone."

The earphone voice said, "Marcus, NOW!"

"That was live from the Oregon Coast at Newport," Marcus cut in. "We haven't been able to contact our media affiliates on the coast north of Newport. The images you are seeing were taken from our news helicopter moments ago above the beach at Lincoln City. The wreckage suggests the scale of the devastation there. Now I believe we have a live radio telephone link with Andy Proudfoot, the skipper of fishing boat at the mouth of the Columbia River. Andy, are you there?"

"Uh —" The sound of static and waves and creaking wood filled the studio.

"Andy?"

"Uh, yeah?"

"Andy, I'm told you rode out the tsunami in your fishing boat. Is that right?"

"Oh, yeah, I guess."

"Andy? What was it like?"

"Oh, the river's changed out here."

"The Columbia River? How has it changed, Andy?" The monitor switched to a file photo of the Columbia River Bridge at Astoria.

"Well, like my dad says, it has its own ideas." Andy's voice sounded a little distant.

"How has the river changed?" Marcus asked. "Tell us what you saw."

"Well, when the tsunami came we found ourselves sailing across solid land, just north of Cape Disappointment, on ten feet of water. We tried to make for Astoria, but no dice. The current turned around and sucked us back out to sea."

"What happened then, Andy?"

"Well, I wanted to steer out the mouth of the Columbia, but it wasn't there."

"What do you mean, it wasn't there?"

"It just wasn't there. The tsunami must have washed sand from Willapa Bay down into the old channel. The old mouth's a sand bar that sticks north to Long Beach. That's where the river goes now, so that's where we ended up."

"So you're at Long Beach?" Marcus asked.

"That's what the instruments say. It's just, there ain't no Long Beach anymore. Like I said, there's nothing here but one big river mouth."

The earphone voice said, "Angela! NOW!"

Angela stared straight at the camera. She wasn't smiling. "Andy? Are you still there? Let's connect with Andy again."

The earphone was shouting at her to move on to the next story, but Angela kept staring straight into the lens. "Andy?" she said.

A moment later Andy was back.

"Yeah?" The river sloshed and a seagull cried in the background.

"Andy, this is the first report we've had from the Long Beach peninsula. My parents have a summer cabin there." Angela's voice caught. "Thousands of people live there in July. Have you seen anything that could tell us if they are all right?"

"Well, ma'am, I'm sorry about your parents, but I don't suppose they are all right," Andy said. "You see, the whole coastline dropped ten feet of elevation, and that's about as high as anything got on the peninsula. The Columbia River runs through here now, and all that's left is debris that's been flushed out to sea. Just like me and my boat, the *Tyee Chinook*."

Even the earphone voice was silent now.

Angela closed her eyes and lowered her head. Before the camera could cut away to Marcus, a tear ran down the makeup on her cheek.

LINCOLN BEACH, 6 am, Wednesday, July 13, 2020.

The Barkers didn't sleep well after all the excitement of the earthquake and the high waves, so they got up early the next morning. The power was still out, and the house was still a mess. Rod ate a bowl of cereal with lukewarm milk while Joan picked books up off the floor.

"We have no idea what's going on in the world," Joan complained. "Even the cell phones don't work, so how are we supposed to find out if the grandkids are OK?

Finally Rod went out to his pickup, partly to get away from Joan. But the more he fiddled with the truck radio, the more puzzled he became. How could every single station still be off the air?

Pretty soon Joan came outside to see what he was doing. As soon as she heard the radio static she announced, "All right, that's it. We're driving into Lincoln City." She got in the passenger side, buckled her seatbelt, and crossed her arms.

"Maybe you're right," Rod admitted. He backed the pickup out of the driveway and took the gravel lane out to Highway 101.

There was no traffic on the highway. None at all. He had never seen anything like it, even at 6:30 in the morning. The lights were off at the Lincoln Beach Sentry—of course the supermarket wasn't supposed to open for another three hours anyway—but a man was already out front, putting letters on the marquee with a pole. So far the man had spelled out, "HELP E".

"What's that supposed to mean?" Rod muttered.

"I don't know," Joan said. "Just drive into town. We'll find out soon enough what's going on."

The earthquake had left so many little cracks and slumps in the asphalt that Rod couldn't drive faster than fifteen miles an hour. Near the turnoff for Gleneden Beach a Subaru passed them going the other way, driving just as slowly, with its lights on.

A quarter mile later Rod was driving down the hill by the Salishan golf course, past the "Entering Tsunami Hazard Zone" sign. But at the bottom of the hill the entire highway simply sloped down into the waters of Siletz Bay.

Rod stopped the pickup, frowning at the water ahead. "For crying out loud."

Either the ground had dropped or the bay had risen. Either way, the highway and the golf course and most of the four-star Salishan Resort seemed to be underwater.

"Is there another way into town?" Joan asked.

Rod scratched his head. "Not unless you've got a boat, I guess."

Just then a bedraggled young man waded up from the swamped woods beside the highway, waving his hands and shouting. "Hey! Hey, you guys! Hey!"

Rod jammed the gearshift into reverse and spun the pickup around. But before he could drive away Joan put her hand on the wheel.

"Rod! That boy looks hurt. Let's find out what he wants."

Rod rolled up his window and locked the door. "All right."

The young man limped up, grabbed the hood of the pickup, and panted. His face was bloody and his hair hung in wet strands. He might have been fifteen, but he looked as strong as a football player.

"Are you all right?" Joan asked loudly through the windshield.

"I—I been going all night," the boy managed to say. "We were at a trailer park up the river. When the flood came I hung onto a tree. I gotta find my folks. And my little sister."

"Well," Joan hesitated. She looked to Rod.

Meanwhile the boy limped around to the passenger door and began yanking on the handle. "You gotta take me to town! To the sheriff or the fire department or somebody!"

Rod took command. "Cut it out! Just shut up and get in the back of the truck!"

"The back?" The teenager stared in the window.

"Yeah, get in back. There's a volunteer fire station in Gleneden Beach. We'll take you there, OK?"

"Oh. Thanks, man." The boy crawled into the pickup bed, curled up against the spare tire, and almost instantly fell asleep.

As they drove up to the Gleneden Beach turnoff, Joan said, "Poor boy. Doesn't he remind you of someone?"

"Not on my side of the family." Rod drove past the Salishack Tavern and the beauty salon to the volunteer fire department. He was surprised to see a crowd of perhaps a hundred people sprawled all over the street in front of the station's big garage.

A fireman in a yellow slicker came up to meet them. "Got another one?" he asked, nodding to the boy in the back.

Rod rolled down his window. "Another what?"

"Tsunami victim. Is he alive?" The fireman picked up the boy's wrist to feel for a pulse.

The boy lifted his head groggily.

Joan leaned over. "He told us he's looking for the rest of his family."

The fireman nodded. "Thanks for bringing him in. Come on inside and we'll see what we can do."

Rod parked the pickup and helped the fireman walk the boy into the one of the station's garage bays. People lay sleeping on tarpaulins and blankets all over the floor. Some of the people had broken legs or hastily bandaged wounds. Through a glass door Rod could see the next garage bay was stacked with bodies.

"Whoa!" Rod said, taken aback.

"I know," the fireman said. "Bodies have been washing up on the beach all night. Here, we've got a bulletin board of everyone who's looking for family. We'll list your boy and see if we can't reconnect him with his people." The fireman paused a moment. "Anything else we can do for you folks?"

Joan asked, "Can we use your phone?"

"Sorry. Official use only."

"Then at least tell us how to drive out of here."

The fireman shook his head. "You can't. The bridges are out at the Siletz River and Depoe Bay. There's no road inland, and the airport's closed by a slide. The state has a few helicopters, but they're busy elsewhere. We're an island, folks. No medical supplies, no power, no nothing until the feds get here."

"For crying out loud," Rod said.

"But maybe there's something you can do for us," the fireman suggested.

"Oh?" Joan asked.

"We've got two hundred homeless people here. Maybe you could take a couple off our hands, give 'em a nice place to stay for a few days?"

The fireman had hardly finished speaking when dozens of refugees began raising their hands, asking to be picked.

Joan shrugged to Rod. "There's always the kids' bedroom."

Rod pointed to the first two people he saw. "Maybe them."

Minutes later the Barkers were driving back to Lincoln Beach with 30-year-old Maria Velasquez and nine-year-old Jeremy Fisher riding in back. Maria, it turned out, had been working as a maid at Salishan Lodge when the tsunami destroyed her house in Cutler City, carrying away her husband and her mother-in-law. Jeremy had been visiting friends at a beach house near the golf course, and wanted nothing more than to get back to his family in Tigard. They had both wound up on the sand at Gleneden Beach, tired but alive.

The sign at the Sentry supermarket now read, "HELP EAT FROZEN FOOD FREE."

Rod pulled into the parking lot. He rolled down his window and called out to a clerk standing by the front door, "Is it really free?"

The clerk took out a shotgun. He clacked the gun open and checked the shells before answering. "Sure, especially ice cream. Not the canned food, of course. And just one turkey or ham per family. But yeah, it's free."

Joan nodded. "I guess we count as three families now, don't we?"

SEASIDE, 10 am Wednesday, July 13, 2020.

Six helicopters had flown over the Sea Queen Resort since the tsunami, but none had responded to the frantic waving of the 23 survivors on the hotel breezeway. Two of the helicopters had been news teams taking pictures. One was an Air National Guard chopper touring the devastation with some bigshot politician. The other three choppers had been in a big hurry to fly someplace else.

Meanwhile Dave and Lynne Engalls had become impromptu gover-
nors of the refugee island, in part because of their children's spectacularly
useful toys. Sam's telescope went from hand to hand as the survivors
scanned the horizon for hope. Makenzie's little solar radio needed no outside power, and when rigged up with an ingenious tinfoil antennae by the
businessmen, succeeded in hauling in startling newscasts from a scratchy
AM station in Portland.

There were also advantages to being marooned on the intact third floor
of a luxury resort. Everyone had a king-size bed. The complimentary re-
frigerator bars offered a surprising diversity of beverages, most of them
alcoholic. The Jacuzzi in Room 307 had been left half full of relatively
drinkable water. For warmth, there were plenty of terrycloth bathrobes.
Despite all this, many of the people at the Sea Queen spent their waking
hours shivering and crying.

Dave had used a notepad from the desk to keep track of the aftershocks
and water levels. Four successively smaller quakes had rattled the walls
in the past eighteen hours. Three additional tsunami surges had arrived
at forty-minute intervals. Since then a pattern had begun to emerge. After
the final tsunami wave, the water level had slowly dropped until about 10
pm. By then moonlight had cast a weird gleam across the mudflats that
had once been Seaside's streets. The surf had retreated to the Promenade's
seawall. Then the water had slowly risen until four in the morning, when
waves rolled waist-deep through the streets once again.

"These are just tides," Dave announced over a breakfast of tortilla
chips and V-8 juice.

"Tides?" Lynne asked. "Then why is the city underwater?"

"I don't know. The ground must have dropped in the earthquake.
Anyway, now the water just rises and falls every six hours, like ordinary
tides."

Lynne thought for a moment. "You're saying the ocean won't ever go
away."

"That's right. The streets emerge for about an hour at low tide. Otherwise, Seaside might as well be Atlantis."

Lynne walked to the window. "So low tide is our chance to get out. We
could walk inland without being swept away by some giant wave."

"Maybe." Dave tapped his juice can on the desk. "The problem is, I
think there's a river channel between us and Highway 101. It might have a
bridge, or it might be out. I don't know. Even if we get to the far shore, the
radio says the highway's closed. People over there are cut off too."

Lynne sat on the bed. "Then let's not tell the others we could hike to dry land. As long as our supplies hold out, we're better off waiting for help here."

Sam hugged his mother's legs. "Mama? I want to go home."

"I know, honey. I know."

PORTLAND, 5 pm Saturday, July 16, 2020.

"Are you really ready for this, Angie?" Marcus asked.

Angela Flint took a long breath. "I think so. I want to get it over with." She closed her eyes and wagged her finger with the "go ahead" signal.

"Taping Marcus in five," said the voice in their earphones. "Three, two."

"Four days have passed since a great earthquake and tsunami struck the Northwest," Marcus said, lowering his eyebrows at the camera. "In those heartbreaking days the official toll of the missing has risen to more than twenty thousand. The confirmed death toll now stands at half that number. Heroic stories of rescue and survival have been keeping hopes alive. But increasingly, we have had to accept that many of the missing will never be found. Tonight, we pay homage to Oregon's lost, in the hopes that they will find rest."

The camera cut to a golden sun slowly descending toward the sea.

Angela's voice held steady as she spoke, "Congressman Lawrence T. Ryan of Milwaukie."

Marcus said, "Bishop Lucinda Diaz of Vancouver. Senator Marion Waller of Seaside. Mayor Nancie Matsushita of Newport."

Angela continued, "Philanthropist Harold Myers III of Lake Oswego. Fashion designer Emily Blass of Portland. Singer-songwriter Harmony Train of Eugene."

"Marcus added, "State Librarian Marla Mann of Salem. Astronaut Jonathan Lowe of Roseburg. Commodore Nils Bergstrom of Florence. Blazers star William P. Jefferson."

The sun was setting in a ball of fire. A vast list of names in small white letters appeared on the ocean, scrolling slowly toward the horizon. A harp strummed a long chord.

"We cannot list all of the thousands who have been lost," Angela said. "But we will remember them forever in our hearts."

The harp strummed again. Then Angela added quietly, "Including my own parents, Gregory and Christine Flint."

"Perfect," the voice in their earphones said. "Thank you both. Angela, you can take forty until the six o'clock. Marcus, your guests are wired for the business interview."

Angela peeled the miniature microphone from her ear. Her eyes were not damp. She had cried enough in the past days that there weren't many tears left. Sometimes she wondered if anything important was left.

"Are you going to be all right?" Marcus asked.

She nodded. "I'll just wait in the green room. It'll be a nice change to watch for a while."

Marcus gave her hand a squeeze. Then he crossed the room to the interview set and began introducing himself to his guests.

Angela drifted out of the studio, walking slowly past the black backdrops, taped cables, and dangling lights. Somehow the low, brightly lit corridor outside always reminded her of a hospital basement. Even the green room looked more like the waiting room for a morgue than for a broadcast station. The room was yellow, anyway, not green, and no one could tell her how it had gotten its name. The vinyl easy chairs had cigarette burns on their arms. There was a tray of donuts and a stack of tired-looking *People* magazines. And of course a television that couldn't be turned off.

Angela felt like she was looking for something, but she didn't know what. Maybe hope? She poured herself a mug of black coffee and sat down to watch Marcus at work.

"With us on Business Today are three distinguished guests to discuss the long-term impacts of the earthquake." Marcus held out his hand to the people lounging in overstuffed chairs beside him. "Dr. Ana Johnston of the U.S. Geological Survey office in Vancouver, Port Authority director Barbara Hsu of Astoria, and mayor Walt Dorland of Coos Bay. Welcome."

The guests on the screen nodded seriously. Marcus continued, "Let's begin with Dr. Johnston. Have you been surprised by the changes in sea level? The earthquake seems to have permanently lowered the North Coast by ten feet and raised the South Coast by twenty. Was that something you could have predicted?"

Dr. Johnston crossed her legs and straightened her skirt. "Well, first let me say I'm not in the fortunetelling business. Earthquakes will always be unpredictable. But if you're asking whether I'm surprised at the scale of ground deformation, the answer is no."

"No?" Marcus lifted his eyebrows—and Angela realized, once again, that those expressive, bushy eyebrows were by far his most telegenic feature.

Dr. Johnston continued, "The geologic record shows that previous subduction earthquakes on the Cascadia fault changed the landscape just as much. The event in 1700 lowered the coastline from Crescent City all the way to Canada, leaving drowned forests in estuaries, particularly in Puget Sound. The uplift of the southern Oregon Coast also has geologic precedent. All of the seafront terraces at Cape Blanco and Shore Acres were originally flattened by wave action. That region has been falling and rising for at least a million years."

"But you still couldn't have predicted the uplift?" Marcus asked.

"Well, no." Dr. Johnston looked uncomfortable. "Not precisely."

The Coos Bay mayor practically jumped out of his seat. "Do you geologists have any idea what this means for us down there? Coos Bay just spent ten years and two billion dollars building a container shipping port, and now it's useless! We've got six miles of mudflats between our docks and navigable water. Five giant freighters are lying on their sides in the mud. They'll have to be cut up and hauled away as scrap. Don't you think you could have warned us just a little?"

"We did warn you," Dr. Johnston replied. "In the feasibility study for the container port the USGS noted that a subduction event would almost certainly occur within a two-hundred-year time frame. The report not only itemized the tsunami danger, but it also specifically mentioned the possibility of coseismic ground deformation. I think that's pretty clear."

The mayor turned aside in evident disgust.

Marcus quickly shifted gears, as Angela knew he would. "Let's turn now to Barbara Hsu of Astoria's Port Authority. Although the earthquake may have drained Coos Bay's port, it seems to have made yours even deeper. What are Astoria's plans at this point?"

"Astoria is still a city in chaos," Ms. Hsu said. "The loss of life on the northern Oregon Coast has been staggering. Although Astoria itself escaped with relatively light damage, we now have two thousand refugees in the city. They're hungry, hurt, and desperate. There's no way to get them to Portland because the roads across the Coast Range are still closed. There are only a few helicopters, and the hospitals are all full. It's hard to plan very far ahead when you don't even have drinking water."

Marcus nodded. "I understand the Navy is sending ships down from Bremerton to serve as floating hospitals. FEMA has rented several Alaskan cruise ships that should arrive in a few days. The cruise ships are supposed to take refugees to San Francisco, outside the damaged area. The question is, will ships like that be able to dock at Astoria's port?"

Ms. Hsu shook her head. "All of our waterfront facilities are damaged or underwater. Until we can rebuild we'll have to access the bigger ships with shuttles. Moving the refugees is going to be slow."

"But eventually you plan to rebuild the port?" Marcus asked.

"Eventually, yes. Of course."

"What is your long-range vision for Astoria?"

Ms. Hsu sat back. "Well, it's still too early to make predictions, but we'll obviously come out of this in a better position than Coos Bay. With ten feet more water in the harbor, and if the new Columbia channel can be kept clear, I think Astoria could eventually rival Seattle as a port."

"Ambitious indeed." Marcus turned to the geologist. "About the Columbia's new channel, Dr. Johnston. Do you think the river mouth will move back south?"

Dr. Johnston spread out her hands. "It could, but probably not for several hundred years. Geologically, the Columbia mouth has been everywhere from Newport to Willapa Bay. The trend, however, has been to the north."

Marcus raised his eyebrows. "Looks like our state's getting bigger. If Cape Disappointment stays attached to the Oregon shore, is there any chance Astoria will be asking the state to annex it?"

Angela knew Marcus was trying to lighten up a grim conversation. But no one smiled.

The Astoria port director cleared her throat. "Actually, we're talking about raising money for a monument at Cape Disappointment. I think the tens of thousands who are missing deserve a memorial. And I think all the rest of us need a symbol of hope. People are looking for a sign."

A sign! The words struck Angela like a lightning bolt. Yes—that's what she had been looking for. She stood up, put down her coffee, and marched out of the green room, suddenly sure of herself.

No one was allowed in the producer's control room, but Angela no longer cared. She walked down the corridor, went up the stairs, and opened the door labeled, "THE GREAT AND POWERFUL OZ. Do Not Enter!"

Lit only by the flicker of little television monitors, an overweight young man swiveled his chair toward her. "Angela? Can't you see we're live?"

She knew the producer's voice so well from the earphones, but it still surprised her whenever she saw him in person. He was only 27, with spiked hair and a torn Grateful Dead T-shirt.

"I'm sorry, but this is important," Angela said. "I want us to follow up on the story about the angel."

The producer rolled his eyes. "The angel? Marcus hated that story. Everybody did. It's been four days and people are tired of earthquake stuff. Go back to the studio and get ready for the six o'clock."

Angela shook her head. "I'm not leaving until you agree to let me follow up on the story."

"Oh, for —"

"I'm serious."

The producer sighed. "Look, that angel woman was obviously nuts, saying she'd been rescued by a guy who flew away."

"That's not what her daughter said," Angela pointed out. "Remember? The little girl kept saying they'd been rescued by a man, an ordinary man. It's just that no one listened to her. She said if we go back to the same spot one week later, he'd be there again."

"One week later," the producer mimicked her words with a satiric lilt. "Right there on the bike path. I suppose if we send a news team to the riverbank an angel will swoop down and say hi. Yeah, sure."

"Just let me do it. Please?"

The producer narrowed his eyes at her. "Don't tell me you're into this angel stuff because of your parents. Or is it because your name's Angela?"

She wanted to hit him. She wanted to quit. She had never been so angry. But somehow she managed to say in her steadiest on-air voice, "Get me a camera crew for Tuesday afternoon. We all need something to believe in."

LINCOLN BEACH, 3 pm Monday, July 18, 2020.

Six days had passed since the tsunami, and the Barkers were beginning to think the world had forgotten their corner of the Oregon Coast, when a white miracle appeared.

"A ship! There's a ship outside!" Maria cried, waving Rod and Joan toward the front door. Maria had lived with them for five days. In that time she had not only tidied up the house, but she had also made tortillas on the woodstove, done the laundry by hand, and generally kept the neighborhood from falling into chaos. Still, this was the first time she had shown genuine enthusiasm.

"Did she say *ship* or *sheep?*" Rod asked Joan, looking up from his mystery novel. He had never gotten the hang of Maria's accent.

"I don't know." Joan shrugged. "Let's take a look."

"Well, I hope it's a sheep," Rod said. "We've used up the frozen meat."

When they got outside, Maria pointed toward the ocean. "You see? A beautiful one!"

A big, beautiful white cruise ship was indeed sailing past Lincoln

Beach. Seven stories of balconied apartments towered above the waves. A sleek white prow speared ahead. The giant blue logo painted on the side portrayed a dolphin with a champagne glass. Modern antennas whirled above a dramatically finned tower that read, *The Northern Star*.

"For crying out loud," Rod muttered. Then he called across the street, "Hey, Ernst!"

The bald cabinetmaker came out of his garage, followed by Jeremy. The nine-year-old castaway had become a kind of apprentice, learning to use hand saws, block planes, and glue clamps.

Rod waved them over. "Come get a load of this boat!"

Maria told Joan, "I worked on a ship like this for two years in the Caribbean. There were swimming pools, shops, theaters, restaurants, everything!"

Ernst and Jeremy joined them on the lawn. The cabinetmaker scratched his head. "Never seen one of those here before."

"Nobody cruises the Oregon Coast," Rod agreed. "No exotic ports of call, I guess."

Joan suggested, "Maybe they're rich tourists, come to gawk at the locals. You know, to see how we're surviving, cut off from the world by the earthquake."

"Look! They're flashing a light," Maria said, pointing again.

"Anyone know Morse code?" Rod asked. No one raised a hand.

"Maybe they've come to rescue us," Jeremy suggested.

"In a cruise ship?" Rod wrinkled his brow.

The boy shrugged. "I don't know. It's kind of close to shore, like they're planning to stop nearby. Maybe we could follow along in the pickup and see."

Everyone looked at each other. They had been without power or telephones or flush toilets or televisions or refrigerated food for an awfully long time. A cruise ship would have all of that and more.

"Let's meet at the pickup in five minutes," Rod said.

"Right," Ernst said. "I just need to get a few things and lock the house."

"Last one out, turn off the lights," Rod added with a smile.

A few minutes later all five of them were barreling down Highway 101 in the Barkers' pickup. Maria and Jeremy bounced in back whenever the truck hit a bump. From time to time they would catch a glimpse through the trees of the beautiful white ship, sailing surprisingly close to shore.

The highway ended at Depoe Bay by a sign announcing *World's Smallest Harbor*. The graceful concrete bridge that had once crossed the entrance to that harbor was gone, but the broken edge of the highway on either hand was packed with a crowd of perhaps two hundred people.

Rod parked the pickup near a whale statue by the seawall. By then the cruise ship had anchored in the bay. A crane on the ship's side was already lowering a shuttle boat.

The Barkers got out of the pickup and started walking toward the broken bridge.

"Let's stick together," Rod suggested. He didn't have to say that the crowd ahead might be dangerous. The entire area had been without law for almost a week.

A woman in the doorway of the Sea Hag Lounge nodded to them, casually tucking a pistol into her apron. Across the street at the observation gift shop, a man with a rifle leaned against a *Whale Watching Spoken Here* sign.

Just before the crowd at the bridge a tough-looking man stepped out to block their way. "Hold it right there, folks."

"We just want --" Rod began.

The man cut him short. "Are you refugees?"

"Yeah, I suppose."

"We'll need your names and addresses. Signatures if you decide to sell."

Joan asked, "Then the ship really is here to rescue us?"

"Sure, sure," the man said. "A week's cruise to San Francisco, courtesy of Uncle Sam. Bus tickets from there wherever you like, or you can live on board for a month. Just talk to the guy at the table first."

Rod looked to Joan. "I don't know. You want to go on a boat to San Francisco?"

Joan asked the man, "Will they have telephones?"

"On a cruise ship? Sure."

"Then let's go," Joan told Rod. "I've been so worried, not being able to get through to the kids."

Rod nodded. But he was also beginning to worry about an earlier phrase he had heard: *If you decide to sell.*

"Parker! Rod Parker, isn't it?" The guy at the card table extended his hand and flashed a big smile.

"It's Barker, actually." Rod shook the man's hand cautiously. "Aren't you McCullough, the real estate guy?"

McCullough laughed. "That's me! Say, this has been a tough week. I don't blame you for wanting to leave. Let me just look you up on the tax lot register. Lincoln Beach, wasn't it?" He thumbed through a pile of papers. "Here you are, 4040 Mina Street."

"That's right," Joan said, surprised.

McCullough shook his head. "You had a nice little property there, but what with the earthquake, I'm afraid I can only offer you $3000 for it."

Rod stared at him.

"In cash, of course," the man continued. "That could come in handy in San Francisco."

"We're not interested in selling," Rod said. "Besides, our house is worth a lot more than that."

"I can offer $5000, but that's my absolute limit." McCullough held out his empty hands. "Take it or leave it, Rod."

Rod looked at the real estate man askance. "You're not really with the government, are you?"

McCullough shrugged. "Did I say I was? I'm just here to help." He looked past the Barkers and spotted Maria. "Say, how about you? What's your name, ma'am?"

"Maria Velasquez."

McCullough leafed through his papers. "I've got a Diego and Maria Velasquez at 125 Pine Street."

Maria reddened, but she nodded.

"Well, Cutler City was hit pretty hard by the tsunami. I assume the house is gone?"

Maria nodded again, tight-lipped.

"I can give you $200 for the bare lot, as is. Interested, Maria?"

She shrugged. "I guess."

"Good. My secretary at the next table will draw up the papers, and the man with the rifle has the cash." McCullough turned to Ernst. "Say, how about you?"

"Not so fast," Rod interrupted. "What's your game here, McCullough?"

"Game?"

"Yeah. A week ago you were selling houses in the tsunami zone for millions of dollars. Now you're buying back the empty lots for hundreds. How do you expect to find anybody fool enough to build out there again?"

Ernst stood by Rod's side. "That's right. What are you trying to pull?" Joan, Maria, and Jeremy joined ranks, watching the real estate man suspiciously.

McCullough frowned. "Move on, Parker, you're blocking customers."

Rod planted his hands on the table. "We're not going anywhere until you tell us what you're trying to pull."

The real estate man sighed. "Oh, hell with it, you're leaving anyway." He waved them closer, leaned forward, and whispered, "Look, folks. Everyone knows we have tsunamis every three hundred years. I've always been upfront about that. Sure, I'm sorry some people made the choices they did. But now the Big One's come and gone. Understand?"

Rod shook his head. "I'm not sure I do."

McCullough raised his eyes in exasperation. "They say these big earthquakes let off steam that's been building up for three hundred years. It stands to reason we won't have another big tsunami for three centuries! Hello? Beachfront land is safe for another *fifteen generations*. The county commissioners are going to declare most lots buildable again. I'm just—"

A whistle blast from the shuttle boat drowned out his words. A loudspeaker on board announced, "Your attention, please! This is Raoul Nichols, first mate of *The Northern Star*. The government has authorized me to offer tsunami refugees free passage to San Francisco, as well as free housing for a month. Please don't push! We'll be taking several shuttle trips so everyone has room."

Joan said, "Let's get our things from the truck."

Rod told Maria, "Don't listen to that real estate man. If you need money, you can borrow from us."

"Are you certain?" Maria asked.

"Sure." Joan said, taking Maria by the arm.

McCullough waved them away. Then he smiled to the next couple in line. "Say, how about you?"

PORTLAND, 3:45 pm Tuesday, July 19, 2020.

The voice in the earphone said, "Live in five. Three, two."

Marcus lowered his eyebrows. "This is Marcus Hampton, with the Week of the Wave, a live report of people and places exactly seven days after the earthquake that devastated western Oregon and Washington. Coming up, the heart-warming story of one family still praying for the return of their guardian angel. But first we'll revisit the tragic scene from Salem that's been burned into our memory. One week ago, the dome of the State Capitol collapsed, killing twelve members of the Lincoln High School choir. Across the street, visiting tourist Mark Daniels of California captured the moment on video."

As soon as the *ON AIR* light turned off, Marcus put his hand over his earphone. "Please tell me we're never going to show this clip again. For Pete's sake, the kids are in there dying."

The light signaled *ON AIR*. Marcus immediately lowered his eyebrows. "Our correspondent Pat Logan is live on the scene, where cranes are now salvaging the golden pioneer statue for use in a memorial. Pat?"

Marcus took a long breath, waiting. At the signal he said, "Thank you Pat. Of course the earthquake that shook the state exactly one week ago also launched a tsunami, a surge of water that left 20,000 dead or missing along the coast. One lucky group of survivors, however, was rescued just yesterday morning from the third floor of a Seaside hotel. In a dramatic scene, helicopters plucked 23 people from the ruin where they had ridden out the waves."

The monitor briefly switched to a shaky view of two people dangling from a helicopter. In the background, open sea stretched a mile west across what had once been Seaside.

"Where are those survivors now?" Marcus asked, raising his eyebrows. "The helicopter took them directly to the luxury cruise ship *The Northern Star*. Let's go there now to meet survivor Dave Engalls. Dave, can you hear me?"

Marcus shrank to an inset at the upper corner of the monitor while an image of a thirty-year-old man whirled in to fill the bulk of the screen.

"Uh, yeah, hi." Obviously Dave had never been on TV before. He was so nervous that he held Sam up to the camera and made the little boy's hand wave.

Marcus smiled. "Is that another of the survivors with you there?"

"Yeah, it's my son Sam." Dave looked around. "And this is my daughter Makenzie and my wife Lynne."

"A beautiful family. Tell me, how did you manage to survive for those six long days?"

"Well, uh, we ran out of water and food. We were about to try wading to shore for help, but I'm not sure all of us could have made it. Fortunately, Makenzie here had a little solar radio, and we picked up a broadcast about the cruise ship."

"How did the rescuers find you?"

"That was Lynne's idea. We waved sheets from the roof."

A voice in Marcus' ear told him, "Keep it short! Angela's ready."

Marcus asked, "So Dave, where are you headed now?"

"San Francisco!" Dave and the others were laughing. "It's not where we wanted to go, but with the highways still closed in the Coast Range, I guess it's the only place they can take us."

"Where's home for you, Dave?"

"Baker City. I'm supposed to get back there to my cattle. Hey Don, if you're listening, feed 'em hay for another couple days, OK?"

"I think you've earned a vacation, Dave." Marcus turned to look at a different camera. "Now let's turn to another story of survival—a story that's still full of mystery. One week ago, almost to the minute, Portland's Marquam Bridge collapsed into the Willamette River. Thirty-two people died, but one lucky family was rescued from their sinking van by what one woman still insists was an angel. On the scene with the rescued woman and her daughter is our own Angela Flint. Angela?"

The monitor cut to Angela, standing on a bike path with a microphone. In the background, broken bridge piers protruded from the river like stumps.

"Marcus, I'm here at what used to be the Interstate 5 freeway bridge with Susan Barker and her daughter Miranda. Susan, can you tell us what happened here one week ago?"

An attractive woman with freshly coifed blond hair smiled at the camera. "Well, I was driving Miranda from her grade school in Tigard to a science program at OMSI when all of a sudden the road ahead just disappeared. Before I could do anything we'd gone off the edge. Once the van hit the water I don't remember anything until I was awakened by an angel."

"An angel?" Angela asked.

"Yes. He was—he was surrounded by light. He kissed me to wake me up. And then he was gone."

"Why do you think he was an angel?"

"He just was. Our van crashed into the river and sank. I was dead. Only an angel could have lifted my daughter and me to safety and brought me back to life."

"Thank you, Susan." Angela turned to the camera. "But there was one other survivor, and one other witness to that crash in the river. We're here today, exactly one week later, because of her."

Angela crouched on the bike path to hold the microphone to a pretty seven-year-old girl in a lavender summer dress. "Miranda, can you tell me what happened after your van fell into the river?"

Miranda tilted her head. "Well, my Mom believes in angels."

"Do you?"

"I don't know. But I remember being rescued by a man."

"A man? How could anyone have lifted you and your mother out of a sinking van?"

Miranda shrugged. "He pulled us out, but then he only took my Mom, because that's what I told him to do. I had to swim by myself."

"Could you really swim that far in a river, all by yourself?"

"I guess I did."

Angela looked at the little girl uncertainly. "Miranda, are you sure it couldn't have been an angel?"

The girl stamped her foot. "Angels are only if you don't believe in *people!*"

"What do you mean?"

"Just that! People can be full of good too. People can do miracles. You just have to believe in them. Like that man who saved us. Everybody says it wasn't possible. Well I don't care! I don't believe in angels. I believe in *him!*"

Angela looked up at the camera, her eyes damp. "Here's one seven-year-old girl who believes so strongly, you can almost hear the click of her ruby slippers."

Angela put her arm around the girl's shoulder. "Miranda, for the past seven days you've been saying that if you came back to the same spot one week later, you'd find your mysterious rescuer."

"Yeah." Miranda bit her lip. "I keep wishing he'd come back."

Angela looked at her watch and glanced around, blinking to keep back a tear. "I'm sorry, honey, but I'm afraid time has run out for that wish."

"No!" Miranda shouted, pointing. *"There he is!"*

The camera jerked crazily past the Starbucks porch.

"Who? Where?" Angela looked up desperately. The barista? The bum on the lawn? The kid on the bike?

PORTLAND, 3:54 pm Tuesday, July 19, 2020.

Seth had been so busy with his Japanese immersion class that he hadn't had time to read newspapers or watch TV for the past week. Sure, everyone talked about where they had been and what had happened when the earthquake hit, but he had just listened and nodded. Even today, bicycling back from Portland State as usual, his mind was elsewhere—imagining a new window in his Macadam Street loft, trying to remember the Japanese Kanji character for shoe, looking forward to a chance to lie down and rest. He had been so tired since the earthquake.

And so he was taken by surprise when a roadblock of television cameras stopped his bicycle in front of the Starbucks patio. He pushed back his helmet and looked around to see what everyone was pointing at.

"Sir?" A smiling woman with way too much makeup was holding a microphone.

"Who?" Seth asked. "Me?"

A little girl was jumping up and down, squealing. "It's him! It's him!"

Suddenly Seth recognized the girl, despite her party dress, and he laughed. "You! The swimmer!"

"I knew it!" Miranda said.

Angela held the microphone to him. "Sir, what's your name?"

"Um—I'm Seth. Seth O'Neil."

"Mr. O'Neil, are you really the one who rescued a mother and her daughter from the river here last week?"

He fumbled for words, "Well, I—I guess."

"Then you're Portland's missing angel?"

"No." Seth shook his head firmly. "Sorry. I'm just a guy."

Angela laughed. She had never laughed live on national television before, and it felt wonderful. "Next you're going to say, 'I only did what anyone would have done.'"

Seth shrugged. "But it's true."

"And that's the story from the riverfront bike path," Angela said. "Hope is alive and well in Portland, Oregon. The angels we've been wishing for have been among us all along. Back to you, Marcus."

Acknowledgments

This book would not have been possible without the work of many Oregon scientists, writers, and reporters. In particular I would like to thank those who reviewed the manuscript: Mabel Armstrong, Martha Bayless, Talbot Bielefeldt, Joe Blakely, Oregon State University forestry researcher Daniel Donato, Alan McCullough, Rebecca Morales, Bill Sarnoff, Janell Sorensen, and Oregon State University tsunami researcher Harry Yeh.

Most of the photographs are by the author, but others deserve special credit and are identified by page number.

Hugh Ackroyd, Ackroyd Photography Incorporated: 132.

Associated Press: 56, 156.

Bear Creek Press of Wallowa, Oregon: Back cover (Heppner flood), 106, 108, 110.

Forest Service Employees for Environmental Ethics, 168, 174, 179, 257, 258.

The Mazamas, 205 (top: Coe Glacier by Harry Fielding, 1901; bottom, Collier Glacier by Fred Kiser, 1910).

National Oceanic & Atmospheric Administration: 2 (lightning), 6, 157, 161.

National Park Service: cover and 254 (painting by Paul Rockwood, original in Crater Lake National Park Museum and Archives Collections).

Oregon Historical Society: cover (Portland Flood of 1984, OrHi5578), pages 131 (OrHi56002), 134 (OrHi67766), and 182 (OrHi55030).

The Oregonian Publishing Company: 40, 90.

Oregon State Library: 2 (Portland flood), 123, 124, 125, 127, 145.

Oregon State University Archives: 150.

David Rydivik: 43.

Salem Public Library: 137, 160.

Janell Sorensen: 264.

Orma Burdick Sullivan: 38.

United States Army: 9.

United States Forest Service: 85, 178.

United States Geological Survey: 45, 52, 53, 54, 64, 92 (eruption).

Randy Wilson: 4, 91.

Bibliography

Chapter I: Ice Age Floods

Allen, John Eliot; Marjorie Burns and Sam C. Sargent. *Cataclysms on the Columbia.* Portland: Timber Press, 1986.

Alt, David. *Glacial Lake Missoula and its humongous floods.* Missoula: Mountain Press, 2001.

Benito, G. and J. E. O'Connor. "Number and size of last glacial Missoula floods in the Columbia River valley between the Pasco Basin, Washington, and Portland, Oregon." *Geological Society of America Bulletin, Vol. 115.* Denver, Colorado: Geological Society of America, May, 2003.

Carter, D. T.; L. L. Ely; J. E. O'Connor; and C. R. Fenton. "Late Pleistocene outburst flooding from pluvial Lake Alvord into the Owyhee River, Oregon," *Geomorphology, Vol. 75.* Amsterdam: Elsevier Science, May, 2006.

Normark, W. R. and J. A. Reid. "Extensive deposits on the Pacific plate from Late Pleistocene North American glacial lake outbursts," *Journal of Geology, Vol. 111.* Chicago: University of Chicago Press, November 2003.

Waitt. "Case for periodic, colossal jökulhlaups from Pleistocene glacial Lake Missoula," *Geological Society of America Bulletin, Vol. 96.* Denver, Colorado: Geological Society of America, 1985.

Chapter II: Tsunamis

Atwater, Brian. "Evidence for great Holocene earthquakes along the outer coast of Washington State." *Science, Vol. 236.* 1987.

Atwater, Brian, *et al. The Orphan Tsunami of 1700.* Reston, Virginia: USGS, 2005.

Charland, James W., and George R. Priest. *Inventory of critical and essential facilities vulnerable to earthquake or tsunami hazards on the Oregon coast.* Salem: Oregon Department of Geology and Mineral Industries, 1995.

Kelsey, H. M., *et al.* "Plate-boundary earthquakes and tsunamis of the past 5500 years, Sixes River estuary, southern Oregon." *Geological Society of America Bulletin.* Texas: Assoc. Engineering Geologists Geological Society, March 2002.

Kelsey, H. M., *et al.* "Tsunami history of an Oregon coastal lake reveals a 4600 year record of great earthquakes on the Cascadia subduction zone." *Geological Society of America Bulletin.* Boulder: Geological Society of America, July-August 2005.

Leonard, L. J., *et al.* "Coseismic subsidence in the 1700 great Cascadia earthquake: Coastal estimates versus elastic dislocation models." *Geological Society of America Bulletin.* Denver: Assoc. Engineering Geologists Geological Society, May-June 2004.

Losey, Robert J. "Native American vulnerability and resiliency to great Cascadia earthquakes." *Oregon Historical Quarterly, Vol. 108.* Portland: Oregon Historical Society, Summer 2007.

McAdoo, B. G. and P. Watts. "Tsunami hazard from submarine landslides on the Oregon continental slope." *Marine Geology.* Amsterdam: Elsevier Science BV, January 2004.

McMillan, Alan D. and Ian Hutchinson. "When the mountain dwarfs danced: Aboriginal traditions of Paleoseismic events along the Cascadia subduction zone of western North America." *Ethnohistory, Vol. 49.* American Society for Ethnohistory, winter 2002.

Nelson, A. R., *et al.* "Great earthquakes of variable magnitude at the Cascadia subduction zone." *Quaternary Research.* San Diego: Academic Press, May 2006.

Oppenheimer, D. H., *et al.* "The seismic project of the National Tsunami Hazard Mitigation Program," *Natural Hazards.* New York: Springer, May 2005.

Oregon Department of Geology and Mineral Industries. "Tsunami hazard maps for the Oregon coast and community evacuation brochures." Web site: *www.oregongeology.com/sub/earthquakes/Coastal/Tsumaps.html.*

Oregon Department of Geology and Mineral Industries. *Tsunami warning systems and procedures: guidance for local officials.* Salem: State of Oregon, 2001.

The Oregonian. "Not so high and dry after all." Portland: March 9, 2008.

—. "Waves lash into Crescent City with awesome knockout force." Portland: March 29, 1964.

—. "Big Wave Floods Cannon Beach." Portland: March 28, 1964.

Phillips, Patricia W. "Tsunamis and floods in Coos Bay mythology." *Oregon Historical Quarterly, Vol. 108.* Portland: Oregon Historical Society, Summer 2007.

Satake, K., K. L. Wang, and B. F. Atwater. "Fault slip and seismic moment of the 1700 Cascadia earthquake inferred from Japanese tsunami descriptions." *Journal of Geophysical Research: Solid Earth.* Washington, DC: American Geophysical Union, November 2003.

Schlichting, R. B. and C. D. Peterson. "Mapped overland distance of paleotsunami high-velocity inundation in back-barrier wetlands of the central Cascadia margin, USA." *Journal of Geology.* Chicago: University of Chicago Press, September 2006.

Weldon, Ray. "Big tsunami hit Oregon in 1700—and will again." *The Register Guard.* Eugene, Oregon, December 28, 2004.

Witter, R. C., *et al.* "Great Cascadia earthquakes and tsunamis of the past 6700 years, Coquille River estuary, southern coastal Oregon." *Geological Society of America Bulletin.* Denver: Assoc. Engineering Geologists Geological Society, October 2003.

Chapter III: Earthquakes

Allen, John Eliot. "Risk of earthquakes in Oregon very low." *The Oregonian*. Portland: November 3, 1983.

Atwater, Brian F., compiler. "Geology of Holocene liquefaction features along the lower Columbia River at Marsh, Brush, Price, Hunting, and Wallace Islands, Oregon and Washington." U.S. Geological Survey Open-File Report 94-209, 1994.

Herald and News. "Quake bashes basin." Klamath Falls: September 21, 1993.

Liberty, L.M., M.A. Hemphill-Haley, and I.P. Madin. "The Portland Hills Fault: uncovering a hidden fault in Portland, Oregon using high-resolution geophysical methods." *Tectonophysics*. Elsevier Science BV: Amsterdam, June 2003.

The Oregonian. "Quake could collapse half of Oregon schools." Portland: May 22, 2007.

—. "Big quake takes a toll." Portland: March 1, 2001.

—. "Aftershocks ripple through K Falls." Portland: September 22, 1993.

—. "The Spring Break Quake." Portland: March 26, 1993.

—. "Research finds powerful earthquake possible in NW." Portland: May 13, 1984.

—. "Vicious earthquake stuns Alaska." Portland: March 28, 1964.

—. "Sharp earthquake jolts NW Oregon." Portland: November 6, 1962.

—. "Quake rocks Northwest, killing seven." Portland: April 14, 1949.

Priest, George R. *Tsunami Hazard Maps of the Oregon Coast*. Oregon Department of Geology and Mineral Industries, 1995.

Sokolowski, Thomas J. "The great Alaskan earthquake & tsunami of 1964." Web site *http://wcatwc.arh.noaa.gov/64quake.htm*, 2007.

Statesman-Journal. "Earthquake in Oregon." Salem: March 26, 1993.

The Sunday Oregonian. "Powerful earthquake rocks West Coast." Portland: November 9, 1990.

Vinson, Brian and Thomas H. Miller. *Pilot Project: Eugene-Springfield Earthquake Damage and Loss Estimate Final Report*. Oregon Department of Geology and Mineral Industries, 1999.

Wang, Yumei and J. L. Clark. *Earthquake Damage in Oregon: Preliminary Estimates of Future Earthquake Losses*. Oregon Department of Geology and Mineral Industries: 1999.

Chapter IV: Volcanoes

Bacon, Charles R. and Marvin A. Lanphere. "Eruptive history and geochronology of Mount Mazama and the Crater Lake region, Oregon." *Geological Society of America Bulletin*. Boulder: Geological Society of America, November-December 2006.

Bishop, Ellen Morris. *In Search of Ancient Oregon*. Portland: Timber Press, 2003.

Dzurisin, Daniel. *Living With Volcanic Risk in the Cascades*. Reston, Virginia: United States Geologic Service, 2003.

—. "Results of repeated leveling surveys at Newberry Volcano, Oregon, and near Lassen Peak Volcano, California." *Bulletin of Volcanology*. New York: Springer Verlag, July 1999.

Dzurisin, Daniel, et al. "Geodetic observations and modeling of magmatic infla-
    tion at the Three Sisters volcanic center, certal Oregon Cascade Range." *Jour-
    nal of Volcanology and Geothermal Research*. Amsterdam: Elsevier, 2006.
Harris, Stephen L. *Fire & Ice: The Cascade Volcanoes*. Seattle: The Mountaineers,
    1980.
Jones, J. and S. D. Malone. "Mount Hood earthquake activity: Volcanic or tec-
    tonic origins? *Bulletin of the Seismological Society of America*. El Cerrito: Seismo-
    logical Socity, June 2005.
Matz, Stephan E. "The Mazama tephra-falls: Volcanic hazards and prehistoric
    populations." *Anthropology Northwest: Number 5*. Corvallis, OSU, 1991.
Nathanson, Manuel, C.R. Bacon and D.W. Ramsey. "Subaqueous geology and a
    filling model for Crater Lake, Oregon." *Hydrobiologia*. Dordrecht: Springer,
    January 2007.
The Oregonian. "Volcano threat is never over." Portland: May 18, 2005.
— . "Mud dams lake, imperils 3 towns." Portland: May 20, 1980.
— . "Eruption decapitates St. Helens; at least 9 die; Spirit Lake gone." Portland:
    May 19, 1980.
— . "Mount St. Helens spews out ash as sleeping volcano awakens." Portland:
    March 28, 1980.
Scott, W. E., et al. *Geologic History of Mount Hood Volcano, Oregon: A Field-Trip
    Guidebook*. Open file report 97-263. Reston, Virginia: USGS, 1997.

Chapter V: Flash Floods

Cutsforth, Cole. "Mitchell floods." *A Second Glimpse of Mitchell Magic*. Mitchell:
    Mitchell Elementary School, 1996.
Highberger, Mark. *Days of Sorrow: The Story of the Heppner Flood of 1903*. Wallowa,
    Oregon: Bear Creek Press, 2003.

Morning Oregonian. "Fly to the hills: Mitchell people escape cloudburst." Portland: July 13, 1904.

The Oregonian. "Famous ride of warning in Heppner recalled." Portland: June 14, 1949.

The Sunday Oregonian. "50-foot flood hits Mitchell." Portland: July 15, 1956.

— . "Big flood recalls Heppner disaster." Portland: July 10, 1927.

Wilson, Julia Carroll. "Mitchell Floods" (undated letter). Prineville: Crook County Historical Society, Bowman Museum.

Chapter VI: River Floods

Anderson, Ryan. *Flooding and Settlement in the Upper Willamette Valley.* Eugene: University of Oregon thesis, 1974.

Corning, Howard McKinley. *Willamette Landings.* Portland: Binfords & Mort: 1947.

The Daily Oregonian. "City: The freshet and its effects." Portland: December 6, 1861.

Ellis-Sugai, Barbara and Derek Godwin. "Why do streams meander?" *Going With the Flow.* Corvallis: Oregon Sea Grant, 2002.

Interagency Hazard Mitigation Team. *February 1996 Flooding, Landslides, and Stream Erosion in the State of Oregon.* Salem: Oregon Emergency Management Division, 1996.

Lewis, Terry, project coordinator. *The Cascades West Region of Oregon and the February Flood of 1996.* Albany: Oregon Cascades West Council of Governments: 1996.

Lucia, Ellis. *Wild Water: The Story of the Far West's Great Christmas Week Floods.* Portland: Overland West Press, 1965.

Maddux, Percy. *City on the Willamette.* Portland: Binfords & Mort, 1952.

The New York Times. "Thousands flee their homes in Northwest Oregon floods." New York: February 9, 1996.

The Oregonian. "Staying above it all: New flood maps for Vernonia serve as a warning to other cities." Portland: February 16, 2008.

— . "Flood fund bails out same few." Portland: December 16, 2007.

— . "Misery drenches western Oregon." Portland: December 4, 2007.

— . "Cry of disbelief: 'There's someone on that house'." Portland: February 9, 2006.

— . "Tillamook flooded, no relief in sight." Portland: February 8, 1996.

— . "The rains came . . . and came." Portland: February 7, 1996.

— . "State declared disaster area: Worst flood in history hits Oregon." Portland: December 23, 1964.

— . "Flood crumbles Vanport, heavy death toll feared." Portland: May 31, 1948.

— . "Projected Willamette dams to cut heavy flood losses." Portland: January 7, 1948.

— . "Toll mounts to 6 in Oregon floods." Portland: January 2, 1943.

The Sunday Oregonian. "Venice rivaled." Portland: June 10, 1894.

West Coast Floods, Washington-Oregon-Idaho: December 1964 and January 1965. Portland: U.S. Army Corps of Engineers, 1966.

Chapter VII: Wind and Weather

Eugene Register-Guard. "Storm leaves grim statistics." Eugene: October 13, 1962.
Lynott, Robert E. and Owen P. Cramer. *Detailed Analysis of the 1962 Columbus Day Windstorm in Oregon and Washington.* Portland: U.S. Forest Service, 1966.
The Oregonian. "Twister rips up Clark County." Portland: January 11, 2008.
— . "Disaster leaves Northwest groggy." Portland: December 14, 1962.
— . "17 dead in area's worst storm; guard called out in emergency." Portland: October 13, 1962.
The Oregon Statesman. "Hurricane devastates Oregon." Salem: October 13, 1962.

Chapter VIII: Landslides

Beaulieu, John D. "State not hiding slide risks." Letter to the editor, *The Oregonian.* Portland: January 24, 2008.
Eugene Weekly. "Losers by a landslide." Eugene: February 7, 2008.
— . "An unnatural disaster." Eugene: February 15, 1996.
Loy, William G., editor. *Atlas of Oregon.* Eugene: University of Oregon Press, 2001.
News-Review. "Clear-cut may have aided slide." Roseburg: November 24, 1996.
— . "Grim recovery begins." Roseburg: November 18, 1996.
The Oregonian. "State keeps slide risks to itself." Portland: January 20, 2008.
— . "Past OSU logging a setup for slide." Portland: December 19, 2007.
— . "Spotters search for slide threats." Portland: December 13, 2007.
Orr, Elizabeth L., William N. Orr, and Ewart M. Baldwin. *Geology of Oregon, Fourth Edition.* Dubuque, Iowa: Kendall/Hunt, 1992.
The Register-Guard. "Slide's impact hits hard." Eugene: January 23, 2008.
Scott, W. E., et al. *Geologic History of Mount Hood Volcano, Oregon: A Field-Trip Guidebook.* Open file report 97-263. Reston, Virginia: USGS, 1997.
Solomon, Senior District Judge. *National Wildlife Federation, et al., Plaintiffs, v. United States Forest Service, et al., Defendants.* Portland: United States District Court for the District of Oregon, August 6, 1984.

Chapter IX: Forest Fires

Atzet, Tom. "Complexity in forest ecology: The case of the Biscuit Fire." Starker Lecture Series. Corvallis: OSU, 2003.
Biscuit Fire Recovery Project: Final Environmental Impact Statement. United States Department of Agriculture, Forest Service: June 2004.
Block, Melissa. "Salvage logging increases forest-fire threat." *All Things Considered.* National Public Radio: January 5, 2006.
Chambers, Valerie. "No greater foe than fire" (Masters thesis). Eugene: University of Oregon, 1989.
DellaSalla, D. A., *et al.* "The facts and myths of post-fire management: a case study of the Biscuit Fire, southwest Oregon" (unpublished report). Ashland: World Wildlife Fund, 2006.

Donato, Daniel C., J. B. Fontaine, J. L. Campbell, W. D. Robinson, J. B. Kauffman, and B. E. Law. "Post-wildfire logging hinders regeneration and increases fire risk." *Science:* January 20, 2006.

From Tillamook Burn to Tillamook State Forest. Salem: Oregon State Department of Forestry, 1983.

Halcomb, Erin. "Weathering the academic firestorm." *High Country News:* Colorado, May 28, 2007.

Hansen, Liane. "Pullout of firefighters and other personnel from Oregon now that Biscuit Fire is largely under control." *Weekend Edition Sunday.* National Public Radio: August 25, 2002.

The Hartford Courant. "The costs of salvage logging" (editorial). Hartford, Connecticut: October 18, 2006.

Kemp, Larry J. *Epitaph for the Giants: The Story of the Tillamook Burn.* Portland: Touchstone Press, 1967.

Lucia, Ellis. *Tillamook Burn Country: A Pictorial History.* Caldwell, Idaho: Caxton, 1983.

The Oregonian. "All fire, all the time" (editorial). Portland: May 24, 2007.

—. "Opposing views of Biscuit study hits the stands." Portland: August 1, 2006.

—. "Forestry report draws crowd." Portland: May 25, 2006.

—. "Biscuit logging may light fuse," Portland: March 1, 2006.

—. "Research rattles forestry school." Portland: February 24, 2006.

—. "Bush says forest plan will aid environmental goals." Portland: August 22, 2003.

"Prescribed Fire in Pacific West Parks" (flier). National Park Service: National Park Service Fire Management Program, Pacific West Region (undated).

Register-Guard. "Study: Logging, replanting fuels fires." Eugene: June 12, 2007.

— "Study sheds light on life after fire." Eugene: April 4, 2007.

Sessions, John, *et al.* "Hastening the return of complex forests following fire: The consequences of delay." *Journal of Forestry.* Bethesda, Maryland: Society of American Foresters, April-May 2004.

Smith, Senator Gordon. "Smith releases progress report on Biscuit Fire recovery" (press release). Washington, DC: March 16, 2006.

Stauth, David. "The clock is ticking on Biscuit Fire restoration" (press release). Corvallis: OSU News & Communication Services, July 17, 2003.

The Sunday Oregonian. "Beast hasn't changed, just its name." Portland: August 11, 2002.

—. "Fire crews a fraternity forged in battles' heat." Portland: August 11, 2002.

Thompson, Jonathan R., Thomas Spies, and Lisa Ganio. "Reburn severity in managed and unmanaged vegetation in a large wildfire." *Proceedings of the National Academy of Sciences: www.pnas.org,* June 11, 2007.

"Wildland fire in National Parks" (brochure). National Park Service: National Interagency Fire Center, Idaho (undated).

Chapter X: Beyond the Cycles

Gore, Albert. *An Inconvenient Truth.* Emmaus, Pennsylvania: Rodale Press, 2006.

Levy, Sharon. "The giving trees." *OnEarth.* New York: Natural Resources Defense Council, spring 2008.

The New York Times. "Feeling warmth, subtropical plants move north." New York: May 3, 2007.

The Oregonian. "A region's vitality, melting away: Why Mount Hood's glaciers matter." Portland: February 11, 2008.

— . "Culprits in a hotter West: People." Portland: February 1, 2008.

— . "Extinction by comet?" Portland: October 31, 2007.

— . "Mazamas aid glacier study from air." Portland: October 17, 2007.

— . "As the climate warms, gentler plants move in." Portland: May 6, 2007.

The Register-Guard. "Ocean 'dead zones' may be permanent." Eugene: February 15, 2008.

— . "Experts in climate change estimate rising sea levels." Eugene: February 4, 2008.

— . "Oregon's Collier Glaicer retreating rapidly." Eugene: October 24, 2007.

— . "Reports warn of warming's effect on wildfires, fish." Eugene: May 18, 2007.

The Sunday Oregonian. "Climate change: It's real, it's here." Portland: November 18, 2007.

— . "Natural 'feedbacks': Scientists test 'the gorilla at the door.'" Portland: September 9, 2007.

General Oregon Resources

Alt, David D. *Roadside Geology of Oregon.* Missoula: Mountain Press, 1978.

Battaile, Connie Hopkins. *The Oregon Book: Information A to Z.* Ashland: 1216 Tolman Creek Road, 1998.

Bishop, Ellen Morris and John Eliot Allen. *Hiking Oregon's Geology.* Seattle: Mountaineers, 1996.

Friedman, Ralph. *Oregon for the Curious.* Caldwell: Caxton, 1979.

— *Tracking Down Oregon.* Caldwell: Caxton, 1978.

— *A Touch of Oregon.* Reprint, Sausalito: Comstock, 1974.

Holbrook, Stewart. *Far Corner: A Personal View of the Pacific Northwest.* New York: Ballantine, 1952.

Loy, William G., editor. *Atlas of Oregon.* Eugene: University of Oregon Press, 2001.

McArthur, Lewis A. *Oregon Geographic Names.* Portland: Oregon Historical Society, 1996.

Orr, Elizabeth *et al. Geology of Oregon, Fourth Edition.* Dubuque: Kendall/Hunt, 1995.

Glossary

basalt - a dark volcanic rock that usually originates as lava flows. Basalt has a relatively low silica content, so it forms lava flows that are runny.

caldera - a large crater formed by the collapse or explosion of a volcano.

Cascadia subduction zone - the 1100-mile-long fault line off the coast of Oregon and Washington where the North American plate is ramming itself on top of the Pacific Ocean plate, pushing down (subducting) the seafloor.

clearcut - a forest area where all trees are cut.

continental plate - the bedrock of a continent, composed of relatively light rock that floats on the Earth's liquid interior.

coulee - a dry rivercourse.

dacite - a light gray volcanic rock that contains more silica than basalt, and thus forms lava flows that are slower and less runny.

dendrochronology - the science of measuring the age of wood by counting the annual growth rings of trees.

epicenter - a point on the Earth's surface directly above the origin of an earthquake.

erratic - a rock transported by a glacier or a glacial flood.

estuary - the broad, lower part of a river influenced by tides, including mudflats and marshes.

fault - in geology, a crack along which ground movement occurs, causing earthquakes.

fault zone - a collection of faults, often arranged roughly in a line, where ground movement and earthquakes cluster.

fire interval - the average number of years between natural fires for a given forest type.

flood crest - the highest elevation of water during a flood, measured from a river's bed.

flood plain - the region covered with water during a river's larger floods, excluding the effect of dikes and dams.

glacier - a permanent field of ice so large that it moves downhill.

ice age - a period of global cooling, occurring on average every 30,000 years.

intraplate earthquake - a deep earthquake caused by the breakup of subducted seafloor rock underneath a continental plate.

jökulhlaup - a glacial flood caused when a glacier dams enough melt-water that the ice floats and suddenly releases a flood.

lahar - a dangerous, fast-moving flow of volcanic ash and mud.

lava dome - a large mound of rock that rises slowly from a volcanic vent and cools in place, usually in a crater.

meander - the looping curve of a slow-moving river.

megafauna - large animals, particularly those larger than people.

obsidian - black volcanic glass, formed when silica-rich lava cools quickly.

plate - in geology, one of the moving sections of the Earth's crust that forms either a continent or part of an ocean seafloor.

pumice - a light, silica-rich volcanic rock infused with so many air bubbles that it can usually float on water.

pyroclastic flow - a dangerous, fast-moving flow of gas and hot rock from a volcanic eruption.

Richter scale - a measure of earthquake severity in which each larger whole number represents a 32-fold increase in power.

riprap - boulders placed along a beach or riverbank in an attempt to stop erosion.

seismic sea wave - a powerful ocean wave created by an earthquake, volcano, landslide, or asteroid impact.

seismograph - a machine that records the ground movement of earthquakes.

shield volcano - a broad volcano composed largely of runny basalt lava flows, forming a mountain that resembles a Roman warrior's shield.

silica - the element in glass, white beach sand, obsidian, and pumice.

silver thaw - a storm that coats trees and other surfaces with a layer of ice.

subduction - in geology, the process whereby an oceanic seafloor plate is overridden by another plate and forced down into the Earth's interior.

temblor - an earthquake.

tsunameter - a device for measuring the pressure of tsunamis at sea.

tsunami - a powerful ocean wave created by an earthquake, volcano, landslide, or asteroid impact. See seismic sea wave.

understory - the brush and small trees growing in the shade of a forest canopy.

volcanologist - a scientist who studies volcanoes.

wetland - an area that is marshy or underwater only during floods.

Index

About the Author

William L. Sullivan is the author of a dozen books and numerous articles about Oregon, including an outdoor column for the Eugene *Register-Guard*. A fifth-generation Oregonian, he received his English degree at Cornell University, studied linguistics at Germany's Heidelberg University, and completed an M.A. in German at the University of Oregon.

In 1985 he set out to explore Oregon's wilderness on a 1,361-mile solo

William L. Sullivan

backpacking trek from the state's westernmost point at Cape Blanco to Oregon's easternmost point at the bottom of Hells Canyon. His journal of that two-month adventure, published as *Listening for Coyote*, was chosen by the Oregon Cultural Heritage Commission as one of Oregon's "100 Books." Since then he has written a series of *100 Hikes* guides describing the trails of Oregon. The most recent of his novels is *The Case of Einstein's Violin*.

Sullivan's hobbies include backcountry ski touring, playing the pipe organ, and promoting libraries. He and his wife Janell Sorensen live in Eugene but spend summers without roads or electricity in a log cabin they built by hand along a wilderness river in Oregon's Coast Range. Sullivan's memoir of his adventures at that cabin retreat is entitled *Cabin Fever: Notes From a Part-Time Pioneer*. A complete list of Sullivan's books and speaking engagements is available at *www.oregonhiking.com*.